Great Golf Tournaments – Volume 1

Len Ferman - The Sports Time Traveler

Paperback ISBN 979-8-9915012-2-4

Ebook ISBN 979-8-9915012-3-1

Published by The Sports Time Traveler, LLC

DEDICATION

To my beautiful bride Heather who had the idea for this book, and encouraged me throughout the process.

To my three incredible children and their amazing spouses. You are a constant source of happiness and inspiration.

To my dad for instilling in me a love of sports. And in particular, for taking me to see my first PGA TOUR event when I was just 10 years old.

To my mom, a published author herself, who has provided me with constant support for all my writing.

To my father-in-law Tony, whose positive feedback, when I first started The Sports Time Traveler, gave me the reinforcement to continue on this journey. May his memory continue to be a blessing to us all.

To my cousin Sandy who reads all my stories and tells me how much she loves them.

To my nephew Ben for his valuable advice that led to getting my stories published on Substack.

To my best friends from New Jersey, an incredible group of guys who have been like my brothers for the past 45 years. Thank you Bill, Charlie, Glenn, Greg and Mark for being avid readers of my work.

Thanks also to my friend Matt who I played golf with growing up and who reviewed several of the chapters.

And finally, to my young grandson and granddaughter, who I hope one day may find enjoyment in the game of golf as well as these stories.

Contents

FOREWORD

BY MG ORENDER - 33RD PRESIDENT OF
THE PGA OF AMERICA, MEMBER OF THE
2005 PGA HALL OF FAME CLASS AND
PRESIDENT AND CEO OF HAMPTON GOLF

When Len asked me to write the foreword for his next Sports Time Traveler book, and shared the table of contents, I was excited about the opportunity. After reading his first Sports Time Traveler book, "The 1973 Mets- You've Got to Believe," I couldn't wait to see what he had in mind for some of the great and not-so-great moments in golf.

Though all of the subjects are of interest in "Great Golf Tournaments – Volume 1," I was particularly keen on his coverage of the 1975 Masters, Joe Louis receiving a sponsor's exemption and playing in the 1952 San Diego Open, Hogan's 1953 Season, Palmer's trip to the British Open in 1962, and the Great Walter Hagen. I will opine in chronological order, starting with Walter Hagen.

Walter Hagen may have been Golf's Greatest Showman. He said, *"I don't want to be a millionaire, just live like one."* He came along when professional golf was in its early development and professionals were not considered gentlemen. In fact, at many of the venues hosting professional events, they were not allowed in the clubhouse. The Jigger Inn at St. Andrews has pictures of old-time golfers on the walls. The next time you're there, note the names of the golfers in the captions. Most names start with "Sir" or "Mister," while some only have a first and last name. The latter are professionals, and hence, not gentlemen, and do not get titles before their names.

Sir Walter Hagen ("Sir" was just a nickname) had an amazing career, he was the first American-born professional to win a PGA Championship, which he won 5 times, tied only by Jack Nicklaus. In total, he won 11 Majors at a time when there was no Masters. He won 5 PGA Championships, 4 British Opens, and 2 U.S. Opens. He loved the PGA. Our old conference room in Palm Beach Gardens had a painting of him, paddling a canoe at his home in Michigan. That painting, along with the proceeds of the sale of his home, were donated to the PGA by his estate.

In 1952, the San Diego Open gave a sponsor's exemption to Joe Louis, one of the great heavyweights in the history of boxing and a very good golfer. This was at a time when the Caucasian-only clause was in effect. This set up a classic showdown between a championship boxer and the leadership of the PGA. Joe showed he could be competitive and help open doors for some very talented African-American players.

The debate about non-white golfers competing was not new. The U.S. Open at Shinnecock was held in 1896, and two players in the field that qualified were John Shippen, an African-American caddie and greenskeeper, and Oscar Bunn, a member of the Shinnecock tribe. The other players met and signed a petition that they would not play if these two competed. To his credit, the USGA President at the time, Theodore Havemeyer, basically said, 'we will miss you.'

Fast forward to 1934, and the PGA voted to ban non-white players, a ban which effectively stayed in place until 1961, even though some positive changes were made as a result of Joe Louis's efforts in 1952.

Hogan's comeback was one for the ages. After his car accident in 1949 nearly claimed his life, and he was told he may never walk again, he began the journey back. He eventually made it back to the top of the golf world. The several chapters in this book on Ben Hogan can serve as an inspiration for everyone in overcoming a challenge.

Arnold Palmer's trip to the 1962 Open Championship in Scotland further shined a light on the Oldest Championship, and due to its rising popularity, it forced the PGA Championship to be moved later on the calendar in 1965, to August, so it would not interfere with those wishing to play in both the Open and the PGA.

Finally, the 1975 Masters is special to me. It was the first time I walked on that sacred ground. The tournament was a battle of titans, between Jack Nicklaus, Johnny Miller and Tom Weiskopf. While Arnold drew an enormous amount of interest to the Masters, Jack shined a spotlight on it. Never more so than his incredible 1986 victory to win his 6th Master's title and his 18th Major. While that alone is amazing, the record people do not discuss and should is Jack Nicklaus's 19 runner-ups in majors.

I highly recommend Len's book which covers so many special days and events in the history of the game. Enjoy the trip back in time to some of the greatest golf tournaments.

INTRODUCTION

I have a been a huge golf fan since I was 10 years old in 1974, when my dad took me to see my first PGA TOUR event. It was the Westchester Classic, which at that time had the largest purse of the year at $250,000. The winner received $50,000. That was enough, in those days, to get all the top players to come out. We saw Arnold Palmer, Jack Nicklaus, Gary Player, Johnny Miller and Sam Snead. I was hooked. I started following the PGA TOUR, watching as many tournaments as I could when they were on television in the late afternoons on weekends.

It was one of the great eras in golf. "The Big Three" were all still competitive, while younger players, that I idolized, like Johnny Miller and Tom Weiskopf, were playing at a sensational level – some of the best golf ever played in my opinion.

For decades I have missed that experience of following those great players. I wished I could somehow have that experience again.

I did follow the next generations of players. I enjoyed the meteoric rise and dominance of Tiger Woods as much as anyone. And I'm a big fan of many current players on the PGA TOUR, and continue to watch each week.

But that still doesn't diminish the feeling that I would love to follow the great players of the past, both those I remember from the 1970s, as well as those who were long before my time that I never got to experience. It would have been very special to experience some of the all-time greats like Ben Hogan, Byron Nelson, Walter Hagen and Bobby Jones.

This problem gnawed at me for a long time.

And then a few years ago, I came up with a solution.

I call it "virtual time travel." I devised a method by which I could create the feeling that I was back in time experiencing my favorite golfers playing tournaments that took place 50 – 100 years ago.

In 2022, I began a personal journey to travel back in time virtually and experience great golf tournaments from the past. I did this by pointing my "sports time travel machine" back to a specific date that was just prior to the start of a golf tournament I was interested in, and then parking myself there. I would read the newspapers of that time each day. And I followed the cardinal rule of sports time travel – never look ahead. For example, when I was following the 1973 U.S. Open at Oakmont, and I was finished reading the 3rd round coverage in the June 18, 1973 newspapers, I didn't open the June 19, 1973 papers, to find out about the conclusion of the tournament, until the next day.

In this manner I was doing two essential things: 1) I was having the same experience someone would have had at that time as they tried to follow the golf tournament through the newspapers; and 2) I was mimicking the cadence of real life, since I would only read the newspapers for that day and wait a day to read the next day's paper.

Where it was available I would supplement this experience with YouTube videos of the tournaments. Consistent with the rules of sports time travel, I would not watch those videos until I had reached the time that corresponded with where I was in the newspaper coverage.

This method successfully achieved the goal for which I had long sought. It made me feel like I was actually back in time following these great golfers as though I was really there.

It's the closest I will ever get to actual time travel. And this method has delivered so many great experiences for me that I feel compelled to share them with you via this book.

In Great Golf Tournaments – volume 1, I share with you my favorite stories of golf time travel trips that I made over the past 3 years. Most of the time travel trips were made precisely 50, 60 or 70 years prior to the present moment at which

I was writing the story. For example, I made my trip back to the 1973 U.S. Open in 2023.

Some of the stories I covered in this book I was familiar with but didn't know all the details. And the details were absolutely fascinating. Other stories were ones I never knew about, but now feel grateful to have learned about them. And then there is a third category of stories that have become very special to me. They're stories I never expected, that I wasn't searching for, in which I made "discoveries" that few people in the present time seem to know about since I could find little to nothing about them in books or the internet.

Collectively, the stories in volume 1 provided me with such excitement that I plan on continuing the journey. There are many, many more golf tournaments from the past that I can't wait to "go back in time" and cover for you over the next couple of years. The stories of those tournaments will eventually make their way into volume 2.

For now, I hope you enjoy the experience reading volume 1.

NOTE: In each chapter the datelines of the stories represent the date I read the newspapers. Since most newspaper accounts report on the prior day's news, the actual date of the tournament play will be one day prior to the dateline.

CHAPTER ONE

The Comeback at Hogan's Alley

THE 1950 LOS ANGELES OPEN

INTRODUCTION from The Sports Time Traveler

Before I tell the story of my virtual trip back in time to the 1950 Los Angeles Open, I must provide some background for those of you who are reading this in the mid-21st century.

2 years earlier, in 1948, Ben Hogan won the U.S. Open at Riviera Country Club in Los Angeles with a record score of 276. It was a popular victory that led sportswriters to begin referring to Riviera as Hogan's Alley, since he had won the two prior Los Angeles Opens on the same course.

The 1948 U.S. Open was Hogan's 2nd major of the year and his 3rd overall. Bantam Ben, as the press liked to call him, had just solidified his status as the world's best golfer.

By the end of 1948, Hogan had won an astounding 30 tournaments in 3 seasons. He was 36 years old and on top of the golf world.

And then it all crashed, literally. Ben Hogan was in a horrific car accident on the morning of February 2, 1949. The car he was driving was hit head on by a Greyhound bus in foggy conditions. The bus was in Hogan's lane at the time of the accident. Ben had been driving home to Ft. Worth, Texas from Arizona, with his wife Valerie, after he had lost the Phoenix Open in a playoff. Just prior to the collision, Hogan threw his body over his wife heroically saving her from injury.

Hogan's recovery from the accident was long and difficult with life threatening complications. It was assumed he would never walk again, but he did walk.

It was then assumed he would never be able play golf again. On September 28, 1949, nearly 8 months after the accident, an AP article indicated that Hogan told reporters that he had, *"not swung a club since the accident."*

But he did play. On December 11, 1949, the Fort Worth Star-Telegram ran an article with a headline, *"FLASH! HOGAN PLAYS 18 HOLES AT COLONIAL."* Hogan had played a round of golf at the Colonial Country Club in Fort Worth. It was the first report that Hogan had even hit a golf ball. Hogan told the newspaper that he had hit his first few practice balls just the prior week.

The next day The Fort Worth Star-Telegram reported, *"Ben Hogan played another 18 holes of golf at Colonial."* The paper also noted, *"observers said he looked sharp as of old... unofficial reports gave his scores as 71 and 72 over the par 70 layout."*

Although he was playing, it was assumed he might never return to tournament golf. In the December 15th Fort Worth Star-Telegram, Jack Murphy revealed that in the 2 practice rounds over the past weekend Hogan had been, *"riding from hole-to-hole on a motor scooter."* Murphy asserted, *"Hogan is still a sick man... His underpinning is shaky. His legs still are encased in binding rubber stockings."*

Murphy asked Hogan if he will return to playing PGA tournament golf. Hogan replied, *"I honestly don't know."*

But then came the news 2 weeks later on December 28th that Hogan and his wife Valerie were heading to California to escape the cold weather and prepare for a possible comeback. Murphy speculated that Hogan might try to play at the Bing Crosby tournament in mid-January. Hogan was going to be staying at Bing's house.

If not the Crosby, then Murphy thought Hogan might play in the Phoenix Open at the end of January. It had been announced that the tournament was being re-named the Ben Hogan Open.

Hogan told Jack Murphy, *"There's a possibility that I'll play. But right now I can't say. I honestly don't know myself... just don't know if my legs will stand up for 18 holes a day."*

On Sunday, January 1, 1950, Charles Curtis of the Los Angeles Times revealed that 2 days earlier, Hogan had played a practice round at Riviera Country Club and shot a 69. With the Los Angeles Open starting the following Friday, there was now speculation that perhaps Hogan might enter the tournament on the course where he had such celebrated success.

The next day, Curtis didn't have a further update on Hogan's status for the Los Angeles Open, but he did have a classic quote from Sam Snead. Slammin' Sammy said, *"Only three things I fear on a golf course, lightning, a downhill putt and Ben Hogan."*

One day later on Tuesday, January 3, 1950, Bob Lee of the Los Angeles Daily News had the big news of the day. The headline of his article read, *"HOGAN ENTERS L.A. Open Tourney * * * Ben launches comeback campaign."* Lee noted that, *"it was believed his golfing career had ended."* But he, *"surprised the experts by several sensational practice rounds."*

So Ben Hogan was going to give it a go at the Los Angeles Open.

Now here are my reports from the 1950 Los Angeles Open. The bylines for the reports include the dates on which I read the newspapers on my virtual journey back in time.

PRE-TOURNAMENT – Riviera Country Club, Los Angeles – Friday, January 6, 1950

Charles Curtis of the Los Angeles Times set the stage on this opening day of the tournament. His article on page 1 of the sports section started with this, *"Ben Hogan launches the most ambitious comeback attempt in the history of golf."* And then he went on to make his pick for who would win the tournament. Perhaps it was based on the great practice rounds that had been reported, perhaps it was the proximity to Hollywood and a dose of wishful thinking, perhaps it was the desire to see a fantasy come true, but Curtis picked Ben Hogan to win the tournament.

Or perhaps in his pick, Curtis was playing to the frenzy among the fans. In the article he noted, *"The excitement all centers around Hogan and every stroke he plays will be followed by golf fans throughout the world with avid interest."*

The public eagerly anticipated the return of the great golfer. 2 days ago, Los Angeles Daily News writer Bob Lee wrote an article with the headline, *"Sports World Roots for Hogan Comeback."* The first sentence read, *"Bantam Ben Hogan, the little man who just wouldn't call it quits, will carry the hopes and good wishes of the entire sports world."*

Coming back to Curtis's picks to win the tournament, his 2nd, 3rd and 4th choices to win were Dr. Cary Middlecoff, Sam Snead and Jimmy Demaret. Needless to say the field was loaded for this tournament which is the most lucrative on the *"winter slate."*

I can't wait for the 1st round today. Ben Hogan tees off at 12:03pm.

1st ROUND – Riviera Country Club, Los Angeles – Saturday, January 7, 1950

The Los Angeles Times reported on the front page that, *"a long throng"* followed Hogan on the course in the 1st round.

The front page of the sports section had a picture that covered the entire top quarter of the page. It showed Hogan making a birdie putt on the 2nd hole. The caption read, *"Ben Hogan, the center of attraction at Riviera yesterday as he attempted one of the most heart-warming comebacks in sports annals."*

In the Long Beach Independent, George Lederer described the scene when Ben Hogan stepped onto the 1st tee, *"Welcome him back they did with a spontaneous round of applause that echoed throughout Santa Monica Canyon... Hogan's tee shot, a sizzling drive, carried straight down the middle 270 yards. Hogan had come back!"*

Hogan wasted the great drive when he 3-putted for a bogey on the 1st hole. But on the 476 yard 2nd hole, Hogan nearly holed out his 3-iron shot which stopped just a foot from the pin. He went around the opening 9 in a 1 under 34.

But he had a little struggle on the back 9. He started with another 3-putt green at 10. Then after not missing a fairway on the first 12 holes, Hogan hit into the trees at 13 and 15 and had a wayward tee shot on 18 into the rough. He took a 3 over 39 on the back 9. That gave Ben a 2 over par 73 in the 1st round which put him 5 shots off the lead and in a tie for 16th place.

Sportswriters were in awe. Fred Delano of the Long Beach Press-Telegram remarked in his column, *"It was not until this very week that anyone dreamed he could possibly return to the tournament trail."*

The coverage focused more on Hogan than the leader Ed Furgol who had shot a 3 under par 68, taking only 9 putts on the back 9 during which he made 6 birdies and fired a 32.

Notable Scores in the 1st round:

-3   **Ed Furgol**

-2   **Jerry Barber**

Even   **Sam Snead**

+2   **Ben Hogan, Jimmy Demaret and Dr. Cary Middlecoff**

After the round Hogan told Fred Delano, *"I'm terribly, terribly tired."* Delano also made note of an incredible statistic. One year earlier, prior to the accident, Hogan had shot one shot higher in the 1st round at 74. That led Delano to comment, *"Think about that 73 of yesterday and what has happened to the guy in the last 11 months."*

2nd Round – Riviera Country Club, Los Angeles – Sunday, January 8, 1950

Ben Hogan drew almost the worst possible set of starting times for the first 2 rounds. He was in one of the last groups to tee off for the 1st round Then in yesterday's 2nd round he had one of the earlier tee times at 9:35am. This worked against Hogan whose damaged legs are severely stressed walking the 18 holes. But fortune struck when there was a vacancy in the 10:43am tee time. And Hogan was able to move to that time slot.

Hogan made the best possible use of that extra hour to prepare. It also gave time for more fans to arrive on the course to see Bantam Ben.

Chuck Panama of the Pasadena Independent followed Hogan on the course. He was one of many. Panama wrote, *"The majority of the 12,000 in the crowd trailed him."*

Charles Curtis described Hogan's play in the 2nd round in The Los Angeles Times. On the 1st hole his drive went far right behind a tree. He took a 4-wood and hooked it around the tree and reached a sand trap near the green on the par 5.

From the trap Hogan blasted to one foot from the cup for a birdie. Curtis wrote, *"It was the old Hogan in action."*

Hogan bogeyed the 2nd hole, but parred the 3rd. Then Curtis marveled at Hogan's tee shot at the 245 yard par 3 4th hole, *"he drilled one on the green."* That helped Hogan maintain par through 8 holes. On the 9th he canned a 12 foot birdie putt to give him a 1 under 34 on the front 9 for the 2nd day in a row.

It looked like it might be a repeat of his back 9 woes from Friday when he 3-putted the 11th. But he made up for it when he dropped his longest putt so far in the tournament, a 60 footer on 14 for his 3rd birdie. Curtis described the putt as, *"a sweeping arc as it cut across the vast green and plunked into the cup."*

Hogan notched another birdie at 17 and finished with a 2 under 69. That led Chuck Panama to open his article with this, *"The comeback attempt of Bantam Ben Hogan to professional golf hit a new high yesterday."*

In a UP article Hogan said he felt a lot stronger after the 2nd round than he did after Friday's 1st round, but he didn't consider it to be a good round.

Although he scored 4 better than the 1st round, Hogan still ended the day 5 shots behind the leader. Jerry Barber, of nearby Pasadena, fired a 68 to go with his 1st round score of 69 for a 2 round total of 137, which incidentally is 1 less than Hogan's 138 in the first 2 rounds of the 1948 U.S. Open. Barber benefitted from sinking 4 putts of at least 18 feet, including a 30 footer at 16.

Leading Scores through 2 rounds:

-5   **Jerry Barber**

-3   **Henry Ransom**

Even   **Ben Hogan and Ellsworth Vines**

+1   **Sam Snead, Ed Furgol, Otto Greiner, Eric Monti, Charles Congdon**

3rd ROUND – Riviera Country Club, Los Angeles – Monday, January 9, 1950

Something unthinkable back in the 2020's happened here in 1950 today. After two-thirds of all the players had completed the 3rd round in the rain, flooding on the course forced the cancellation of the round. But rather than simply picking up play the next day, the rules in effect here in the 1950 Los Angeles Open call for the entire day's scores to be nullified. Scores will revert to what they were at the end of the 2nd round and all the golfers will begin the 3rd round again tomorrow. This was the 1st time this has happened in the Los Angeles Open in the 24 year history of the tournament.

For most of the golfers this rule made sense. Bruce McCormick, one of the nation's top amateurs shot a 92 in the rain. Ed Furgol, the 1st round leader, had finished with an 80.

But the cancellation didn't help 2nd round leader Jerry Barber. Barber, in spite of the cold rain, shot a 73 yesterday, the best round of any who had finished. And among players who had finished their 3rd round of play, Barber had a 10 shot lead.

Ben Srere in the Riverside Daily Press described the conditions on the greens during play yesterday, *"The course was swept by a heavy downpour, which started before the opening threesome teed off... Riviera's greens are normally among the trickiest in the world. The rain made them almost impossible."*

Ben Hogan was among the golfers that called for the cancellation after they could not navigate the creek that had sprung up on the 11th fairway. Charles Curtis wrote, *"It was dangerous for the players to attempt to cross."*

Jack Tobin in the Los Angeles Mirror comically wrote, *"There were many incidents that brought about the ultimate cancellation... but it was little Ben Hogan's inability to swim that finished things off."*

When play was stopped, Hogan, who was 4 over par for the day, was offered a ride back to the clubhouse, but he said, *"I'll walk in like the rest. I'm not asking any favors."*

3rd ROUND AGAIN – Riviera Country Club, Los Angeles – Tuesday, January 10, 1950

Today the golfers were able to complete the entire 3rd round. Although it was cold, a high of just 52, the conditions were deemed to be ideal for scoring.

Jerry Barber had a relatively early tee time. He shot 1 stroke better in this version of the 3rd round than he did the day before in the rain, navigating Riviera in a 1 over 72.

Meanwhile, Ben Hogan was just finishing the front 9 when Barber completed the round. Al Wolf in the Los Angeles Times described the unceasing support for the comeback man, Ben Hogan, calling him *"a greater gallery god than ever."*

A UP article declared, *"So completely does the gallant Texan dominate attention that... there is only one word around the fairways. It's 'Hogan'"*

Spurred on by the crowd, Hogan had a magnificent front 9. He made a 30 foot birdie putt on the 3rd. On the 7th he hit his 7-iron approach shot to 3 feet and made another birdie, and then a 12 foot birdie on 8. He made the turn in 32, and that put him in 2nd place just 1 shot behind Barber.

But on the back 9, Hogan was erratic with 2 birdies but 3 bogeys and he came home in 37. Still, Ben Hogan had just shot 69 for the 2nd consecutive round (that counted). And he was just 2 shots back in 2nd place at the end of the day.

Charles Curtis asked Hogan if his legs were tired after the round. *"Plenty tired,"* Hogan shot back. And now thanks to the aborted round yesterday, Hogan would have to tee it up for a 5th day for today's final round.

Leading Scores through 3 rounds:

-4   **Jerry Barber**

-2   **Ben Hogan**

-1   **Jack Burke**

Even   **Ellsworth Vines**

+1   **Sam Snead and Henry Ransom**

4th Round – Riviera Country Club, Los Angeles – Wednesday, January 11, 1950

One of the oddities of tournament golf here in 1950 is how the groupings are set up in the final rounds. Yesterday, Ben Hogan, who started in 2nd place, was not in the final group with leader Jerry Barber. Instead he started 37 minutes ahead of Barber in a group with Ellsworth Vines, who was in 4th place after 3 rounds and Henry Ransom who was tied for 5th.

Sam Snead, who was tied with Ransom in 5th was put in the final group with Barber and Jack Burke who had started in 3rd.

Hogan got off to an excellent start when he reached the par 5 1st hole in 2 and 2-putted for a birdie. That immediately put him just 1 shot off the lead.

When Jerry Barber bogeyed the 1st hole, Ben Hogan vaulted into a tie for the lead at -3 for the tournament.

Hogan played rock steady and parred the 2nd through 7th holes. When Barber bogeyed number 5, Ben Hogan assumed the lead in the Los Angeles Open. Hogan then increased the lead to 2 strokes when he sank a 12 footer for birdie on the 8th. After a par on 9, Hogan had gone out in 33.

Barber continued to buckle under the pressure. He *"fell apart"* on the 7th hole according to Maxwell Stiles in the Los Angeles Mirror. Jerry ended the front

9 with a 41. He had fallen off to +2 for the tournament. Effectively Barber was out of contention.

Hogan lost a shot on 11 when he hit 2 bad woods on the par 5 hole. Pete Kokon in the Valley Times wrote, ***"Hogan skied his tee shot on the 11th hole which only traveled 180 to 200 yards."*** Although Hogan bogeyed the hole he was still in the lead at -3.

A couple of holes behind him, Jack Burke had completed the front 9 in 35 and Sam Snead, who birdied the 1st and parred the rest, finished the front 9 with a 34, and was suddenly a factor.

At this point, the leaderboard looked like this:

Leading Scores mid-way through the final round:

-3   Ben Hogan (through 11 holes)

-1   Jack Burke (through 9 holes)

Even   Sam Snead (through 9 holes)

Hogan recovered from his bogey on 11 to post pars on 12, 13 and 14. But when Burke playing behind Hogan, birdied 10 and parred 11 that pulled Burke to within a shot of Hogan.

Up ahead, Hogan hit his approach shot at the 15th to at least 50, maybe 75 feet from the hole. It was a long curling putt according to Maxwell Stiles. It was the type of situation where you could easily 3-putt. But Hogan knocked it in! That got him back to –4 for the tournament. He stayed at -4 shooting pars on 16 and 17.

At 18, Hogan's second shot came up well short of the green. But he hit a great chip shot from 75 yards to just 3 feet from the cup and holed the putt to par the finishing hole. He was the leader in the clubhouse at -4.

Hogan had shot 69 for the 3rd consecutive day. While his playing partner Ellsworth Vines had shot a 72, putting him 5 shots back of Hogan. And his other partner, Henry Ransom, had carded a 77 to finish 11 behind Hogan.

Only Jack Burke and Sam Snead had any chance of a catching Hogan.

And just before Hogan finished, Slammin' Sammy Snead got hot. He birdied 12 and 13 to pull into a tie with Burke for 2nd at -2.

Leading Scores when Hogan completed the final round:

-4   **Ben Hogan (through 18 holes)**

-2   **Jack Burke (through 13 holes)**

-2   **Sam Snead (through 13 holes)**

When Snead and Burke got to the 14th tee, Charles Curtis noted that Snead knew Hogan had finished with a 72 hole score of 280 (-4 for the tournament). *"He knew too, that he needed two birdies in the last five holes to catch Hogan."*

But neither Snead nor Burke could manage a birdie at 14, 15 or 16. They each parred all 3 of those holes.

When they reached the 17th tee, both Snead and Burke were still in need of two birdies to catch Hogan.

Bob Myers of the AP was following Snead and wrote that on the long par 5 17th hole Snead, *"banged his third shot high and straight, ten feet from the pin."* Myers and the gallery then heard Snead say to Burke, *"We gotta knock a couple of these in to get that little man."* Myers wrote, *"The fans howled. They had never seen Snead so relaxed."*

Snead made the putt and pulled to within a single stroke of Hogan. But Burke missed his 10-foot birdie putt. That kept him 2 shots back with 1 hole to play and effectively ended his run at the title.

The 18th hole at Riviera is a 455 yard par 4. Snead needed a birdie to tie Hogan and force a playoff. Despite being a long driver, Snead needed a 2-iron on his second shot. Myers wrote, *"Snead's approach shot sailed true, but left him with a fifteen-foot putt."*

Snead was generally regarded as the game's best player besides Hogan prior to the accident. But he was a notoriously bad putter. The UP article went further, in an article this morning their writer asserted that Snead was, *"one of the game's worst putters although he was 1949's golfer of the year."*

This putt had to go in to tie Hogan and force an 18-hole playoff the next day.

George Lederer of the Long Beach Independent wrote, *"More than 8,000 fans surrounded the 18th green and another 3,000 trailed the Snead threesome watching history being made."*

Curtis wrote, *"fans clung to the hillside, perched in trees, clambered on clubhouse railings."*

Myers noted that Snead, *"studied the greens for four minutes."*

Lederer penned, *"He paced the carpet like an expecting father while surveying the situation."*

Lederer then continued, *"Snead stroked the ball, saw it roll true to the cup, and a second later the victorious 'kerplunk' was completely drowned out by the hysteric throng."*

Sam Snead had done it. He had tied Hogan by scoring birdies on the last 2 holes to shoot a stunning 66, the lowest round of the entire tournament.

Frank T. Blair, sports editor of the Long Beach Press-Telegram wrote, *"Seldom has a tournament packed such thrills and drama."*

Lederer wrote, *"Slammin' Sammy sank the greatest putt of his life and simultaneously ruined the greatest sports story of the year,"* which was a reference to Hogan not being crowned the outright victor, and instead having to go to a playoff.

But in the clubhouse Snead was quick to note that this was not the most crucial putt he ever made. Coy Williams in the Los Angeles Mirror quoted Snead, *"I sank a 20-footer in the 1947 National Open to tie Lew Worsham. Lew won the playoff."*

While the fans loved the idea that the 2 top players in the world would have to come back to the course again for an 18-hole playoff, Hogan's wife Valerie was distraught. Coy Williams noted that he saw her sitting in the far corner of the clubhouse close to tears. She told him, *"I almost wish Snead had won it. This is so hard on Ben, having to play another day. He's tired. His legs swell after each round. Just think – six straight days of this! We didn't dream he would do this well. But how can he go on?"*

Ben Hogan echoed his wife's sentiment. He told Coy Williams, *"I don't feel bad about Sam tying me. I just don't want to play another round. I'd rather Sam had won. I'm tired, dead tired."*

Leading Scores after 72 holes:

-4   **Ben Hogan and Sam Snead**

-3   **Jack Burke**

+1   **Ellsworth Vines**

+3   **Bob Hamilton**

+4   **Jerry Barber and Jimmy Demaret**

The Playoff Postponed - Riviera Country Club, Los Angeles – Thursday, January 12, 1950

Yesterday, for a 6th consecutive day, Ben Hogan had to prepare to play 18 holes at Riviera. Even though there was heavy rain, tournament officials wanted to proceed with the playoff. Neither player wanted to play in these conditions and just 10 minutes prior to the 12:30pm tee time the tournament chairman, George Dann, announced the postponement of what he called, *"The golf match of the century."*

Hogan was very thankful for the decision. He told Chuck Panama, *"I never felt more tired than I did after finishing yesterday's round. My legs bothered me more than at anytime since I returned to the links."*

Due to commitments for Hogan and Snead to play in the Bing Crosby Pro-Am at Pebble Beach, the playoff has been rescheduled for a week from now.

The Playoff - Riviera Country Club, Los Angeles – Thursday, January 19, 1950

Last Friday in the New York Times, Arthur Daley wrote, *"There probably hasn't been anything in sports for the past half century that made folks tingle all over with a sense of warm satisfaction as did the incredible comeback of Ben Hogan."*

That sums up the impact that Ben Hogan has had on the public over the past week.

Last weekend, Sam Snead tied for first again, this time at the Bing Crosby Pro-Am at Pebble Beach, while Hogan finished 9 shots back. Unlike the Los Angeles Open there is no playoff at the Bing Crosby. So both players had 2 days to get ready for their head-to-head playoff.

In Monday's newspapers, after the Bing Crosby Pro-Am, an AP reporter described Hogan as looking *"drawn and pale."* Hogan admitted, *"It's just too much for me. I can't keep up the pace."*

Hogan indicated he will play in the Los Angeles Open playoff, and he will play in the Phoenix Open, January 26 – 29 and then he will go home to Fort Worth, TX, *"for a good long rest."*

Across America, anticipation has been building for the playoff. Charles Curtis noted that this was the first time Ben Hogan and Sam Snead had ever met in a playoff.

Maxwell Stiles wrote yesterday, *"EPOCHAL is the word for today's playoff between Ben Hogan and Sam Snead for the Los Angeles Open championship. Hogan's comeback has caught the fancy of newspaper editors, sportswriters and radio and TV men throughout the country. Eastern papers have asked press associations to file stroke by stroke coverage of the match – just as if this was a world championship fight between Joe Louis and Jack Dempsey... I can recall no single golf match, man against man, that has attracted as much national interest as this."*

Here in Los Angeles, fans could listen to the playoff live on the radio on KMPC starting at 12:30pm yesterday.

Charles Curtis reported that the gallery was rooting for Hogan.

HOLE 1 (513 yards par 5) – The playoff did not begin well for Ben. He hooked his opening drive, although he salvaged par. But Snead came away with a birdie.

HOLE 2 (476 yard par 4) – Both players were down the middle on their drives, but Hogan's 2nd shot carried over the green, while Snead's ball landed 35 feet from the hole. Ben bogeyed while Snead parred and Sam was 2 shots ahead after just 2 holes.

HOLE 3 (415 yards par 4) – Both reached the green in 2 shots and parred the hole.

HOLE 4 (245 yards par 3) – Fog became a problem. Snead couldn't see the pin from the tee, so a greenskeeper raised a red flag. Snead got into trouble when his tee shot on the par 3 plugged in the sand trap. He needed 2 shots to get out of the trap and took a double bogey, while Hogan reached the green and two-putted from 40 feet for par. The match was back to even.

HOLE 5 (432 yards par 4) – Both men needed 3 shots to reach the green and two-putted for bogey. The match remained tied.

HOLE 6 (166 yards par 3) – Both missed the green. Each of them put their 2nd shots close and putted in for par.

HOLE 7 (402 yards par 4) – Both hit long, straight drives. Hogan's approach landed 18 feet from the pin. Snead got his approach to 15 feet. Both missed the putts and took par. The match was still tied.

HOLE 8 (375 yards par 4) – Hogan hit his drive down the middle. While Snead was left and nearly out of bounds. But both players put their approach shots to about 12 feet from the hole. Hogan missed his birdie putt. But Snead made his to take a 1 stroke lead..

HOLE 9 (422 yards par 4) – Fog was a problem again. It was not possible from the tee to see where the players' drives landed. But both were in the fairway and landed their approach shots on the green within 15 feet. Snead 2-putted, but Hogan took 3 putts and Snead's lead grew to 2.

Scores after 9 holes

+1   Snead

+3   Hogan

HOLE 10 (315 yards par 4) – Snead missed the green on his approach shot to the right while Hogan landed on the green. Snead chipped to within inches and parred the hole. Hogan just missed his birdie putt and also took par.

HOLE 11 (569 yards par 5) – Snead was straight and long, while Hogan hit into the crowd on the right and had to hit a shot back into the fairway. And his 3rd shot went right again. Snead was on the green in 3 shots only 10 feet from the pin. Hogan needed 4 to get on the green and even then was 40 feet from the hole. He needed 2-putts for a bogey. Snead missed his birdie putt, but picked up another stroke with his par. Snead now led by 3.

HOLE 12 (445 yards par 4) – Both players had good drives. And both were on the green in 2 and within 30 feet from the cup. Both players 2-putted for par.

HOLE 13 (440 yards par 4) – Both hit good drives again. Hogan hitting first put his shot 15 feet from the pin. Snead's shot also landed on the green a little farther away than Hogan's. Again, both 2-putted for par.

HOLE 14 (180 yards par 3) – Fog was an issue again. Hogan hit 30 feet to the left of the hole while Snead hit 20 feet to the left. Both nearly holed their putts and took pars. Snead continued to lead by 3.

HOLE 15 (440 yards par 4) – Snead had another straight drive. But Hogan's drive went left and landed under a tree. His second shot sliced and left him off the green behind a trap. Snead put his approach shot on the green 25 feet from the pin. Hogan pitched to within 5 feet. But Hogan missed the putt for par, while Snead 2-putted for par. Snead opened up a 4 shot lead with just 3 holes to play.

HOLE 16 (145 yards par 3) – Both put their tee shots 30 feet from the pin and 2-putted for par. Snead's lead remained at 4 shots with 2 to play.

HOLE 17 (585 yards par 5) – Both hit down the middle on their tee shots. Both hit good second shots, but Snead was 30 yards closer to the green. Hogan's 3rd shot was 30 feet short of the pin. Snead landed his 3rd shot 20 feet away. Both 2-putted. Now Snead led by 4 going into the final hole.

HOLE 18 (455 yards par 4) – Both hit good drives. Hogan's iron into the green was 15 feet from the pin. Snead hit to 20 feet away. Both men 2-putted for par.

Final Scores

+1 Snead

+5 Hogan

Hogan was not happy with his play telling Curtis it was *"damned bad golf."* And he refused to make any excuses. He told Maxwell Stiles, *"My legs didn't bother me."* But he also said, *"Had I known it was going to go for this long I would have never entered."*

Pete Arthur in The Valley Times, summed it up this way, *"The greatest golf comeback of all time didn't quite hit its peak... A tired Hogan, still recuperating, was beaten by a sharper golfer."*

Sam Snead had the kindest of words for Hogan. He told Arthur that Hogan, *"was terrific. He's the same old Hogan. He scares you to death."*

POSTSCRIPT

The miracle comeback didn't end with a Hollywood finish. But later that year Hollywood took care of that.

20th Century Fox made Ben Hogan one of the only golfers ever to have his life chronicled in a major Hollywood movie with A-list stars.

The movie was called "Follow the Sun," and starred Glenn Ford as Ben Hogan, and Anne Baxter as Hogan's wife Valerie. Baxter was an academy award winning actress prior to the making of the movie, and Ford was one of the top box office draws at the time.

You can watch the entire movie for free on YouTube at this link:

https://www.youtube.com/watch?v=CaKy9TcPCnA&t

Or just type "Follow the Sun movie" into the YouTube search bar.

In the movie, there are some interesting highlights:

At the 30:20 mark you can see a spectacular view of the 18th hole at the Pebble Beach Golf Links in 1950.

The movie concludes with the playing of the 1950 Los Angeles Open at the Riviera Country Club.

At the 1:19:45 mark you can see Glenn Ford, portraying Hogan, wearing the wrap around his legs that he needed to walk a golf course.

At the 1:20:20 mark you can see 2 of the biggest golf stars of the 1950s, Cary Middlecoff and Jimmy Demaret, playing themselves teeing off at the 1st hole of the Riviera Country Club for the Los Angeles Open.

Sam Snead also plays himself, and has several appearances in the movie. You see Snead in the locker room at 1:18:15.

Then Snead sinks the putt on 18 to tie Hogan and force the playoff at the 1:27:40 mark.

And at 1:28:10, Snead sinks a putt to win the 1950 Los Angeles Open. Snead then shakes hands with actor Glenn Ford, playing the part of Ben Hogan.

Ben Hogan's comeback was certainly incredible. But he wasn't done playing championship golf. In the next chapter we'll continue following Hogan as he plays the 1950 U.S. Open.

CHAPTER TWO

The Miracle at Merion

THE 1950 U.S. OPEN

INTRODUCTION from The Sports Time Traveler

Following his unexpected comeback at the 1950 Los Angeles Open, Ben Hogan played as planned in the newly named Ben Hogan Open in Phoenix at the end of January. After opening with a spectacular 65, he shot mediocre rounds of 73, 73 and 72 and finished 14 shots behind the winner Jimmy Demaret and 13 shots back of 2nd place Sam Snead.

Hogan then headed home telling reporters he had no future golf plans. Ben and his wife Valerie took the train home to Fort Worth instead of driving as they had the prior year when he suffered the near fatal car accident.

On February 2nd, Jack Murphy, sports columnist for the Fort Worth Star-Telegram spoke with Hogan seeking an update. Ben said to him, *"Why write anything else. It's all been said before. I'm tired of reading about myself, and I know everybody else must be too."* Regarding his future, Hogan told Murphy, *"No plans. I'll stay around here until I have the urge to go somewhere. Haven't decided about anything."*

Murphy finished his article with this, *"So if you see Ben Hogan around town... don't bother to tell him he's lucky to be alive."*

Hogan was spotted around town 3 weeks later. On February 25th, the Star-Telegram reported Hogan had played 18 holes at River Crest Country Club and tied the course record of 64.

On March 4th it was announced that Hogan would play a tournament again in Palm Beach, Florida at the Seminole Pro-Am starting on March 13th. In the first round, Hogan shot just 79. The Palm Beach Post reported that Hogan, *"was off his game all the way and faded on the back nine."*

Hogan improved to 71 and 70 in the final 2 rounds, but finished 13 shots back of the victor, Dr. Cary Middlecoff.

Hogan remained in the Southeast playing in exhibitions and a one-day Pro-Am in South Carolina where he shot a 73. The State newspaper in Columbia, SC reported that Hogan was, *"playing a game of golf that lacked the old Hogan touch."*

In the beginning of April, Hogan went to Augusta to begin practicing for the Masters. Once there he seemed to be back to the old Hogan. On April 3rd, Sterling Slappey, writing for the AP, in an article that appeared in the Columbus, GA Ledger, indicated that Hogan shot practice rounds in 72, 68 and 66 over the past 3 days. Hogan told him, *"I want to win a Masters. I've been here 6 days getting as much practice as I could take without getting too tired for the tournament."*

The next day the Atlanta Constitution reported Hogan had shot a 67. Adding his 4 scores from his practice rounds, Hogan would have had a 273, which would be a Masters record. The record at the time was 279.

When the tournament started on Thursday, April 6th, Hogan could only muster a 73. But in the 2nd round, Hogan came back with a 68 and ended the day in 2nd place 4 shots off the lead. He shot 71 in the 3rd round and that kept him in 2nd. But on Sunday he faded to a 76 and finished 5th, 5 shots shy of Jimmy Demaret. Gene Gregston in the Fort Worth Star-Telegram wrote, *"he was miserably off."*

Gregston then pontificated on Hogan's future, *"The performance of Ben in the Masters produced two trends of thought. One is that Ben will never regain his former mastery because of the severe physical punishment he has undergone. The other is that Ben does not now have the mental force, the ability to concentrate, he once had."*

Valerie, Ben's wife, told Gregston that Ben has no tournaments planned until the Colonial in Fort Worth at the end of May.

But Hogan decided to go to West Virginia in the beginning of May to play in Sam Snead's tournament at The Greenbrier. In the 1st round, Hogan showed up Snead by carding a 64 to Snead's 66. The next day Hogan scored 64 again. Snead playing in the same threesome with Hogan shot a 68 to fall 6 shots back of Hogan. In the 3rd round Hogan kept up his torrid pace with a 65. It was a remarkable 54 holes for Hogan. Hogan had a 7 shot lead on the field and he was 10 strokes ahead of the host, Sam Snead.

The Roanoke Times noted that Hogan's 54 hole total of 193 was tied for the lowest 54 hole score ever recorded in a PGA tournament.

In the final round, Hogan blistered the course once more for a 66 to finish with a 21 under 259 for 72 holes on the par 70 course. That tied the 72 hole professional record set by Byron Nelson in 1945. And it gave Hogan a 10 shot victory over Sam Snead who also scored 66 to finish 2nd. It was Hogan's first victory against competitive pros since returning. And it was impressive.

Charles Lewis of the AP writing in an article appearing in the Roanoke Times indicated, *"Ben was inclined to shrug off his accomplishment... He said he played better golf during the Masters."*

In fact, Hogan was so nonchalant that he failed to recognize the Duke of Windsor, the former King Edward VIII who congratulated Hogan and presented the winner's check to him. Hogan said to the former King, *"Glad to meet you."* The former King replied, *"We've met. Remember two years ago."* A photo of Hogan and the Duke of Windsor appeared in many newspapers including the Buffalo News.

While Hogan didn't think he had done anything special with his record score, newspapermen disagreed. The Arizona Republic called it, *"One of the greatest comeback performances in sports history."* The Daily Mirror in London ran a story with the headline, *"Ben Hogan Equals World Golf Record."*

Back in Texas, Hogan looked sharp in a practice round at Colonial with Jimmy Demaret a few days before the tournament. In the Fort Worth Star-Telegram, Gene Gregston reported, *"Ben's 69 was the lone sub-par round recorded as 14 of the field of 36 tested the course."*

The biggest crowd in the history of the Colonial turned out to see Ben Hogan compete in Texas for the first time in his comeback.

Sam Snead though was determined to outduel Hogan to make up for his embarrassing 10 shot defeat at The Greenbrier. In the first 3 rounds of the Colonial, Snead shot 66, 72 and 66 and took a commanding 5 shot lead. Hogan was 8 shots behind having fired rounds of 71, 73 and 68.

In the final round Snead and Hogan were in the final threesome together. Sam only shot a 73, but it was enough to win the tournament. While Hogan closed with a 70 to finish 5 shots behind Snead in 3rd place. But Hogan was never close to Snead. In fact he had been 8 shots back with just 2 holes to play before Snead bogeyed the 16th and 17th. So each man had won handily on the other's home course.

With the Colonial finished, Ben Hogan took aim at the U.S. Open to be held at Merion Golf Club outside of Philadelphia beginning on Thursday, June 8th.

Now I begin my daily reports from my virtual trip to the U.S. Open in 1950 at Merion.

PRE-TOURNAMENT – Thursday, June 8, 1950

Maury Fitzgerald of the Washington Times Herald reported on the betting odds for the two favorites at this 50th playing of the U.S. Open that is set to begin today.

Odd to win the 1950 U.S. Open

8 to 1 – Sam Snead

9 to 1 – Jimmy Demaret

The 38-year-old Snead has never won the U.S. Open. Fitzgerald wrote that Snead told him, *"Merion is built for him and if he doesn't win this year he might just as well quit."*

Absent from that short list of favorites was Ben Hogan. Hogan is considered a big question mark for the U.S. Open because of the tournament format that requires the golfers to play 36 holes on the final day on Saturday. Fitzgerald noted, *"Even Hogan isn't sure his scarred up legs can stand the grind of the championship's two finishing rounds."*

John Webster of the Philadelphia Inquirer called Hogan, *"the sentimental favorite of nearly everybody... his return to the fairways and the greens already has established himself as the most courageous of athletes."*

Webster went on to predict, *"If the next three days should take a storybook course to see the tight-lipped Texan crowned the champion... his comeback would be the greatest of all-time and the most popular."*

Webster also reported today on his interview with Ben Hogan. Discussing the 36 hole grind ahead on Saturday, Hogan said, *"Yes, I expect that'll really wear me down – if I'm still in there by Saturday... Yes, I'll be tired."*

Webster finished his article with this interesting anecdote, *"Hogan will have many a rooter, including Joe Horgan, an ancient, wrinkled ex-caddy."* Horgan had been the caddy for the 1st U.S. Open winner, Horace Rawlins in 1895 and had also caddied for Gene Sarazen. Horgan was quoted, *"After Ben's wonderful comeback from that accident, I gotta root for him."*

165 golfers will be teeing off today. The first will be Dick Mayer at 8am.

Here are the tee times for the most notable players:

9:36am   Lloyd Mangrum

10:08am   Dr. Cary Middlecoff

11:04am   Gene Sarazen

12:40pm   **Sam Snead**

1:36pm   **Ben Hogan**

2:40pm   **Jimmy Demaret**

1st ROUND – Friday, June 9, 1950

The golf world was shocked this morning to learn that an unknown and unemployed golf pro from Alabama shot a 64 yesterday, the lowest score in the history of the U.S. Open. 26-year-old Lee Mackey Jr. had the round of his life and took a 3 stroke lead going into today's 2nd round. It was the lowest score he ever recorded on any golf course. Even more shocking was the fact that only 6 golfers broke par which is 70 here at Merion.

Mackey is only here because he earned the final spot in the qualifying round in Birmingham 2 weeks ago. His biggest career victory coming into the 1950 U.S. Open is the 1949 Michigan Assistant Pro tournament. In that event he was the only player to break par.

Yesterday, Mackey was 6 under par on the par 70 layout. And he was the only player to take less than 28 putts. He made 7 birdie putts in all, 2 of them over 25 feet on the back 9.

Sam Snead, the pre-tournament favorite, found himself 9 shots behind after round 1. Snead hit 4 balls into sand traps on Thursday and also 3-putted from just 10 feet on the 5th hole in carding a 73.

Ben Hogan and Jimmy Demaret both shot 72s, leaving them 8 shots behind. Hogan had a terrible start shooting a 39 on the front. Ben came back in 33, highlighted by a 45 foot birdie putt at 12. But other than that long putt, it was his putter that did him in on Thursday. Hogan told the AP, *"I must have missed nine putts under 12 feet. I was puttin' like I had both arms broke."*

1st round scores of the leaders and notable others:

LEADERS:

-6	Lee Mackey Jr.
-3	Al Brosch
-2	Skip Alexander & Julius Boros
-1	Harold Williams & Henry Williams

NOTABLE OTHERS:

+1	Cary Middlecoff
+2	Ben Hogan, Jimmy Demaret, Lloyd Mangrum & Gene Sarazen
+3	Sam Snead

2nd ROUND – Saturday, June 10, 1950

Dutch Harrison, a 40-year-old long time player on the circuit, fired a 67 in the 2nd round to take a 1 shot lead at -1 for the tournament going into today's 36 hole finale.

Harrison easily overtook yesterday's leaders. 1st round leader Lee Mackey Jr., followed up his record round of 64 on Thursday with an 81 yesterday. And Al Brosch, who had been in 2nd with a 67 on Thursday, blew up to an 84 yesterday. Brosch missed the cut which was at +9.

Harrison actually got off to a slow start. He was +1 for the day going into the par 3 9th hole. But at that hole he put his tee shot 7 feet from the pin and sank the putt for his 1st birdie. On the back 9 he had exhibited, *"superb iron play,"* according to Lincoln A. Werden in The New York Times, scoring birdies on 10, 13 and 16.

Harrison told the AP, *"I sure shot me some golf yesterday. No three-putts. No long putts... No mishaps. No headaches."*

Pre-tournament favorite Sam Snead had plenty of headaches. He shot a 75 and barely made the cut by a single shot. Werden reported, *"Snead was hitting tee shots off line and the three-putt bugaboo that has so often followed him in these championships was there again at two holes."* Snead goes into the final day trailing the leader by 9 shots.

After the round, Snead told Grantland Rice, *"If I can lead the field in the PGA tournament, and win more than my share of $15,000 tournaments, the Open ought to be easy. But you keep remembering the mistakes you made in the past that cost you an Open title."* Perhaps Snead was thinking about what happened the last time the U.S. Open was played in the Philadelphia area. In 1939, Snead came to the final hole of the U.S. Open at the Philadelphia Country Club needing a par to win. He took triple bogey and finished in 5th.

Jimmy Demaret was even worse than Snead yesterday. He shot a 77 and made the cut right on the number.

Another player had a tough finish that cost him the lead. Julius Boros was at -3 for the tournament with 3 holes to go yesterday. He finished bogey-bogey-bogey. But at even par he goes into today's final rounds just 1 shot off the lead.

Like Sam Snead, Ben Hogan also three-putted 2 holes yesterday. But Hogan managed a 2 under par 34 on the front 9 and then hit a, *"stunning pitch to the tenth green where he had a putt of some twenty inches,"* according to Werden. That birdie aided Hogan on his way to a 35 on the back 9 for an 18 hole score of 69, which was the 3rd best round of the day. That put Hogan at +1 for the tournament and good for a tie for 4th place just 2 shots behind the leader Harrison.

Hogan seemed to be loose and easy going during the round. Fred Byrod of the Philadelphia Inquirer was following Hogan. He reported that on the 8th hole in which Ben drove his ball near a vendor's truck, he said to the gallery, *"Here's where we stop for a soda."*

Now comes the real challenge for Ben. The U.S. Open final day requires 36 holes of play.

2nd round scores of the leaders and other notables:

LEADERS:

-1   **Dutch Harrison**

EVEN   **Julius Boros, Jim Ferrier, Johnny Bulla**

+1   **Ben Hogan**

+2   **Dr. Cary Middlecoff, Bob Toski, H.G. Picard, Skip Alexander, Lloyd Mangrum, Skee Riegel,**

OTHER NOTABLES:

+4   **Gene Sarazen**

+5   **Lee Mackey, Jr. and George Fazio**

+8   **Sam Snead**

+9   **Jimmy Demaret**

FINAL ROUNDS – Sunday, June 11, 1950

The Morning 18 – 3rd Round

Dutch Harrison, the U.S. Open leader, was so late arriving for the morning round that he almost forfeited. This may explain why he lost his lead in the U.S. Open on the 1st of the 36 holes of play when he started out with a double bogey. He ended the front 9 with a 40. That opened the door for several other players.

Lloyd Mangrum who started the day at +2, just 3 shots back, made a big move shooting shot a 1 under 69 in the morning round. That was the lowest score of the day. The 35-year-old Mangrum was a formidable competitor having won the U.S. Open 4 years earlier in 1946. He has also finished in the top 8 at The Masters in each of the past 4 years. Mangrum ended the 3rd round at +1 for the tournament, giving him a 1 shot lead over Harrison who collected himself and shot 33 on the back 9 to reach the lunch break at +2.

Three players finished the 3rd round in a tie for 3rd at +3. Cary Middlecoff shot his 3rd consecutive 71. Johnny Palmer shot a 70 to leap over 7 players in reaching +3. And Ben Hogan shot a 72 to get into the +3 group, just 2 shots off of Mangrum's lead. Hogan encountered a myriad of trouble along the way. He was in the rough 7 times and in the trap 3 others. But he had kept himself squarely in contention. If Hogan was hurting he kept it to himself. There were no outward indications of his condition during the morning round.

Now the big test would come for Hogan. He had not played more than 18 holes in a day since his comeback.

3rd round scores of the leaders and other notables:

LEADERS and their 3rd round score:

+1   **Lloyd Mangrum (69)**

+2   **Dutch Harrison (73)**

+3   **Ben Hogan (72), Dr. Cary Middlecoff (71) & Johnny Palmer (70)**

+4   **Jim Ferrier (74)**

+6   **Henry Ransom (73)**

+7   **Julius Boros (77), Bill Nary (74) & George Fazio (72)**

OTHER NOTABLES:

+10   **Lee Mackey, Jr. (75)**

+10   **Sam Snead (72)**

+10   **Jimmy Demaret (71)**

+16   **Gene Sarazen (82)**

The Afternoon 18 – 4th Round

The new leader, Lloyd Mangrum, started the 4th round similar to how Dutch Harrison handled his lead in the 3rd round. He bogeyed the first 2 holes. On the 3rd hole, he had a birdie opportunity on what Bob Drum of the Pittsburgh Press called, *"an impossible downhill putt."* Somehow Mangrum holed the putt. But that didn't save his slide from the top. Lloyd bogeyed the next 4 consecutive holes. He finally righted his ship, getting his 1st par of the afternoon on the short par 4 8th, and he also parred the par 3 9th. But Mangrum had gone out in 41 and was now +6 for the tournament.

Yet Mangrum wasn't the only one in meltdown mode.

Dutch Harrison double bogeyed the 1st hole for the 2nd time in the same day. He shot a 41 on the front 9, that put him +7 at the turn.

Johnny Palmer, who had shot his way into the 3rd place group in the 3rd round, also shot a 41 on the front 9, sending him to +8.

Jim Ferrier, who had reached +4 after 3 rounds, shot 40 on the opening 9, also putting him at +8.

George Fazio who started the round 6 shots back at +7, got wind of the golfers losing strokes around him. He told Fred Byrod after the round, *"I got the idea maybe I had a chance and I began to grind."* He tried to make a 7-footer at the 7th, and hit it too aggressively. *"It was downhill and the ball slipped a couple of feet past."* He 3-putted, and that seemed to end his hopes. He had a 37 on the front 9, sending him to +8.

Playing behind everyone else were Ben Hogan and Cary Middlecoff, the defending champion. Newspaper reports indicate they were an hour behind Mangrum and 2 hours behind Fazio.

Middlecoff, who started the round at +3, was playing with Hogan. After 3 holes, he was still dead even with Hogan, as both men were now at +4 for the tournament. Then the pair reached the beastly 595 yard par 5 4th hole. Middlecoff hit a 300 yard drive and he decided to go for the green. Walter Steward of the Memphis Commercial Appeal wrote, *"A full-fleshed fairway wood might carry the green. Perhaps he remembered Gene Sarazen's double- eagle at the Masters* (in 1935) *... He moved savagely into the ball – saw it burn the crest of the fairway grass – rise too slowly and slam sickeningly into the brow of the bunker... That was the mistake which jolted concentration from its delicate pivot and sent him faltering."*

The defending champion bogeyed that 5th and double bogeyed the 6th. He ended the front 9 with a 39 to put him at +6, tied with Mangrum.

Ben Hogan started the final round well. He made par on the 1st and 2nd holes. He bogeyed the 3rd, but made pars on all the remaining holes on the front 9 for a 37. When he made the turn, Ben Hogan, with scarred and damaged legs, less than 6 months after playing his first round of golf in his comeback, was in the lead of the United States Open by 2 shots.

One more player, who was not among the leaders going into the final round was Joe Kirkwood, Jr. of Australia. Kirkwood shot a superb 2 under 34 on the front 9, and with all the others moving back, suddenly Kirkwood was in the mix at +7. Two years earlier, Kirkwood had the distinction of being half of the first father-son duo ever to make the cut at the U.S. Open. Kirkwood was also a grade B movie star, having been selected in 1946 to star in the Joe Palooka, Champ series of films about a boxer. Kirkwood starred in 7 of these films prior to 1950 and there are plans for 2 more this year.

LEADERS after Hogan and Middlecoff were through 9 holes in the 4th round

NOTE: This is approximated since no one can be certain where each player was located on the course. I have made estimates based on the hole-by-hole scores published in various newspapers and also Grantland Rice's estimates of the scoring when Hogan had 9 holes remaining. Rice's syndicated article appeared in the Miami News.

+4   **Ben Hogan**

+6   **Lloyd Mangrum and Dr. Cary Middlecoff**

+7   **George Fazio, Henry Ransom, Dutch Harrison and Joe Kirkwood, Jr.**

The Final 9 Holes

After the opening 9 holes in the morning, on which Fazio shot a 40, he had been 9 shots behind Mangrum and appeared completely out of contention. But then on the back 9, The Washington Evening Star wrote that he, *"fired pin-splitting iron shots on the long par four 14th, 15th and 16th holes and bang-bang-bang his birdie putts of 15, 7 and 16 feet found the cup."* This propelled Fazio to a 2 under 32 on the back 9 of the morning round. Yet he was still 6 shots back of Mangrum. But then his 37 on the front 9 of the final round put him just 2 behind Mangrum, and 4 behind Hogan.

Fazio was suddenly in contention and playing ahead of the leaders he had a chance to post a score in the clubhouse. On the 10th, 11th and 12th holes he was not able to take advantage of birdie opportunities. But on the short par 3 13th hole his tee shot landed 4 feet from the hole and he made the birdie putt. Fazio was now just 3 behind Hogan.

Fazio, who grew up in the Philadelphia area, started to attract a larger gallery now. The Washington Evening Star wrote, *"He picked up a few hundred well wishers."* They saw him bogey 14, but his 2nd shot on the par 4 15th stopped just 9 feet from the hole and he made the putt for another birdie. Fazio was still only 3 shots behind Hogan. He parred in from there for a brilliant 70. Fazio had played the final 27 holes in 2 under par!

George Fazio, who had been 9 shots off the lead in the morning, was now the leader in the clubhouse at +7 for the tournament. Fazio, has won just 2 PGA tournaments previously, and has never won a major. His highest finish to date was a 5th place at the 1948 PGA Championship.

Dutch Harrison, who had ballooned to a 41 on the front 9, came back with a 35 on the back 9 to finish the Open at +8. Fazio was still the leader in the clubhouse.

Joe Kirkwood was having a fabulous day. After his 2 under 34 on the front 9 had put him just 3 strokes behind Hogan, he birdied the 10th and parred 11, 12 and 13. He came to 14th tee just 2 shots off the lead. But then he 3-putted on 3 consecutive holes and finished at +9 for the tournament. Fazio remained the leader in the clubhouse.

Next in was Lloyd Mangrum. He was an hour ahead of Hogan on the course. After his disastrous first 7 holes of the round, he shot par on the next 7 holes and came to the 15th tee at +6 for the tournament. At this point he was a shot ahead of Fazio and 2 shots behind Hogan. And then he ran into trouble. Fred Byrod wrote, *"He drove into heavy rough and failed to clear a gaping trap in his path."* Mangrum made bogey at 15 to go 3 back of Hogan and into a tie with Fazio for 2nd. Mangrum then parred 16 and 17. On 18 he was in the sand in 2. Grantland Rice reported that he, *"hit a spectacular shot from a deep bunker to get his 4."*

Mangrum had finished the Open at +7. George Fazio and Lloyd Mangrum were now tied for the clubhouse lead.

Cary Middlecoff was playing with Hogan and at the turn he was just 2 shots behind, still very much in the tournament. On the short par 4 10th hole, Middlecoff hit his tee shot in the trap on the right. On his 2nd shot he couldn't get the ball out of the trap. He took a double bogey to fall 4 shots back of Hogan.

Ben Hogan had reached the 10th hole with a 2 shot lead over Middlecoff and Mangrum. Those three men had won the 1946 U.S. Open (Mangrum), the 1948 U.S. Open (Hogan) and the 1949 U.S. Open (Middlecoff). It was set up to be a classic finish.

Hogan took pars at 10 and 11 to remain at +4 for the tournament. He was now about to begin his 30th hole of the day. No one, including Hogan himself, knew how his legs could hold up in this golf marathon that is the final day of a U.S. Open.

It is at this point that Gayle Talbot of the AP described Hogan's condition, *"The first inkling that the bantam, idol of the huge gallery, was facing serious trouble came at the 12th hole... after hitting his tee shot he was seen to stagger and almost fall."* Hogan was seen grimacing in pain. Thousands of fans saw him limping in the fairway.

Charles Einstein, writing in the Miami Herald for INS, confirmed Talbot's observation from the 12th tee. *"The largest gallery in the history of the Open saw him grab his right knee in pain as a sudden cramp seized his leg when he drove off on the 12th tee of his final round... He limped up the 12th fairway. When he got to the green, he could not bend down to mark his ball."*

In an extraordinary show of sportsmanship that I have never heard before in 50+ years of following professional golf, Dr. Cary Middlecoff marked Ben's ball on the 12th green. Some reports indicated that Middlecoff marked Hogan's balls on the greens for the rest of the round.

Hogan was hurting, although he would not admit it. But Talbot observed that for the remainder of the round, *"he never again stooped to pick up his ball on the green."*

NOTE: The statement is not actually not true. In a video link that I provide later is evidence of Hogan picking his ball up after holing a putt late in the round. Perhaps he had several holes where he couldn't bend

down and then started to feel better. The video is clear that late in the round he could bend down without issue. And even Einstein in his article noted that Hogan was able to retrieve a ball from the cup late in the round.

At this time, after Hogan had teed off on 12, both Mangrum and Fazio were in the clubhouse and Hogan was 3 up on both of them.

Hogan's 2nd shot on 12 went over the green, but as reported by Lincoln Werden in the New York Times, the ball hit a spectator and stopped close enough to the green that Hogan was able to putt the ball. Werden noted that if not for the spectator the ball could possibly have traveled out of bounds. But Hogan still lost a stroke on the 12th green when he 3-putted. His lead was now down to 2 strokes.

LEADERS after Hogan completed the 12th hole of the final round

Note this assumes that Mangrum, Fazio and Harrison had all finished their rounds

+5   **Ben Hogan**

+7   **Lloyd Mangrum and George Fazio**

+8   **Dr. Cary Middlecoff and Dutch Harrison**

Fred Byron commented that at this point Hogan was, *"obviously dead tired and limping."* Yet Bantam Ben managed to par the next hole as did Middlecoff. Now as they got to the 14th tee, all the attention on the golf course focused on the twosome of Hogan and Middlecoff. Grantland Rice reported, *"The tremendous gallery braving the blazing heat shut off Hogan and Middlecoff from all outside connection."*

Hogan only needed to play the last 5 holes in +1 to win the tournament. But Rice noted, *"Those five holes are murderous."*

Ben and Cary got their pars at 15. Now Hogan needed to just finish +1 on the last 4 holes to win. While Middlecoff was still 3 shots behind.

But Hogan lost that 1 shot cushion on 15 when he again 3-putted. Now Hogan needed to par in to win. Middlecoff also bogeyed 15 to remain 3 shots behind Ben with 3 holes remaining.

On 16, Hogan again hit a spectator on his approach shot. Fred Byrod indicated that the ball stopped in the rough near the green, but had the ball not hit the spectator it would have been further away. Hogan chipped up close for an easy par.

Middlecoff was not as lucky on 16. His 2nd shot landed against a piece of granite on what is known as the "quarry hole." He ended up taking another double bogey and that dropped Dr. Middlecoff completely out of the picture. Gayle Talbot, of the AP, wrote that Cary, *"found the strain of trying to match shots with Hogan and escaping being trampled by the whooping gallery a little too much."* Cary ended up shooting a 40 on the back 9 and finished at +12 for the tournament.

Now there were 2 holes remaining and Hogan needed to par both to win.

On the long 250 yard par 3 17th hole, Hogan hit his ball into the trap and took another bogey. Ben Hogan had used up his entire advantage.

He now needed a birdie on the 465 yard par 4 18th hole to win and a par to tie Mangrum and Fazio and force a playoff. Rice indicated that Hogan had to drive into the wind, making the hole play even longer. His drive landed perfectly in the middle of the fairway.

On his 2nd shot, it was so far to the green, at least 200 yards on a downhill lie, that Hogan required a 1-iron.

As he struck the ball and assumed his finishing pose, professional photographer Hy Peskin snapped what is perhaps the most famous picture ever taken in golf.

You can see the picture at this link, or type in the words below in a search engine.

Link to the iconic Hogan picture at Merion

Hogan's 1-iron landed on the green 40 feet from the cup.

He now had a putt to win the U.S. Open.

Grantland Rice described the scene on the 18th green, *"The big 18th green at Merion was surrounded by the biggest gallery crowd of all-time."* He wasn't exaggerating. Gayle Talbot, writing for the AP, also indicated that the crowd was now, *"The largest ever to witness a day's play in golf's blue ribbon classic – estimated at over 12,500."*

Rice then described Hogan's putt to win, *"In place of playing for safety, he went boldly for the cup, slipped by at least 5 feet as a stricken groan slipped from the gallery."*

Hogan had missed the putt, and now he had a tough one coming back. He had missed from a shorter distance back at 15. This one he had to make to tie Mangrum and Fazio and get into the playoff. He made it. And the crowd roared.

You can watch the putt at the link below or you can find it on YouTube by searching on "Ben Hogan 72nd green 1950 US Open. Merion."

https://www.youtube.com/watch?v=9zB-ML_36BI

Ben Hogan had finished in a tie with Lloyd Mangrum and George Fazio at +7. There would be an 18 hole playoff the next day.

After the grueling 36 holes of play, John McCafferty of the International News Service interviewed Hogan. He said, *"I have to get me a new putter."* Hogan knew that his poor putting had cost him a victory. He then proactively told McCafferty, *"In case you're interested, I feel fine."* Hogan was answering the question that was on everyone's mind although probably no one believed him.

Regarding the playoff that is scheduled for 2pm today, Guy Butler in the Miami News wrote, *"If little Ben wins it in this playoff then truly when we speak of courage in sports we cannot ever mention anybody's again in the same breath with the tiny Texan's. His brave performance, after most people, including himself, feared he'd never play championship golf again, leaves all other comebacks so far in the background it's no contest."*

4th round scores of the leaders and other notables:

+7   **Ben Hogan, Lloyd Mangrum and George Fazio**

+8   **Dutch Harrison**

+9   **Joe Kirkwood, Jr., Jim Ferrier, Henry Ransom**

Other Notable Players:

+12   **Dr. Cary Middlecoff**

+14   **Sam Snead**

+16   **Jimmy Demaret**

+22   **Gene Sarazen**

18-HOLE PLAYOFF – Monday, June 12, 1950

"I feel fine," declared Ben Hogan before the playoff began. Lincoln Werden heard Hogan say it in an attempt by Ben to ward off any suggestion of an excuse that his legs might be bothering him. Werden wrote, *"He reiterated this statement as he sat in the locker room before starting out."*

HOLE 1 (360 yards par 4) - Mangrum and Hogan made par, but Fazio took a bogey.

HOLE 2 (555 yards par 5) – Mangrum hit his approach shot to just 3 feet and made the putt for a birdie. Fazio had a birdie putt from 20 feet and holed it. Hogan missed the fairway and hit his 2nd shot into the rough. He got on the green in 3 and 2-putted for par.

HOLE 3 (195 yards par 3) – Mangrum missed the green left, chipped up and 2-putted for a bogey, while Fazio and Hogan parred.

Playoff scores after 3 holes

EVEN   George Fazio, Ben Hogan and Lloyd Mangrum

HOLE 4 (595 yards par 5) – All 3 men took par, but Fazio had to scramble

HOLE 5 (425 yards par 4) – All 3 men again took par with Fazio again scrambling with a par saving putt.

HOLE 6 (435 yards par 4) – Hogan and Mangrum took par. Fazio's struggles caught up with him. His 2nd shot went over the green into a trap and this time he couldn't save par.

Playoff scores after 6 holes

EVEN   Ben Hogan and Lloyd Mangrum
+1   George Fazio

HOLE 7 (360 yards par 4) – George Fazio drove his ball out of bounds and Lloyd Mangrum drove into the rough. Hogan was in the fairway and put his 2nd shot 4 feet from the pin and made the birdie putt. Mangrum managed to save par. But Fazio bogeyed his 2nd consecutive hole.

HOLE 8 (367 yards par 4) – Hogan drove into a trap and took a bogey while Mangrum had a routine par. Fazio made a 9-foot birdie putt to pull back to even par for the day. The 37-year-old Fazio, a Philadelphia area native, who has never won a major, was now back within 1 stroke of the two legends, Lloyd Mangrum and Ben Hogan, with 10 holes remaining.

HOLE 9 (185 yards par 3) – All 3 men took par, but yet again, Fazio had to do it by scrambling, this time with a sand save. Fazio had taken just 13 putts on the front 9 to 16 by Mangrum and 17 by Hogan.

Playoff scores after 9 holes

EVEN   Ben Hogan and Lloyd Mangrum
+1   George Fazio

HOLE 10 (335 yards par 4) – Mangrum's drive landed in a trap and he bogeyed the hole. Hogan and Fazio made par. This resulted in Hogan moving into the lead by a stroke over Mangrum and Fazio.

HOLE 11 (378 yards par 4) – Mangrum got back to even with Hogan when he hit his approach shot to 5 feet and sank the birdie putt. Hogan and Fazio had routine pars.

HOLE 12 (400 yards par 4) – Mangrum's 5-iron approach shot sailed out of bounds and completely off the premises onto Ardmore avenue. He took a bogey. Again, Hogan and Fazio had 2-putt pars. The playoff so far had been a thriller with the 3 players separated by a single stroke.

Playoff scores after 12 holes

EVEN   Ben Hogan
+1   Lloyd Mangrum & George Fazio

HOLE 13 (133 yards par 3) – On the short par 3, each player was on the green and 2-putted. With 5 holes to play, Hogan was still ahead of both Mangrum and Fazio by a single stroke.

HOLE 14 (443 yards par 4) – Now the players entered the final 5 arduous holes. The first to crack was Mangrum. He hit his 2nd shot into the trap and 2-putted for a bogey. Fazio was on the green in regulation, but 3-putted for a bogey. Hogan got par and increased his lead to 2 shots over Mangrum and Fazio.

HOLE 15 (395 yards par 4) – Mangrum drove his ball almost, but not quite out-of-bounds. But he hit a magnificent recovery shot to 12 feet from the hole. And he sank the putt for a birdie. Fazio again reached the green in 2 and 3-putted for bogey.

Playoff scores after 15 holes

EVEN   Ben Hogan

+1   Lloyd Mangrum

+3   George Fazio

HOLE 16 (445 yards par 4) – Hogan and Fazio hit their drives in the fairway. Mangrum's tee shot landed in a cabbage patch on the right side. The 16th at Merion is known as the Quarry hole because a limestone quarry existed here before the golf course was built. The quarry guards the left side of the green with what now are a series of bunkers. Mangrum realized he could not fly the green and risk landing in the quarry so he hit a safe shot back into the fairway. He then hit a pitch shot to 15 feet from the pin. He had a putt for par.

Fazio had missed the green to the left, chipped on and was the furthest away from the hole. Hogan was on in 2 and was just 6 feet from the hole. Mangrum marked his ball while Fazio putt.

After Fazio missed his long putt, Mangrum was next up. And here's where the big controversy of the day took place. After he replaced his ball and lined up his putt, Mangrum picked up his ball, without marking it. He then blew on it and put it back down according to Lincoln Werden in the New York Times. The story was confirmed by both Grantland Rice in his syndicated column and Fred Byrod in the Philadelphia Inquirer. Later Mangrum said there was a bug crawling on the ball and he blew it off.

Mangrum then studied hit putt. Gayle Talbot of the AP wrote, *"He curled the long putt into the hole and it looked like a lifesaver."* Mangrum had saved his par. And when Hogan missed his birdie putt, Mangrum had escaped the quarry hole still just 1 shot off the lead as the trio went to the 17th tee.

But before they reached the 17th tee, Isaac Grainger of the USGA informed Mangrum that he had incurred a 2-stroke penalty. Simply put, you are not allowed to lift a ball that is in play and clean anything off of it. Mangrum had broken both rules.

Instead of being 1 stroke back of Hogan with 2 holes to play, Mangrum was now 3 strokes back.

NOTE from The Sports Time Traveler

It may be hard to understand back in the present time how a golfer of Mangrum's stature could have made such a mistake. But back in 1950, many PGA tournaments were in fact allowing players to touch a ball in play. In his syndicated column that appeared today in the Boston Globe, Grantland Rice, perhaps the foremost authority on golf within the sports writing profession, a man who is regarded as the singular newspaperman who popularized golf as a sport of interest back in the 1920s, had this comment, *"The trouble is that amateur tournaments and PGA tournaments have been steadily violating one of the main principles of golf – that the ball must not be touched or cleaned... This rule has been violated steadily, year after year... It was not so much Mangrum's fault as the disintegration of the rules of a great game."*
Now back to 1950.

Playoff scores after 16 holes

EVEN   Ben Hogan
+3   Lloyd Mangrum
+4   George Fazio

HOLE 17 (230 yards par 3) – Hogan teed off first as Mangrum had lost the honor. Ben's shot on the long par 3 landed on the lower level of the putting surface about 50 feet from the hole. The fact that Ben had shot first was the crowd's first clue that something was amiss. It took several minutes for the crowd to learn about Mangrum's 2 stroke penalty on 16.

Next up, Fazio, and finally Mangrum hitting last, both reached the lower level of the putting surface on their tee shots.

Hogan was away and putted first. Lincoln Werden described the action, *"He sighted carefully and hit it well, the ball running up and over a ridge and on into the cup for deuce."* It was a sensational birdie on the long par 3. When Fazio and Mangrum parred the hole it put Hogan up by 4 shots over Mangrum and 5 over Fazio. The tournament was effectively over. It also put to rest any notion that Hogan had benefited from Mangrum's mistake.

Playoff scores after 17 holes

-1	**Ben Hogan**
+3	**Lloyd Mangrum**
+4	**George Fazio**

HOLE 18 (458 yard par 4) – All 3 players approach shots landed on the green, but none of them could hold the green. They all needed to chip. Fazio needed 2 putts and settled for a bogey to give him +5 score of 75 in the playoff. Mangrum made his putt for par to finish +3 with a 73. Then Hogan took his putt. Werden wrote, *"Hogan's putt curled in for the championship. There was a mad rush and several persons were knocked down in the melee. A cordon of police saved Hogan from the happy jam of well-wishers."*

It has to be one of the greatest triumphs in the history of golf. And you can see it on the video at the link below or go to YouTube and type into the search "1950 U.S. Open Highlights."

https://www.youtube.com/watch?v=cM42eqW21ys

Sportswriters all seemed to compete with each other for the most grandiose openings to their stories today. They could unleash all the hyperbole they had ever considered using in the past but held back because they didn't want to oversell the drama. This time, anything they could come up with was deserving. For Hogan had been on the brink of death a year earlier, and now he was the National Open champion. And for each of them it was a rarity, an opportunity to have a story at the top of the front page of the newspaper.

Lincoln Werden wrote this on the front page of the New York Times, *"Hogan completed one of the outstanding feats in the annals of sports to win the trophy."*

Fred Byrod started his page 1 article in the Philadelphia Inquirer, *"Ben Hogan trudged the last weary lap in his march back from death's door to supremacy in professional golf when he won the 50th National Open Championship."*

Walter Stewart was given an opportunity for a front page first column article in the Memphis Commercial Appeal. He started it with this, *"Ben Hogan completed a comeback as great as any the world of sports has ever known."*

The Newark Star-Ledger ran a UPI article across the entire top of page 1. The banner headline read, *"A Story to Cheer the Heart: Ben Hogan Comes Back."* The article began, *"Ben Hogan marched on scarred and aching legs yesterday to a National Open championship triumph almost too amazing to be believed."*

And Gayle Talbot's AP story took the front page first column of the Greensboro News and Record and included this line, *"Hogan climaxed gloriously the most remarkable comeback in the history of sports."*

FINAL Playoff Scores

-1   69   **Ben Hogan**

+3   73   **Lloyd Mangrum**

+5   75   **George Fazio**

After they praised Hogan in the most superlative terms, sportswriters also were quick to note that the Mangrum 2-shot penalty did not affect the outcome of the tournament. Hogan had won by a decisive 4 strokes. And even if Mangrum had not incurred the penalty, he still would have lost by 2 strokes.

Hogan's incredible 50 foot putt on 17 had earned him the victory, not the Mangrum penalty.

Grantland Rice wrote, *"The ruling at Merion costing Mangrum two strokes didn't affect the final result or cost Mangrum a dime."* Rice went on to share the belief that the Mangrum penalty will have a beneficial impact on golf in general, *"From now on both amateurs and pros will begin looking over rule books. I don't think you'll find them picking up their balls, cleaning them and placing them in the general neighborhood of where they belonged."*

Rice also speculated that after the penalty on 16, Hogan had an even greater desire to make the long birdie putt at 17 to make his victory a decisive one.

Mangrum was asked by Fred Byrod if he gave up after he was assessed the penalty. He said, *"I did after Ben got that putt on 17."*

Mangrum also explained to Byrod what happened on the 16th green, *"I had the idea that you could get anything off like a bug or a snake."* Lloyd said he was unaware he was violating a rule.

In the clubhouse, Hogan told reporters that out of all the tournaments and majors he had won before, *"I got my biggest kick out of winning this one."* He also told them he planned to slow down on his tournament schedule and only play in the big ones. And he indicated he would never play 36 holes in one day again. When asked about next year's U.S. Open Hogan replied, *"We'll see about that when the time comes."*

Hogan was also asked by Fred Byrod how come his putting was so much better than the prior rounds. Hogan gave an insightful answer about his thinking process. Now anytime Ben Hogan offers you this type of answer you have to take note. He said, *"I had been taking the club back with my right hand. And yesterday I started taking it back with my left hand. It kept my stroke smoother."* I'm definitely going to try that.

CHAPTER THREE

The Biggest Fight of My Life

BOXER JOE LOUIS TAKES ON THE PGA AT THE 1952 SAN DIEGO OPEN

INTRODUCTION from The Sports Time Traveler

I have now jumped ahead to January, 1952 in Southern California.

I wanted to follow a story that was brewing around the San Diego Open, a PGA tournament scheduled to begin on Thursday, January 17th. Joe Louis, the legendary boxer, had received a sponsor's exemption to play in the PGA tournament, but PGA rules in 1952 do not allow NON-white players.

BACKGROUND:

The first African-American golfer to play in a PGA sponsored tournament was Robert "Pat" Ball who played in the St. Paul Open in Minnesota from July 13 – 15, 1934. On July 16, 1934, The Minneapolis Tribune reported that Ball was, *"The only Negro professional in the United States to play in open competition."*

Ball shot an 80 in the 1st round. But in the 2nd round he shot a 72, the 5th lowest score of the day and he made the cut in the tournament. His 2nd round score beat the reigning U.S. Open champion, Olin Dutra and the legendary Walter Hagen, each of whom scored 73 in the 2nd round.

But apparently Ball did NOT have PGA approval to play in the St. Paul Open. It is quite possible that the tournament organizers in St. Paul did not confer with the PGA about Ball's entry prior to the tournament.

It seems that once the word got out that an African-American golfer had played in the tournament, the PGA took action to prevent NON-white players from competing in the future. In 2023, notable golf historian Robert Trenham reported on his website trenhamgolfhistory.org that, *"At its national meeting in November 1934, the PGA added a 'Caucasians Only' clause to its constitution, concerning membership in its association."*

Trenham also states, *"Robert "Pat" Ball, competing in the 1934 St. Paul Open, may be the reason why the PGA added the Caucasian Only clause to its constitution."*

While Robert "Pat" Ball was the first African-American to play in a PGA tournament, it sadly can't be marked as the breaking of the color barrier in golf due to the ensuing prohibition on NON-white players.

In January, 1952, it seems that Robert "Pat" Ball's appearance in the 1934 St. Paul Open was not known about or had been long forgotten as there was no mention of it any newspaper articles.

And now a little more background on the main subject of this chapter.

Background on Joe Louis

Joe Louis was the heavyweight boxing champion of the world from 1937 to 1949. He successfully defended his title a record 25 times. Here in the present time that remains the record for all weight classes.

And for those of you in the present who don't know too much about Joe Louis, ESPN ranked him as the #11 greatest athlete of the entire 20th century.

You can see the list via a Google search on the phrase below or clicking on the link if you're on a Kindle.

ESPN's Greatest Athletes of the 20th Century

Louis had initially retired from boxing as the champion in 1949, but came back to fight in 1950 and 1951 in high profile matches against Ezzard Charles and Rocky Marciano. He was beaten badly in both bouts. Marciano actually knocked Louis completely out of the ring in their October 26, 1951 fight. This led Louis to retire for good.

Joe Louis was also an outstanding golfer, having taken up the game in the mid-1930s. By 1941, Louis had created his own tournament, The Joe Louis Open in Detroit. It was a way for top African-American golfers to compete and earn money. Louis even put up the $1,000 purse himself and paid for golfers' travel expenses. At that time only white golfers were eligible to play in PGA sponsored tournaments.

With Joe Louis's boxing career over he had more time to focus on golf as the 1952 season began in California.

Now I will share with you the events of the past several weeks, leading up to and including the 1952 San Diego Open.

Tuesday, December 11, 1951

Sports columnist Maxwell Stiles of the Los Angeles Mirror has been on a mission to get the PGA to allow NON-white players in PGA sponsored events.

In today's paper he exposed the unspoken reason why the upcoming Los Angeles Open will not be a PGA sponsored event this year. Stiles wrote, *"A former U.S. Open champion and PGA member said he thought the reason the PGA refused to sign the contract is that they want the right to bar Negro players from playing in the L.A. Open."*

The L.A. Open for several years has allowed African-American players, most notably Ted Rhodes, who finished in a tie last year with the great Jimmy Demaret.

By not signing the contract with the PGA, the Los Angeles Open could continue to allow NON-white players.

Thursday, December 13, 1951

In his column today Stiles discussed the issue with golfing legend Gene Sarazen who told him, *"There should be no racial discrimination in tournament golf."*

Friday, December 14, 1951

The next day Stiles shared his conversation with 1951 PGA leading money winner Lloyd Mangrum who told him he, *"has been foremost in the battle for recognition of Ted Rhodes, Bill Spiller and a few other well qualified players of the Negro race."*

Tuesday, January 1, 1952

The Los Angeles Open is taking place this year once again with NO PGA sponsorship of the event. This means that African-American players may participate.

The Los Angeles Times reported that Joe Louis will be among the 368 golfers playing in the qualifying rounds for the Los Angeles Open that will take place at several courses around the area tomorrow. There will be 64 spots for local qualifiers with the remainder of the spots filled by players that are on the PGA exempt list.

Thursday, January 3, 1952

Joe Louis played in the 36 hole qualifier yesterday. The qualifier was held at 8 different courses. The top 8 at each course qualified to play in the Los Angeles Open.

In the morning round, Louis shot a 73 putting him among the leaders at his qualifying course. But in the afternoon round he could only manage a 79. His 36 hole score of 152 put him 3 shots over the qualifying cut off of 149 at the Western Avenue course location. A top African-American golfer, Bill Spiller, also shot 152 and missed the qualifying.

But 2 African-American players did qualify at Western Avenue. Charlie Sifford shot a 141, and Eural Clark shot 145.

Ted Rhodes was exempt from the qualifying, perhaps based on his finish in the tournament last year. Rhodes will tee it up at 9:56am on Friday at Riviera Country Club.

Friday, January 4, 1952

The Los Angeles Daily News announced that Horton Smith, winner of the 1st Masters tournament, is now the president of the PGA, having taken over leadership at the start of the year. Smith will also be playing in the Los Angeles Open.

Sunday, January 6, 1952

After 2 days of play in the Los Angeles Open, Ted Rhodes not only made the cut, he was just 7 shots off the lead, and tied with 1951 leading money winner, Lloyd Mangrum, and a shot ahead of Jimmy Demaret – 3 time winner of The Masters.

Monday January 7, 1952

Sports columnist Maxwell Stiles wrote an article in the Los Angeles Mirror today in which he shared his personal efforts to get the newly elected PGA president, Horton Smith, to take actions to end the ban on African-American golfers in PGA sponsored tournaments. The tone of the article indicates that Stiles is determined to see the PGA integrate as other major American sports have already.

Stiles wrote that Horton, *"assured this writer under close questioning that he himself will bring before the next national meeting of the PGA a constitutional amendment, that if passed, would remove the PGA ban against the Negro and pass the decision on to the host club."*

Tuesday, January 8, 1952

Ted Rhodes finished the Los Angeles Open tied for 15th and 2 shots ahead of Lloyd Mangrum, the leading money winner in 1951.

Sunday, January 13, 1952

The Long Beach Independent, on the bottom of page 23, had a story on the upcoming San Diego Open that included this sentence, *"Former heavyweight boxing champion Joe Louis will be one of 10 amateurs exempt from qualifying."*

Unlike the Los Angeles Open of the prior week, the San Diego Open was going to be a PGA sponsored event.

The stage was set for Joe Louis to challenge the ban against NON-white players.

Monday, January 14, 1952

An AP article in the Los Angeles Times today announced that in addition to boxing legend Joe Louis, two African-American professional golfers, Bill Spiller and Eural Clark, had also secured sponsor's exemptions into the San Diego Open which begins on Thursday, January 17th.

The article also reported that when Joe Louis arrived in San Diego yesterday, he was informed, *"the PGA rule* (against NON-white players) *would bar him."*

Joe Louis, Bill Spiller and Eural Clark would NOT be allowed to play.

In the article, Joe Louis said he was going to bring the issue of the ban against NON-white players, *"into the open."*

Louis was livid. The Times wrote, *"He declared it was the first time in sports he had encountered racial discrimination."*

Tuesday, January 15

The Pasadena Independent ran a UP article in which Louis declared his battle with the PGA was going to be the, *"biggest fight of my life."* That quote was in newspapers across the country.

Louis specifically had harsh words for new PGA president Horton Smith.

Smith who was still at Pebble Beach, site of the recently completed Bing Crosby national tournament, was reached for comment by the UP. He said, *"I do not know the exact situation. We can make no ruling on anyone who wants to play in the tournament until I've talked with the other six members of the PGA Tournament Committee."*

Louis did have the local tournament sponsors on his side. The Los Angeles Evening Citizen News ran a story titled, *"San Diego Open Fights PGA Ban of Joe Louis."*

One of the sponsors released a statement saying, *"We are most anxious that Joe, one of America's true sportsmen, play in our event."*

And Anderson Borthwick, chairman of the San Diego Open, called the situation an *"unfortunate mistake,"* and indicated a ruling by the PGA would be made in the next few days.

But the *"mistake"* comment seemed to be at odds with a report in the Los Angeles Daily News this morning that the PGA was considering pulling out as a sponsor of the San Diego Open. If the PGA pulled out, then the San Diego Open could proceed as planned with Louis, Spiller and Clark playing, similar to how the Los Angeles Open got around the ban. But losing PGA sponsorship also means losing significant funding for the tournament.

Meanwhile the tournament operators had decided to allow Bill Spiller and Eural Clark to play in the qualifying rounds yesterday, *"subject to official PGA acceptance."* Clark did not qualify, but Bill Spiller did. Louis' sponsor exemption did not require him to qualify for the tournament.

The matter was not yet settled, and that led The Los Angeles Mirror to run a banner headline across the entire top of the sports section that read, *"ACTION DUE ON LOUIS CASE."*

And sports columnist Bob Panella in the Los Angeles Evening Citizens News wrote a long article concluding that since all other sports have lifted their NON-white bans, *"There's no reason whatsoever that golf alone should make a mockery of fair play."*

Wednesday, January 16

Southern California residents opened their newspapers this morning to a bevy of headlines that signaled a resolution to the matter.

The Los Angeles Times sports section contained a headline reading, *"PGA OKAYS LOUIS IN SAN DIEGO GOLF."*

A banner headline across the top of the sports section of the Long Beach Independent declared, *"Louis in San Diego Open."*

An AP article headline in the Los Angeles Daily Breeze declared, *"Joe Louis Scores Major Victory in Golf World."*

Joe Louis had received PGA approval to play in the San Diego Open. The AP article by Norman Bell indicated, *"Louis claimed it made him the first Negro, amateur or professional to gain such approval."*

And it is likely that Joe Louis was correct in that statement. There is no record of any prior African-American player receiving the express approval of the PGA to play in a PGA sponsored tournament.

But it was not a knockout of the NON-white ban that Joe Louis was seeking. Rather it was what could be called a technical knockout. The PGA had made a somewhat back handed ruling. They indicated that Joe Louis could play because he was an amateur. However, Bill Spiller, the professional African-American golfer who had qualified for the tournament, could NOT play because the ban on NON-white players applied to professionals.

An unsatisfied Joe Louis indicated that he would play in the tournament but vowed to continue the fight to allow African-American professionals to play.

The AP article also noted Louis, *"received many wires backing him in his stand, one of them from Brooklyn Dodgers baseball star, Jackie Robinson."*

Thursday, January 17

On the morning of the first day of the tournament, The Los Angeles Times reported that Joe Louis was scheduled to tee off at 9:27am in a threesome with PGA president, Horton Smith, and another member of the PGA Tournament Committee, Leland Gibson. Whatever the rationale was for putting this threesome together, it was an opportunity for Joe Louis to tee off not just on the golf course, but on the PGA leadership.

In a United Press article appearing in the Escondido Daily-Times, Louis said, **"I've just begun to fight."** He would not take off his gloves until the PGA would allow African-American professionals to play in a PGA sponsored tournament.

But while Louis was not celebrating, another United Press article which appeared in newspapers across America proclaimed, *"it is the first time a Negro ever has been allowed to play in a PGA sponsored golf tournament. It is the first evidence of the racial barrier breaking down in the game of professional golf."*

The story ran as far east as the Portland Press Herald in Maine, as far north as the Great Falls Tribute in Montana, and as far south as the Birmingham News in Alabama.

Friday, January 18

Yesterday, at 9:27am, when his threesome teed off at San Diego Country Club, Joe Louis, playing as an amateur, became the first African-American player in a PGA sponsored tournament with the approval of the PGA.

Louis played admirably shooting a 76, the same score as 1952 PGA championship winner Jim Turnesa, and better than many other PGA professionals including Jerry Barber (who later won the 1961 PGA Championship).

Only one shot ahead of Louis was a young player who was still a few years away from the 1st of his 51 PGA victories – Billy Casper.

Horton Smith shot a 73.

According to the January 18th Los Angeles Times, Smith told Louis, *"You hit like a pro, Joe,"* when he watched Louis hit a 250 yard drive on the opening tee shot.

Later when Louis hooked his tee shot into the left rough on the 3rd hole, Smith said to him, *"The only place a left hook is good is in the ring."*

Saturday, January 19, 1952

Louis didn't fare as well the next day and shot 82 to miss the cut. He still had managed to post a better score than 6 professional players.

But that was inconsequential to Louis who was less interested in the score on his card than the score he had to settle with Horton Smith, the PGA president, with whom Louis spent another day walking the course.

Perhaps Louis ruffled Smith a bit, as the PGA president ballooned to a 78 in the 2nd round (2 shots worse than Louis had shot the day before). And Smith also missed the cut by one stroke.

But not only did Joe Louis knockout Horton Smith from the San Diego Open, apparently he changed Smith's mind on the NON-white professional ban.

The Los Angeles Mirror ran a story with the headline, *"Easing of PGA Negro Ban Nears."* The article stated that Horton planned to announce a decision that had already been agreed to by long distance telephone, *"whereby the PGA seven-man tournament committee would approve a plan to ease the bars against Negroes."*

Joe Louis was satisfied calling it a, *"good move."*

Sunday, January 20, 1952

Today the Los Angeles Times ran a story titled, *"Ruling Lifts Ban on Negroes in PGA Events."* The story detailed a new rule voted on by the PGA Tournament Committee in which, *"permission for Negroes to compete would be subject to approval by local sponsors and host clubs."*

Monday, January 21, 1952

Yesterday the San Diego Open concluded without Louis or Smith, who had both missed the cut on Friday.

Ted Kroll captured his 1st PGA tournament victory. Kroll put the tournament out of reach when he sank a 20 foot birdie putt on the 16th hole, putting him 3 shots ahead of Jimmy Demaret with 2 holes to play. The 32 year old New Yorker earned 3 Purple Hearts during World War II, serving in the infantry in Africa, Italy and France. He's been playing the PGA circuit for the past 3 years.

But Kroll's victory was not the big news at the San Diego Open.

A United Press story that appeared in newspapers across the country today, including the Brooklyn Eagle, declared, *"The big news was the end of the Negro ban."*

And the Los Angeles Daily News reported that the next tour stop in Phoenix would be where, *"the Negroes make their first appearance under the new Professional Golfers' rules."*

The article gave the credit for the victory to Joe Louis, *"who led the fight to have Negroes compete in PGA co-sponsored events."*

So celebrated was this conquest that Ed Sullivan, host of the CBS television show, "Toast of the Town," reported on Joe Louis's achievement in his nationally syndicated entertainment column today that appeared in the New York Daily News and other newspapers across the country. Sullivan wrote how Joe Louis coerced the new PGA president, Horton Smith to get the, *"PGA board of governors to take a telephone vote and rescind the ban on Negro competitors which is in the best tradition of American sportsmanship and common sense."*

POSTSCRIPT from The Sports Time Traveler™

Joe Louis was the first African-American to play in a PGA sponsored tournament with PGA approval.

But even more important to Joe Louis was the lifting of the PGA ban on NON-white professionals which he secured. This leads me to the conclusion that the Joe Louis – Horton Smith match in the first and second rounds of the 1952 San Diego Open was the most important bout of Joe Louis's career. You could call it a 2 round technical knockout.

It's still just a technical knockout because it still took another 9 years until African American golfer Charlie Sifford became the first full-fledged member of the PGA TOUR with no restrictions.

Following the San Diego Open, Joe Louis played in the qualifying rounds at the Phoenix Open but failed to post a qualifying score.

On January 24, 1952, it was announced that Louis had received an invitation to play the following week at the Tucson Open. This time his invitation came with an exemption that did not require him to play in the qualifying rounds. The next chapter shares the thrilling story of the 1952 Tucson Open.

CHAPTER FOUR

Joe Louis Belts an Uppercut on the PGA

THE FORMER HEAVYWEIGHT BOXING CHAMP MAKES HISTORY AGAIN AT THE 1952 TUCSON OPEN

INTRODUCTION from The Sports Time Traveler

The Sports Time Traveler™ has gone back in time to watch the 1952 Tucson Open, a PGA sponsored tournament here at the El Rio Golf & Country Club.

The purse is $10,000 with $2,000 going to the winner. That's the standard money for PGA tournaments here in 1952.

All the greatest players on tour are here with the exception of two - Sam Snead and Ben Hogan.

Ben Hogan of course is chronically limited in his ability to play due to the near fatal auto accident he sustained in 1949. Hogan only competes in about 6 tournaments a year now.

Sam Snead is not here this week because of a commitment in Florida. Snead is headlining the Greater Miami Sports and Vacation Show alongside baseball legend Bob Feller.

Despite missing two of the premier players in golf, attendance at the Tucson Open is on pace to break the all-time record for the event.

Joe Louis is in the Tournament

The large galleries in Tucson this week are mostly due to an unexpected entrant - former world heavyweight boxing champion, Joe Louis.

Joe Louis is playing here in 1952 in Tucson as an amateur on a sponsor's exemption.

It's his 2nd PGA sponsored tournament.

His 1st one, the San Diego Open, in mid-January, 1952, was monumental as reported in chapter 3. Joe Louis, playing as an amateur, became the first African-American to play in a PGA sponsored tournament with PGA approval. Louis also secured from PGA president Horton Smith an agreement that African-American professionals could play in PGA sponsored tournaments to which they were invited by the host sponsors & clubs.

The following week, Joe Louis went to the Phoenix Open. He did not qualify to play, but he watched his friend, Ted Rhodes play. At 8:28am on Thursday, January 24, 1952, when Ted Rhodes teed off in the 1st round, he became the 1st professional African-American golfer to play in a PGA sponsored event with PGA approval. Also, playing that day, teeing off at 10:55am, was Bill Spiller, another African-American professional golfer. A 3rd African-American golfer, Eural Clark, was also in the field, officially playing as an amateur.

A week later Joe Louis also had an invitation to play in Tucson, as an amateur invitee, and this time Louis was exempt from playing in the qualifying rounds.

Now here are my reports from the 1952 Tucson Open.

The PRO-AM – Thursday, January 31, 1952

Yesterday, 18 foursomes played in the pro-am for the 1952 Tucson Open. The foursome with the largest gallery following them was the one that included Joe Louis. Skibo McKay was following the group for the Tucson Daily Citizen. He wrote, *"A crowd watched Louis's every move."*

Louis's group shot a best ball score of 68, putting them 8 shots back of the winning group. Louis himself recorded a 74 on the par 70 course that measures 6,402 yards.

A large photo appeared on the front page of the sports section of Tucson Daily Citizen today of Joe Louis lining up a putt on the 6th green with the other members of his pro-am foursome standing behind him.

Lloyd Mangrum, winner last week at Phoenix, and defending champion here at Tucson and leading money winner from 1951, is the overwhelming favorite to win again this year when the tournament gets underway today. The 37-year-old Mangrum told Ray McNally of the Tucson Daily Citizen, *"I'm going all out to win this one. But from the looks of things here, these kids are going to make it tough on me."*

Mangrum may have been referring to two golfers almost a decade younger than him, Jimmy Clark and Jack Burke, Jr. Clark shot a 62 in the pro-am to tie the course record. While Burke shot a 29 on the back 9, to equal that record.

McNally noted that Clark missed 6 putts of 5 feet or less. It sounds like Clark could have easily broken 60 if he had a hot putter.

Clark told McNally, *"It was one of the greatest rounds I've ever shot in my life."*

1st ROUND – Friday, February 1, 1952

Yesterday, Joe Louis teed off in the 6th group of the day at 9:05am. On the opening 9 holes he shot a 1 over par 36. Not a bad start for an amateur.

But on the back 9, Joe Louis played like a champ. He fired a brilliant 2 under par 33 to finish the day with a 1 under par 69.

When Joe Louis completed his round, he was just 1 shot off the best score posted at that point, a shot behind Jack Hardin who had posted a 68.

When all the scores were in for the opening round, Louis's 69 still looked astonishing. Out of 150 golfers, in a field that included most of the best players in the world, Joe Louis was in 17th place and just 4 shots off the lead.

Here were the leading scores after round 1:

-5 **Dr. Cary Middlecoff and Jimmy Clark**

-3 **Frank Champ, Doug Higgins, Fred Hawkins and Max Evans**

-2 **Lloyd Mangrum and 9 others**

-1 **Joe Louis, Ted Kroll and 5 others**

Joe Louis was tied with the man who had won the San Diego Open 2 weeks earlier. And he was just a shot behind Lloyd Mangrum, the 1951 leading money winner.

Louis was ecstatic with his round. Only 5 of the 150 golfers in the field shot better on the back 9 than Joe Louis. He told Ray McNally, *"If I have another 69 tomorrow I'd like to take this course home with me."* The Arizona Daily Star reported that Louis was, **"tickled to death"** with his round of 69.

When looking at just the scores of the amateurs in the field, Joe Louis had the BEST score of the day. This was an amateur field which included Frank Stranahan, perhaps the best amateur player in the world. Stranahan had posted a 71. Stranahan had finished 2nd in both The Masters and the British Open in 1947.

The biggest shocker of round 1 came from one of the biggest names in the field, Jimmy Demaret – 3-time Masters champion and 2-time winner of this tournament. Demaret came to the dog leg par 5 18th hole 1 under par on his opening round (tied with Louis).

Demaret, as he always does at the El Rio course, tried to cut the corner of the dog leg on his drive.

But his drive went out of bounds.

Then in an unimaginable sequence he proceeded to hit 4 more drives out of bounds.

Jimmy Demaret finished the 18th hole with a 14! That gave him a score of 78, leaving him virtually certain to miss the cut.

Demaret took it very well and was laughing when he told a reporter from the Arizona Daily Star, **"That's the highest score I've taken on one hole in my life."**

NOTE from the Present Time

I went back to the present time to research the highest score ever posted on a single hole in a PGA sanctioned event. I found it interesting that a 2021 Golf Week article on the "highest single-hole scores in PGA TOUR history," failed to include Demaret's 14, even though the article cited scores as long ago as 1925. Demaret's score would have ranked as tied for the 7th worst score on a single hole.

2nd ROUND – Saturday, February 2, 1952

The Tucson Daily Citizen, in a page 1 article, noted that the crowd, *"gave Joe Louis the best hand of the day."*

But Louis was *"kayoed"* as the leading amateur, wrote Abe Chanin in a front page article in the Arizona Daily Star.

There was no shame in this for Louis, because Frank Stranahan demonstrated why he might be the best amateur in the world, and one of the best golfers anywhere, in yesterday's 2nd round.

Stranahan stood over a 20 foot putt on the 18th hole.

Up to that moment he had taken only 58 shots.

That's right, Frank Stranahan had a putt for a 59!

The front page of the Arizona Daily Star has a photo of the putt. In the photo the ball is on its way to the hole and appears on line.

If the putt goes in, Frank Stranahan would become the first player ever to break 60 in a PGA event.

Abe Chanin, described the action as Stranahan stroked the putt for history, *"Instead of playing it safely with an approach putt, Stranahan went for the cup and the record. The ball rolled past the hole, a few inches off line."*

Stranahan had barely missed the 59.

Another NOTE from the Present Time

It was startling to learn about this near miss of a 59 in 1952. It will be another 25 years until Al Geiberger becomes the first player in a PGA event to shoot a 59 in 1977.

Now back to 1952.

Stranahan's putt for a 59 had slid 3 feet past the hole. And he missed the 3 footer coming back.

Despite 3-putting the final hole, Frank Stranahan had himself a 9 under par 61.

That was good enough to wrest the amateur lead from Joe Louis, and also to move into a tie for 1st place in the Tucson Open at the halfway mark.

Stranahan and Skee Riegel both stood at 8 under par 132.

Stranahan had also broken the course record for the front 9 with a 28. Abe Chanin believed that might be the PGA record for 9 holes. And it meant that Stranahan only needed a 31 on the back 9 to break 60.

If Stranahan had broken the 60 barrier, few fans would have seen it. That's because the largest crowd of the day was following the former boxing champ, Joe Louis.

Joe Louis played well again in the 2nd round. He came to the 18th hole poised to remain under par for 36 holes. But he required 2 shots get out of the sand trap on the 18th and finished the day with a 2 over par 72.

Joe Louis' 36 hole score was a 1 over par 141, tied for 39th.

And that was good enough to make the cut which was at 144.

An All-Time Great Athletic Achievement

I'm interrupting this article yet again to come back to the present and ponder the magnitude of what Joe Louis did in the 2nd round of the 1952 Tucson Open.

The fans who followed Joe Louis that day saw something unprecedented, something astonishing.

On February 1, 1952, Joe Louis became the only athlete from another sport of his stature to make the cut in a PGA event. As noted in the last chapter, Joe Louis was ranked the #11 greatest athlete of the 20th century by ESPN.

I have also found a ranking by the Associated Press that ranks Joe Louis as the #7 greatest athlete of the 20th century.

No one else in that top 100, whose primary sport was not golf, ever made the cut in a PGA event.

Think about that.

Joe Louis made the cut at the Tucson Open!

How great an accomplishment was this?

Consider the company Joe Louis was in by making the cut at 141:

He was tied with multiple major champions Jack Burke, Jr. and Lawson Little.

He was ahead of several players who won major championships in their careers including, Tommy Bolt, winner of the 1958 US Open, Vic Ghezzi, winner of the 1941 PGA Championship, and Dick Mayer, winner of the 1957 US Open.

I'm just totally blown away by this.

There is no parallel with any other great athlete of Joe Louis' stature making the cut in a PGA event.

I did quite a bit of research on this, and it seems that the next closest athlete in stature from another sport to make the cut in a PGA event is Ellsworth Vines. You're probably asking right now, *who is Ellsworth Vines?*

In 1931 and 1932, Ellsworth Vines was the world's best tennis player. He won the men's singles title in the U.S. Open in both of those years and he won the singles title at Wimbledon in 1932. He later became a professional golfer and made the cut many times at PGA events. He never won on the PGA TOUR but he did finish 3rd in the 1951 PGA Championship.

But Vines was not in the same category as Joe Louis. Vines did not make the ESPN or AP top 100 list. And even in his own sport, Wikipedia lists Vines as the #64 tennis player of all-time.

Joe Louis made the cut in a PGA event.

It's mind boggling.

And just as astonishing is that almost no newspapers at the time made note of the fact that Joe Louis had made the cut.

Besides the local Tucson papers, the New York Times simply mentioned, *"Louis qualified for tomorrow's play."*

And nothing was ever mentioned again about it.

The achievement seems to have been lost in history.

And now back to 1952.

Here were the leading scores after round 2:

-8   **Frank Stranahan and Skee Riegel**

-7   **Dave Dougles, Henry Williams, Jr., Joe Moore, Jr.**

-5   **Dr. Cary Middlecoff and Ralph Blomquist**

-4   **Jimmy Clark and Ed Furgol**

-3   **4 players tied**

-2   **Lloyd Mangrum and 5 others**

-1   **Ted Kroll and 7 others**

E   **Ted Rhodes and 9 others**

+1   **Joe Louis and 6 others**

3rd ROUND – Sunday, February 3, 1952

Apparently Joe Louis never fathomed he would make the cut at the Tucson Open and have a commitment to tee off at the El Rio Golf & Country Club on Saturday.

Louis had made a previous commitment for Saturday morning at 8:30am to be the highlight of a youth safety program in downtown Tucson.

The Tucson Daily Citizen reported on Friday, ***"Louis will appear on the stage of the Fox-Tucson theater during the safe-teen club program... during his appearance Louis will present an award to the city's Junior Citizen of the Week."***

There had also been advertisements in the newspapers in Tucson during the week for this event. The ad appeared in the Tucson Daily Citizen and read, *"Hey Kids JOE LOUIS in person. Ex-heavyweight champ of the world. On stage at the Fox-Tucson theater. Saturday morning kid show."*

Reading those ads, the prior day, I wondered if Louis was going to make good on the youth program appearance, since after making the cut it was announced he had an 11:42am tee time in the 3rd round of the tournament.

It turns out he did make it to the theater 3 hours prior to his tee time just as planned. A large photo of Joe Louis at the youth program appeared this morning on page 32 of the Arizona Daily Star. The caption read, *"Joe Louis, former world's heavyweight boxing champion, handed out awards at yesterday's meeting of the Safe-Teen club at the Fox-Tucson theater.*

Louis was pictured with the club's citizen of the week, young Lloyd Bell. Louis presented Bell with a set of boxing gloves. And a little boy, Tommy Gibbons, received a camera from Louis.

At the golf course, Joe Louis teed off on time at 11:42am in a twosome with Jack Burke, Jr. Ray McNally wrote, *"Once again Joe Louis lured the largest gallery of the day."*

But things did not start out so well for Louis in the 3rd round.

The winds were gusting to over 40 miles per hour and on the 1st hole the former boxing champ's tee shot, **"went high and the wind carried it out of bounds,"** according to the report from Ray McNally.

Louis finished the front 9 in 39. His playing partner, Jack Burke Jr. was only 1 shot better at 38.

The back 9 was no easier for Louis. He shot another 39 for a total of 78.

But many of the top players also saw their scores soar on Saturday. Frank Stranahan, the 36 hole co-leader, shot 17 strokes higher from Friday to Saturday as he posted a 78, just like Louis.

Ted Rhodes and Ted Kroll both also shot 78.

Only 4 golfers broke par on the day.

Henry Williams, who started the day in 2nd place at -7, was 3 over par after 3 holes. But somehow he managed to shoot 3 under the rest of the way to come in at even par 70 on the day. The was good enough to put him in sole possession of 1st place going into the final round. Williams has never before won a PGA tournament.

Unfortunately, Louis's 78 dropped him to 16 shots off the lead and well out of contention at +9 for the tournament. Yet Louis could take some consolation in the fact that he was just 2 shots behind San Diego Open champion Ted Kroll through 54 holes.

Here were the leading scores after round 3:

-7   **Henry Williams, Jr.**

-5   **Ralph Blomquist**

-4   **Skee Riegel**

-3   **Ed Furgol**

-2   **Lloyd Mangrum and Johnny Bulla**

-1   **Dr. Cary Middlecoff and 4 others**

4th ROUND – Monday, February 4, 1952

The final round didn't go well for Joe Louis. Abe Chanin's front page article mentioned this, *"Boxer Joe Louis got in too much trouble on the course and picked up. He didn't turn in his scorecard."*

Ray McNally wrote, *"Joe Louis, who made such a good first day start, dropped out after nine holes yesterday."*

I can't find any other mention of Joe Louis in the final round of the 1952 Tucson Open. So the mystery of why Louis didn't finish out the tournament is unknown to this writer.

A shake up at the top of the leaderboard took place after Louis dropped out. Dr. Cary Middlecoff, who started the day 6 shots back, shot a 31 on the front 9 to get within 2 shots of the 54 hole leader, Henry Williams, Jr.

But Middlecoff ran into trouble on the 10th hole when his ball hit a tree and lodged inside the tree. He ended up with a double bogey and never contended after that.

Williams played conservatively the rest of the way and shot a 71 to win by 2 strokes for his first ever PGA victory.

Here were the final scores of the top finishers at the 1952 Tucson Open:

-6   Henry Williams, Jr.

-4   Cary Middlecoff

-2   Skee Riegel

-1   Lloyd Mangrum, Frank Stranahan and Joe Moore Jr.

E   Ralph Blomquist

-1   Dr. Cary Middlecoff and 4 others

Immediately after the tournament, for Cary Middlecoff and Joe Louis there was still more golf to play. Both of them plus, golf stars Jimmy Demaret, Lloyd Mangrum, Tommy Bolt and Jack Burke Jr., were invited back to Los Angeles to play in a unique 18 hole event tonight.

That's right at night!

STARS UNDER THE STARS Night Tournament – Tuesday, February 5, 1952

Last night at Inglewood Country Club near Los Angeles was a unique golfing event. It was called the "Stars Under the Stars" golf tournament. Promoter Jim Walker created the event in which 6 golfers competed over 18 holes on a golf course lit by floodlights. Walker's goal was to *"demonstrate the feasibility of playing golf on an 18 hole course at night,"* according to the AP article that appeared in the Los Angeles Daily Breeze.

The 6 golfers were:

Lloyd Mangrum – The 1951 PGA money leader and winner of the 1946 U.S. Open

Jimmy Demaret – 3-time winner of The Masters

Dr. Cary Middlecoff – The 1949 U.S. Open winner and winner of 20 PGA tournaments to date

Jack Burke, Jr. – Winner of 8 PGA tournaments, including 4 consecutive tournaments earlier this year

Tommy Bolt – Winner of the Los Angeles Open last month

Joe Louis – Former heavyweight boxing champion and a top amateur golfer who made the cut in the Tucson Open

2,000 fans came out to see this unique event which consisted of 2 threesomes. The 1st threesome included Lloyd Mangrum, Tommy Bolt and Joe Louis. The 2nd threesome consisted of Jimmy Demaret, Dr. Cary Middlecoff and Jack Burke Jr.

Every shot was followed by giant floodlights that were mounted oddly on the heads of 8 groundskeepers who rode the course on bicycles. There were also enough permanent lights to provide *"near daylight playing conditions, "* according to the Long Beach Independent.

A picture of Joe Louis teeing off in the dark on the first hole appeared on the front page of the Los Angeles Times sports section today. Behind Louis were 6 eerie looking light bearers, all dressed in the same uniform of long sleeve white shirts, white pants and white helmets, the tops of which hold the giant floodlights that rise high up above their heads. It is a bizarre looking scene.

Charles Curtis of the Times covered the event. He wrote that, *"Tee shots and second shots were brightly illuminated, the spotlights following the flight of the balls without difficulty. But on the green, the lighting was short of perfection and many shadows and moving beams hampered the players."*

The incentive for the 5 professionals was $1,000 for each stroke the winner shot under par. There was no prize money available for Joe Louis who was playing as an amateur.

Dr. Cary Middlecoff, with birdie putts of 6 feet and 12 feet on the 3rd and 4th holes, took the early lead.

After 9 holes the scoring was as follows:

- 2   **Dr. Cary Middlecoff**

- 1   **Lloyd Mangrum**

Even   Jimmy Demaret

+1   Jack Burke Jr. and Tommy Bolt

+5   Joe Louis

On the back 9, Mangrum made the longest putt of the night on the 12th hole, a 20 footer for birdie. And Middlecoff lost 5 shots to par. That enabled Mangrum to win the event with a 1 under par 71.

Final Scores:

- 1   Lloyd Mangrum

Even   Jack Burke Jr.

+1   Jimmy Demaret

+3   Dr. Cary Middlecoff

+4   Tommy Bolt

+9   Joe Louis

POSTSCRIPT

Here is Joe Louis's record in tournaments he played in during the winter of 1952:

Did not qualify – Los Angeles Open

Missed cut – San Diego Open (PGA sponsored tournament)

Did not qualify – Phoenix Open (PGA sponsored tournament)

MADE THE CUT, but did not finish – Tucson Open (PGA sponsored)

"Last Place" – Stars Under the Stars

After the Start Under the Stars event, I cannot find any record of Joe Louis ever playing in another PGA or high level golf event.

CHAPTER FIVE

The Long Layoff

BEN HOGAN PLAYS THE 1953 MASTERS AFTER A 10 MONTH LAYOFF FROM THE PGA

INTRODUCTION from The Sports Time Traveler.

In 2023, I decided to go back in time virtually, precisely 70 years, to experience Ben Hogan's 1953 season.

It wasn't not so much a season as just a few appearances.

Hogan was extremely limited in the amount of golf he could play (similar to Tiger Woods in the 2020's) following his near fatal car crash on February 2, 1949.

The accident had occurred at the height of Hogan's career. By 1949, at age 36, Hogan had won 3 majors and was regarded as one of the best golfers in the world.

Immediately following the accident there was grave concern for Hogan's life. One of the world's leading specialists was called in to perform complex blood clot surgery necessary for Hogan's survival. The surgery was successful.

In the months after the accident it was not expected that Hogan would be able to walk again. But Hogan diligently performed physical therapy and was able to walk in the months following the accident.

And although he suffered with pain for the rest of his life, he even recovered enough to play golf again. One year later, in 1950, Hogan miraculously returned to competitive golf on a very limited schedule. In spite of his condition Hogan managed to win three more majors – the 1950 and 1951 U.S. Open titles and the 1951 Masters.

Hogan's remarkable 1951, double major season, led to an announcement by the PGA (the Professional Golfers' Association) that Hogan had been voted the greatest professional golfer of the last 50 years. The voting was conducted via a poll of the 3,032 PGA members plus 900 sportswriters. The results were made public in the middle of 1952 in an AP (Associated Press) article.

Here were the results of the voting:

522 – Ben Hogan

519 – Walter Hagen

504 – Gene Sarazen

499 – Sam Snead

491 – Byron Nelson

351 – Tommy Armour

304 – Lloyd Mangrum

Note that in the same voting, Bobby Jones had been selected as the greatest amateur golfer of the last 50 years, but received less votes (519) than

Hogan. Thus, Hogan could be thought of as having the crown of best golfer of the last 50 years period.

But while he received that flattering title, in 1952 Hogan was shut out in the majors. He played well, but not like he had in 1951. In the 1952 Masters in particular, Hogan faltered on the final day. He started the day tied for the lead with Sam Snead, but Hogan soared to a 79 on Sunday while Snead shot an even par 72 and won his 2nd Masters by 4 shots.

Coming into the 1953 season, Hogan was 40 years old and permanently damaged. He might have been the best golfer of the last 50 years, however, his greatest days seemed certainly to be behind him.

At this stage, Hogan could not physically endure more than about 6 tournaments a year. Unlike all the other top golfers, Hogan didn't play a single early season PGA event. Coming into the Masters in mid-April, 1953, Ben Hogan had not played in a serious 72 hole tournament since the U.S. Open in June, 1952.

Yes, he had played a few rounds in short pro-am tournaments. He had even carded a 65 in the first round of a 54 hole pro-am in Palm Springs, California in January, and finished 2nd in the tournament to Jimmy Demaret (a 3-time Masters winner). And in March, in Palm Beach, Florida, in a 36 hole pro-am, Hogan had finished 2nd to little known Pete Cooper (and 4 strokes better than Jimmy Demaret).

But pro-ams were not PGA events. And they were not the grueling endurance test that characterizes a 72 hole tournament. The traditional 4 day PGA tournament was excruciating on Hogan's damaged legs.

The Masters in mid-April, was Hogan's first real test in 1953. In fact it was his first true competitive tournament since mid-1952.

And now let's begin the journey through Ben Hogan's 1953 season, starting with the Masters.

Saturday April 4, 1953

The Atlanta Constitution reported that things were very quiet at the Augusta National Country Club yesterday. The Master doesn't get started until next Thursday. But Ben Hogan has already been here in Augusta for a week preparing for the tournament. His preparations are working. 2 days ago he shot a 66.

Only 5 other players had arrived and signed the register as of yesterday. They include Claude Harmon, the 1948 champion and amateur Frank Stranahan, the only amateur ever to come close to winning a Masters in the 16 times it has been contested. Stranahan finished tied for 2nd with Byron Nelson in 1947, just 2 shots behind the winner, Jimmy Demaret.

An AP article this morning announced the results of a poll of 33 touring professionals with their picks for the 1953 Masters.

Here were the top 5 in the voting:

7 votes – Sam Snead (Snead won last year and in 1949)

7 votes – Ben Hogan (the 1951 winner)

6 votes – Lloyd Mangrum (the leading money winner this year)

3 votes – Tommy Bolt (winner of 2 tournaments this year)

3 votes – Julius Boros (the 1952 U.S. Open champion)

It's quite remarkable that a 40 year old that has taken a 10 month layoff from playing PGA events can still be considered so highly. It's also interesting that Sam Snead is 40 as well and Lloyd Mangrum is 37. Golf has become an old-man's game it seems in these post-war years as potential young golf stars lost their foundational years. A generation ago, Bobby Jones retired by the time he was 28. And Gene Sarazen won 5 of his 7 majors by the time he was 30.

Monday April 6, 1953

The Fort-Worth Star-Telegram this morning had some statistics on historical Masters scoring over the 16 times the tournament has been contested since it was inaugurated in 1934. Ben Hogan has the #1 lifetime best scoring average of 71.91. And Hogan is the ONLY golfer that has ever averaged below par across all the rounds they have played in the tournament. Hogan has played in 11 Masters tournaments to date. Since his first time playing in 1938, when he finished 25th, he has never been out of the top 10, although he has only won it once, in 1951.

Here are the lifetime best scoring averages at The Masters through last year, 1952:

71.91   Ben Hogan
72.19   Lloyd Mangrum
72.21   Byron Nelson
72.25   Jimmy Demaret
72.58   Sam Snead

Tuesday April 7, 1953

Gene Gregston, sportswriter for the Fort-Worth Telegram reported on a long distance phone call he had with Ben Hogan yesterday. *"I've been playing pretty good,"* said the normally over-modest Hogan. Then Hogan offered some insights about the practice rounds in an effort to downplay the 66 he had shot, *"These practice rounds don't mean much, especially on this course. They don't cut the green until Wednesday night."*

Hogan also had high praise for the Augusta course, *"This course is just beautiful. The fairways are some of the best I've ever hit a shot off of, simply beautiful."*

Bert Prather of the Atlanta Constitution reported that 45 of the 74 invited golfers had arrived by Monday.

Wednesday April 8, 1953

Prather reported today that Ben Hogan, the 1951 winner, played a practice round yesterday in a fivesome with Jimmy Demaret (winner in 1940, 1947 and 1950), Claude Harmon (winner in 1948), Jack Burke Jr. and Dr. Cary Middlecoff. Hogan and Harmon both shot 69.

Prather also commented about Hogan's long layoff from PGA competition, *"Some are a little afraid that Ben's layoff from the tourney trail... may prove more than even he can overcome.*

NOTE from The Sports Time Traveler

I've come back to the present to tell you that both Dr. Cary Middlecoff and Jack Burke Jr. went on to win Masters titles in 1955 and 1956. That means the fivesome that Hogan played in on April 7, 1953 contained 5 Masters champions. Wow!

Now back to 1953.

Thursday April 9, 1953

The big news in yesterday's final practice round was that Lloyd Mangrum shot a 63. Ed Miles in the Atlanta Journal noted that is the lowest score ever shot at Augusta during or preceding the tournament. The official tournament record is 64 by Mangrum back in 1940.

Miles made an interesting observation about Mangrum's brilliant 63 in the practice round, *"While all golfers here might have envied... the brief fame of the 63,* (all) ***thought of it as wasted in a practice round on the eve of the competition."***

Miles also noted that Ben Hogan did not play a practice round on Wednesday. Instead, Hogan spent all his time practicing on the driving range and the putting green.

Gene Gregston talked to a number of players on Wednesday about Ben Hogan's chances. He reported, ***"Locker room talk has formed the belief that Ben will not be able to stand up under the physical strain and will have another "bad" round like last year's closing 79."***

1st ROUND – Friday April 10, 1953

Ben Hogan opened the tournament with a 70 to put him in a tie for 3rd place, 2 strokes off the lead held by Chick Harbert. Harbert, who has never won a major title, opened the Masters with a bogey on the 1st hole. He then proceeded to make 6 birdies over the final 17 holes, giving back just 1 stroke at number 10, to fire a sensational 68.

Harbert was all smiles after the round. A picture of him with a wide grin as he soaked his sore feet in a tub appeared in an AP article on the first round in the Detroit Free Press, Harbert's hometown.

Hogan was 4 under par through 16 holes, on his way to what could have been a 68 if he parred 17 and 18. But on both of the closing holes, Hogan was in a trap on his 2nd shot and suffered 2 bogeys.

Trailing Hogan by a shot was his long time nemesis, and defending Masters champion, Sam Snead. Snead's official score for the round was a 71. But Snead only took 70 shots. Unfortunately, his playing partner, the great Byron Nelson, wrote "4" on the scorecard for Snead on the 18th hole, even though Snead had actually had a birdie 3. Snead did not catch the mistake before he signed his scorecard, and thus he lost a stroke.

Nelson himself, a 2-time Masters champ in 1937 and 1942, recorded a 73 in his opening round to put him in a tie for 11th with Jimmy Demaret, the only man to ever win the Masters 3 times (1940, 1947 and 1950).

Here was the leaderboard after round 1:

-4 Chick Harbert

-3 Al Besselink

-3 Ed Oliver

-2 Ben Hogan

-2 Milan Marusic

-1 Sam Snead

-1 Tommy Bolt

-1 Bob Hamilton

-1 Ted Kroll

2nd ROUND – Saturday April 11, 1953

Ben Hogan began the day dialed in on the front 9. On the 5th, 6th, 8th and 9th holes he hit approach shots within 5 feet. He made each of the birdie putts and parred the other 5 holes and completed the outward 9 in just 32 strokes.

He came back to Earth on the back 9. On the 11th hole, his 30 foot birdie putt continued 5 feet past the hole. Ed Miles of the Atlanta Journal described the 5 foot par putt, *"he became frigid, stood too long over the ball and jerked it offline."* The result was a bogey 5.

He missed another short putt on 16. The bogeys led him to a 37 on the back 9 for an 18 hole score of 69.

Fortunately for "Bantam Ben" as many newspapermen call him, the first day leaders imploded. Chick Harbert was 5 shots off his 1st round score with a 73. Ed Oliver matched Harbert's score. While Al Besselink could only manage a 75 after his opening round 69. Sam Snead, a heavy pre-tournament favorite, also shot a 75 to put him 7 shots behind Hogan at the halfway mark.

Moving up on Friday was Lloyd Mangrum, the 1946 U.S. Open winner and two-time runner up here at Augusta. Mangrum had caused a stir when he fired a 63 in a practice round earlier in the week. But in the opening round he could only manage a 74. On Friday he came back with the low round of the day – a 68. That moved him up from 26th to 5th.

Also making a move was cigar chewing Bob Hamilton, who had started the day 1 shot behind Hogan. He matched Hogan's 32 on the front 9 and finished with the same score as Hogan with a 69. That kept him a shot behind Ben.

Ted Kroll, who earned 3 purple hearts in World War II, also started the round a shot in back of Ben, and shot a 70 to put him 2 shots off Ben's pace for 36 holes.

As a result, Hogan found himself all alone in front after 36 holes in what Bert Prather of the Atlanta Constitution called, *"the finest and largest field ever to participate in this tournament."*

Here was the leaderboard after round 2:

-5 Ben Hogan

-4 Bob Hamilton

-3 Chick Harbert

-3 Ted Kroll

-2 Ed Oliver

-2 Milan Marusic

-2 Lloyd Mangrum

3rd ROUND – Sunday April 12, 1953

On the 1st hole Hogan scrambled for par. On the 2nd, a par 5, he hit his 2nd shot into the trap and got up and down for a birdie. Then on the 3rd hole, a 220 yard par 3, he put his 4-iron tee shot just 3 feet from the pin and sank another birdie putt. Hogan had started 2 under for the opening 3 holes. On the 8th hole, another par 5, he reached the green in 2 and 2-putted for his 3rd birdie. And on 9, he drained a 60-foot putt for yet one more birdie. Hogan was out in 32.

On the long 470 yard par 4 10th hole, Hogan made it 3 birds in a row sinking a 25 footer. He was now 5 under through 10 holes. Next it was a 6-foot birdie putt on 14 to go to 6 under. And on the par 5 15th hole he his 4-wood 2nd shot ran within inches of the hole before coming to rest a few feet beyond. He made that putt as well to get to 7 under.

He finally gave back a stroke on the par 3 16th, when he 3-putted from 40 feet. He made par at 17 and 18 to finish with a brilliant 66. That tied Hogan for the 2nd best round in the history of the Masters and gave him a record 54 hole score of 205 (11 under par) and a 4 shot lead.

Gregston wrote, *"It's an astonishing performance by one of the game's all-time greats."*

He had shot a 66, and yet, it could have been better as he had two 3-putt greens. It was a near perfect round from the tees and fairways. Gregston asserted that just a single shot all day didn't, *"go where he planned it."* Gregston described that lone wayward shot, *"a 3-wood off a downhill lie on the 555 yard second, it faded a little more than he'd hoped and sanded in to the right of the green."*

Hogan was paired yesterday with Ed Oliver who had a remarkable finish, scoring 5 under on the final 6 holes to shoot a 67. That led Gregston to call the Hogan-Oliver scores, *"two of the grandest rounds ever shot simultaneously in this, or any tournament."*

All the other top players dropped back relative to Hogan's record score. Mangrum shot a 1 under 71, but lost 5 shots to Hogan. Snead also had a 71, but he had started the day 7 shots behind. Now he was a full dozen back. Julius Boros shot 75 to fall far off the pace.

Some sportswriters were ready to award the tournament to Hogan a day early. Gregston wrote, *"It appears that not even a pack of wild horses can keep him away from the 17th Masters championship."*

The AP wrote, *"It will be almost impossible to catch him in tomorrow's final round."*

It didn't hurt Hogan that some of his nearest pursuers just felt lucky to be here. Bob Hamilton, in 3rd place, 5 shots behind Hogan, told Lincoln Werden of the New York Times, *"Shucks. I thought I'd be forty strokes worse than that by this time."*

Meanwhile the normally cautious Hogan admitted to Lincoln Werden of the New York Times, *"This is the best I've played at Augusta."*

Here were the leading scores after the 3rd round and the scores of some of the pre-tournament favorites:

-11   **Ben Hogan**

-7   **Ed Oliver**

-6   **Bob Hamilton**

-5   **Chick Harbert**

-3   **Lloyd Mangrum**

-2   **Tommy Bolt**

+1   **Sam Snead**

+3   **Dr. Cary Middlecoff and Julius Boros**

+12   **Jimmy Demaret**

There was one reporter for United Press that did question Hogan's health going into the final round. An article titled, *"Can Ben Finish?"* appeared in the New York Daily News. The writer noted, *"Ben Hogan was apparently having trouble with his left leg yesterday as he played the last few holes... he had a masseur give him a rubdown in the locker room."*

4th ROUND – Monday April 13, 1953

On Sunday, Hogan was paired with Byron Nelson in the 1:42pm time slot, even though Nelson was +8 for the tournament and 19 shots behind Hogan. They also were not the final group of the today, there were 3 more twosomes after Hogan and Nelson, none of whom were less than 19 shots back. 2nd place Ed Oliver, was playing 42 minutes ahead of Hogan in a 1pm pairing with 5th place golfer Lloyd Mangrum. 3rd place golfer Bob Hamilton was playing 2 hours and 12 minutes ahead of Hogan in the 11:30am time slot with Sam Snead! This is how Masters pairings are made in 1953.

Hogan went around the front 9 in even par. Oliver bogeyed the 11th hole around the time Hogan finished the 9th. At that time, Hogan had a 5 shot lead with 9 holes to play.

On the back 9, he didn't appear to be playing conservatively as he went for the par 5 13th hole, over water, on his 2nd shot. He reached the green and got his 1st birdie of the round.

But on the par 5 15th, he did lay-up and then pitched to within 4 feet for his 2nd birdie.

On 18, with an enormous crowd watching, Hogan put his 2nd shot on the par 4 just 10 feet from the hole. He sank the birdie putt to finish up 3 under on the back 9.

He maintained his 5 shot lead and finished with a record score of -14.

Hogan shot 70 - 69 - 66 - 69. His total score of 274 was 5 shots better than the old record.

Hogan told Lincoln Werden, *"It was the best I have ever played for seventy-two holes."* Werden was astounded by Hogan's accomplishment. He wrote, *"For a golfer who has not played a seventy-two hole tournament since the United States Open last June his performance during the last four days here was all the more remarkable."*

Gene Sarazen, who was in the first group of the day at 10:30am and finished 26 shots behind Hogan, was quoted in the Atlanta Journal saying, *"I've been debating as to what four rounds by a single player were the greatest I ever saw for 30 years. Today, I got my answer."*

2nd place went to Ed Oliver whose 9 under 279 tied the old record.

3rd place went to Lloyd Mangrum, the current leading money winner, who was 8 shots back of Hogan with a 6 under 282. Mangrum also shot a 69 on the final day.

Sam Snead, the defending champion, finished 18 shots behind Hogan at 292, finishing Sunday with a 75.

Byron Nelson shot a 73 playing with Hogan and finished 23 shots back of Hogan. Nelson was interviewed by Gregston after the round. He said, *"At no time before the round, by any stretch of the imagination could you detect a bit of nervousness in Hogan... I believe he has disciplined himself to golf better than anybody else... It's amazing, simply amazing."*

In winning the green jacket Hogan earned $4,000. He also became the first man ever to win the Masters over the age of 40.

Ben Hogan now holds the records for both the Masters and the U.S. Open.

POST TOURNAMENT – Tuesday April 14, 1953

2 days after the tournament ended, Smith Barrier, a sports columnist in the Greensboro News and Record, shared an insightful quote from Hogan. Hogan indicated he had spent 3 weeks at Augusta, *"It's the preparation and planning for the actual competition that gives me satisfaction. I worked hard for*

the Masters. It took three weeks of concentration on this course, and my game, and actually the four days of competition came as an aftermath."

Barrier also shared what Lloyd Mangrum had told him about Hogan's strategy of taking 10 months off from top flight competitive golf, *"I don't believe anybody else could have such a lay-off and still keep his tournament touch at such an effective edge."*

According to Gregston, Hogan now plans to play in the following tournaments this year:

- Pan American Open in Mexico City at the beginning of May

- The Greenbrier in West Virginia the 2nd week of May

- The Colonial in Fort Worth in late May

- The U.S. Open at Oakmont near Pittsburgh in mid-June

It is likely that will be Ben Hogan's entire competitive schedule for 1953.

I will continue to follow Ben Hogan during his limited 1953 appearances.

NOTE: Hogan's bogeys on 17 and 18 in the 1st round of the 1953 Masters prevented him from being the 1st golfer to have all 4 rounds in the 60's at the Masters.

The feat was not achieved until Cameron Smith did it in 2020 with scores of 67, 68, 69, 69.

Chapter Six

A Week at Oakmont

The 1953 U.S. Open

INTRODUCTION from The Sports Time Traveler

Oakmont Country Club lies 30 minutes east of downtown Pittsburgh. Opened in 1903, it is presently ranked as the 5th greatest golf course in America by Golf Digest. It has made Golf Digest's list of greatest golf courses every year in the publication's history going back to 1966.

The lofty status accorded to the course clashes with its several quirky features. There are almost no water hazards. The greens are unusually large, fast and sloping. Many of the bunkers are brutally penalizing, such as the famous "church pew" traps. And since the late 1940s, the Pennsylvania Turnpike has run right through the course.

Despite the oddities, Oakmont has hosted a record 10 U.S. Open championships as of 2025. And many of those U.S. Opens have been true classics featuring the biggest names in the game's history at key points in their careers. So it's very exciting for me to travel virtually back to some of the truly momentous U.S. Opens at Oakmont and find out all the details.

In this chapter we will journey back in time to 1953. In subsequent chapters later in the book we will travel to 1962 and 1973 for two more classic U.S. Opens at Oakmont.

The 1953 U.S. Open took place at Oakmont in the 2nd week of June. In June of 2023, precisely 70 years later, The Sports Time Traveler™ made the virtual trip to cover it.

And now here are my installments on the 1953 U.S. Open.

PRE-TOURNAMENT COVERAGE – June 8, 1953

Ben Hogan is just 40 years old. But he is physically limited to playing about a half dozen tournaments each year. That's because a 1949 car accident nearly killed him and left him with chronic pain in his legs and other ailments that make it difficult to walk a golf course.

After winning the 1953 Masters, Ben Hogan played in just 3 tournaments prior to the U.S. Open.

- He won the Pan American Open in Mexico City by 3 shots on May 3rd

- He finished 3rd at The Greenbrier in West Virginia on May 10th. Hogan finished 4 shots back of the winner Sam Snead, who was playing on his "home course"

- On his "home course" in Fort Worth, Hogan won The Colonial by 5 shots on May 24th

In 4 events played this year, Ben Hogan has won 3 times, by an average of more than 4 shots in each, and finished 3rd in the other.

Despite playing a severely limited tournament schedule each year since his 1949 accident, Hogan has done something unfathomable. He has become the undisputed best golfer in the world. Through the age of 36, prior to the accident, he had won 3 major tournaments and was recognized as one of the game's top stars. Since the accident he has been other worldly. He has played in 7 majors and won 4 of them and finished 3rd, 4th and 7th in the other 3.

The Best of All Time

Now there is talk that Hogan is not just the best golfer in the world right now, but that he is in fact best of all-time. The current June, 1953 issue of the USGA Journal suggested this in an article by the renowned writer Herbert Warren Wind.

So it's no surprise then that Ben Hogan has been pegged as the favorite to win the 1953 U.S. Open here at Oakmont Country Club. He has already captured 3 U.S. Opens, his 1st in 1948 and 2 more since his accident in 1950 and 1951. He also won this year's first major, the Masters. A win this week would tie Hogan with Willie Anderson and Bobby Jones for the record of 4 U.S. Open victories.

The Projected Runner Up

The man who is considered the 2nd favorite to win is Sam Snead. Snead, 41 years old, has won 6 majors, most recently the 1952 Masters, last year. Yet Slammin' Sammy has never won the U.S. Open, finishing 3 times as the runner up.

Qualifying for the U.S. Open

Despite their prodigious achievements and stature in the game, both Hogan and Snead, must still qualify for the U.S. Open, along with everyone else, except for Julius Boros. Boros is the one man who is automatically qualified as he won the Open last year in 1952.

Sectional rounds earlier this year resulted in 299 players earning spots in the 36 hole qualifying rounds that take place here on Tuesday and Wednesday. The top 149 players, in addition to Boros, then qualify for the official 1st round of the U.S. Open that starts Thursday.

The Practice Round — June 9, 1953

All the golfers played a practice round on Monday and the big excitement came from a total unknown. Bill Collins, a 1st year assistant club pro from Long Island, shocked the golf world by posting a record 29 on the front 9 at Oakmont. Oakmont's front 9 is an unusual par 37, so Collins was 8 under par. He eagled the 1st hole by striking his 2nd shot on the 497 yard par 5 just 10 feet from the pin. He then got to 6 under after 6 holes by posting 4 consecutive birdies on holes 3, 4, 5 and 6. His 29 broke the front 9 record by 3 shots.

On the par 35 back 9, Collins, a 24 year old ex-Marine, only managed a 39 to finish his round at 4 under par 68.

Ben Hogan did not play a practice round at Oakmont yesterday, but did spend time on the practice range

Qualifying Round Day 1 - June 10, 1953

On Tuesday, in the 1st round of qualifying, the massive number of golfers had to be split up across 2 courses. 149 golfers played the shorter Pittsburgh Field Club while the other 150 played Oakmont. Players then traversed the opposite course on Wednesday to finish the 36 hole qualifying.

In Tuesday's round another record was set as Chick Harbert, a 2 time runner up at the PGA Championship, scored a 66 at the par 71 Field Club. A noted long driver, he blasted one 350 yards on the par 5 11th hole on the way to one of his birdies.

Also playing at the Field Club was Monday's sensation Bill Collins. He managed only a 75, but still put himself in good position to qualify for the 1st round.

Experts are suggesting that a score of 157 or 158 for the 36 holes will be required.

Another player at the Field Club on Tuesday was a 23 year old amateur from nearby Latrobe, Pennsylvania by the name of Arnold Palmer. Palmer shot a 74 to put him well within the mix to qualify.

At Oakmont, a longer and more difficult course, the low score was posted by Dr. Cary Middlecoff with a 3 under 69. Middlecoff won the U.S. Open in 1949.

Ben Hogan's 1st Qualifying Round

The favorite, Ben Hogan, had a disappointing and concerning day. He managed only a 77 at Oakmont, putting him in some jeopardy of not qualifying, although he would probably have to shoot 80, at the easier Field Club, to miss the qualifying.

But more alarming is the fact that he pulled a muscle in his back on the 7th hole and struggled around the course the rest of the way. He told the Pittsburgh Post-Gazette that he planned to have a masseur work on the back that night.

Sam Snead, the other pre-tournament favorite, fared somewhat better with a 73 at the Field Club.

In spite of Hogan's poor 1st round, and his aching back, the Pittsburgh Post-Gazette's sports department is still picking Ben Hogan to be the winner of the U.S. Open. But as they noted in the Wednesday, June 10th paper, *"That's like picking the Yankees to win the pennant again."*

Qualifying Round Day 2 - June 11, 1953

Yesterday, in the 2nd qualifying round, the Oakmont record of 66 was equaled by another ex-marine, Jimmy Clark of Laguna Beach, CA. His 36 hole score of 138 was the low qualifying score overall, earning him a gold medal and $250 for winning the qualifying rounds.

Dr. Middlecoff had the 2nd lowest qualifying score of 140 after shooting a 71 at Oakmont yesterday.

The qualifying cut line ended up being lower than predicted at 156. Sam Snead was safely in at 145 after an even par 72 at Oakmont.

Ben Hogan was also well inside the cut line, shooting 73 at the easier Field Club to give him a 2 day score of 150. Hogan said he feels much better after the masseur put 2 vertebrae back in place on Tuesday night.

First day low scorer Chick Harbert could only manage an 82 at Oakmont, but combined with his 66 on day 1, his score of 148 got him a qualifying position.

And the practice round sensation, Bill Collins, shot a 74 at Oakmont to give him a 149, a stroke better than Ben Hogan, and a qualifying spot in today's 1st round.

Arnold Palmer, the young amateur from Latrobe, could only muster an 81 at Oakmont today, but his 155 was 1 stroke inside the cut line meaning he too will also tee it up today in his first U.S. Open.

Unfortunately for Jimmy Clark, Cary Middlecoff and other low scorers in the qualifying rounds, their handsome 36 hole scores won't count when the tournament begins in earnest today.

Today all the scores go back to even par. Qualifying round scores don't count. And just 150 golfers will play today in the official 1st round of the U.S. Open at Oakmont where all 4 rounds of the U.S. Open will be played.

1st Round - June 12 , 1953

The U.S. Open tournament's official 1st round took place yesterday with 150 players, who had survived the 36 hole qualifying rounds, teeing it up at Oakmont.

In the 2nd group of the day at 8:08am was the amateur, Arnold Palmer, making his first appearance in a major tournament. He started the tournament well. He was even par after 5 holes. But then he bogeyed 6 and 7 and triple bogeyed 8. A birdie at 9 gave him a 4 over par 41 on the front 9.

Things went south quickly however on the back 9 with a quadruple bogey 8 on the 10th hole. And then another double bogey on 15 led to a 12 over par round of 84.

Palmer's hometown Latrobe Bulletin had this to say about him and another proud Latrobe resident, Frank Kiraly, who shot 81, *"Despite what they do in the National Open championship rounds Frank Kiraly and Arnold Palmer have proved that they are among the better golfers in these United*

States. Just qualifying for the Open as they did this week was a tremendous achievement."

Perhaps the marquee group of the day teed off an hour later at 9:04am. It consisted of Gene Sarazen (the 1922 and 1932 champion), Jimmy Demaret and Dr. Cary Middlecoff. Demaret was 2 under at the turn, Middlecoff was even par, but the 51 year old Sarazen was 5 over with a 42.

Demaret shot 1 over on the back 9 to finish with a 71. Middlecoff could only manage 76. And Sarazen shot a score that put him on path to miss the cut at 82.

Ben Hogan was the next big name to tee off 10am. New York Times reporter Lincoln Werden followed Hogan on the course, and reported that, *"He walked jauntily to the 1st tee and his manner and poise constantly reflected buoyant confidence."*

Ben wasted no time taking control of the U.S. Open. He birdied the par 5 opening hole by sinking a 30 footer. Then he birdied holes 4, 6 and 7.

He was 4 under at the turn and added another birdie at the 16th to go to 5 under. At the 18th, he missed a 12 foot putt to tie the course record. Instead he finished with a brilliant, bogey free 67.

Hogan was rarely in trouble all day. He only landed in one trap. He was only in the rough twice. One fan on the course lamented, *"What's the use of watching him. He never makes a mistake."*

One striking thing about Hogan's score is that he shot 10 strokes better than he had in the 1st of the qualifying rounds 2 days ago. When asked how he did it, he explained to Harry Keck of the Pittsburgh Sun-Telegraph, *"You never get up for the qualifying the way you do for the championship."*

Sam Snead didn't tee off until 2pm, just around when Hogan was finishing. Snead was in a group with Ed Oliver and Jim Turnesa. Snead was playing with an injured left wrist. But some sportswriters, including Will Grimsley of the Norfolk Virginian-Pilot referred to it as a broken hand. Slammin' Sammy still managed to shoot even par 72.

Hogan was the only golfer to break 70

Hogan's 67 stood in stark contrast to the rest of the field as no other golfer broke 70.

Tied at 70 were 3 golfers, none of whom is felt to have a chance to catch Hogan: George Fazio, Walter Burkemo and an amateur, Frank Souchak.

The popular Jimmy Demaret, winner of 3 Masters, was 1 of 2 golfers at 71.

And Sam Snead, a winner of 6 majors, was 1 of 4 players at even par 72.

Other notable scores from the 1st round included:

Julius Boros, the defending champion from 1952 - 75

Bill Collins, the unknown who set the front 9 record in the practice round - 76

Jimmy Clark, the gold medalist from the qualifying rounds - 77

Gene Sarazen Writes About Ben Hogan

Gene Sarazen wrote an exclusive article for the Pittsburgh Sun-Telegraph that appeared in this morning's paper. He gave an exalted account of Hogan's performance. He started it out with this: ***"Ben Hogan who, in the 1st round of the National Open golf championship, more than lived up to the name his contemporaries like to know him by. The Hawk they call him, and hawk he was yesterday... For the hawk, as you know, flies around aimlessly while waiting for the kill."***

When he finished 5-5-5 the day before in the qualifying... there could be no doubt of his tactics. He was soaring high in order to go into his swoop, and the result was a 33-34-67 for the best round ever played at Oakmont, meaning a 67 in the actual championship, a far different thing from the 66 with which Jimmy Clark won the qualifying medal. It left Hogan's competition badly in arrears.

Leading scores after round 1

-5   **Ben Hogan**

-2   **Walter Burkemo, George Fazio, Frank Souchak**

-1   **Jimmy Demaret and Bill Ogden**

Even   **Sam Snead, Jerry Barber, Jay Hebert, Lou Barbaro**

2nd Round - June 13, 1953

George Fazio was the first of the leaders to tee off at 9:28am. He went out in 1 under 36 and shot even par on the back 9 for a 1 under par 71. For the 40 year old Fazio, whose best finish in a major is 3rd at the 1950 U.S. Open (in which he was last in the 3 man playoff), he had to be a thrilled to keep himself in contention with a fine round.

Sam Snead teed off at 10:24am. He birdied the 1st hole and made the turn at 1 under for the round. He putted well all day, and picked up another birdie on 17 to get to 2 under for the day.

On the final hole he got into trouble. He missed the fairway on his first shot and left his second shot off the green about 80 feet from the hole.

Jack Sell wrote in the Pittsburgh Post-Gazette, *"Just as Snead stepped up to chip, a youngster perched on a rooftop nearby yelled 'you're not going to make it, Sam.' The Slammer stopped abruptly, looked up at the lad and it's pretty certain the latter's ears burned."*

Snead then holed the 80 foot chip for a birdie which gave the crowd a thrill! Snead had finished with a 69.

Arnold Palmer teed off at 11:35am. He improved 6 shots over Thursday to post a 78. But his 2 day score of 18 over par 162 left him 9 shots over the cut line. Arnold Palmer had missed the cut in his 1st major tournament appearance.

Hogan has another great start

Ben Hogan teed off at 1:28pm and got off to a great start again in the 2nd round. He was 3 under after 4 holes. But he gave 2 shots back with bogeys on 5 and 8, to go out in 36. Then 2 more bogeys and 1 birdie on the back 9 left him with another 36 for a 2 day score of 5 under par 139.

This was good enough to give Hogan a 2 shot lead over Snead.

Leading scores after round 2:

-5   **Ben Hogan**

-3   **Sam Snead and George Fazio**

-1   **Lloyd Mangrum**

Even   **Jay Hebert**

Chick Harbert, the gold medalist from the qualifying round, made the cut at 152.

But Bill Collins, the practice round sensation missed the cut at 156 (77-79) as did Gene Sarazen at 161.

PREVIEW OF TODAY'S FINAL ROUNDS

Sam Snead, just 2 strokes behind Hogan, has to feel both great opportunity and great pressure going into today's final rounds. Snead won the PGA Championship on this course 2 years ago. And a win today would be the crowning achievement of his career as it would complete the career grand slam. He has won 3 PGA championships, 2 Masters and 1 British Open.

But the U.S. Open has eluded him. He has been very close before. Painfully close.

In the 1939 U.S. Open he came to the par 5 final hole needing just a par to win. He carded a triple bogey 8 and lost.

In the 1947 U.S. Open, Snead tied for 1st with Lew Worsham and lost the 18 hole playoff by a single stroke.

In the 1949 U.S. Open Snead again lost by just 1 shot.

Snead's Advantage

Sam Snead has a big advantage today and this creates a huge opportunity for him to capture his 1st U.S. Open title. The final day calls for 36 holes to be played. 18 in the morning and 18 in the afternoon after a very short break of just a few minutes.

For Ben Hogan, 36 holes in one day is exceedingly difficult since his near fatal car accident in 1949.

Al Abrams, in the Pittsburgh Post-Gazette, wrote this about Ben Hogan, *"Pain and fatigue wrack his spare, wiry frame when he overdoes his golf game. It must be remembered he set the pace in last year's open in Dallas by 4 strokes at the halfway mark only to drop by the wayside when the heat of 36 holes was too much to take. Had the open rules called for 18 holes today and the same on Sunday, the 40 year old Hogan would be a shoo-in."*

Abrams is referring to the 1952 U.S. Open in which Hogan started the final 36 hole day with twice the margin he has right now. Hogan led by 4, but ended up losing by 5. On the first 2 days he shot 69 - 69. But on the final day, covering 36 holes he shot 74 - 74.

But Hogan said after yesterday's round, *"I feel better than a year ago and I'm not tired."*

FINAL ROUNDS - June 14, 1953

The final day of the tournament consisted of 36 holes as is the custom in the U.S. Open at this time. The golfers had to play 18 holes in the morning and 18 in the afternoon with a very short break in between.

Here were the tee times for the leaders:

George Fazio started round 3 at 8:00am and round 4 at 12:30pm. His playing partner for both rounds was defending champion Julius Boros who started the day tied for 9th place at +3.

Ben Hogan started round 3 at 9:00am and round 4 at 1:30pm. His playing partner was Dick Metz who started the day in 6th place at +1.

Lloyd Mangrum started round 3 at 9:30am and round 4 at 2pm. His playing partner was Jerry Barber who started the day tied for 9th place at +3

Sam Snead started round 3 at 10am and round 4 and 2:30pm. He played with Jimmy Demaret who started the day tied for 9th place at +3.

NOTES From The Sports Time Traveler

In 1953, tee times in the U.S. Open final rounds were not based on position in the tournament. Thus, Hogan and Snead did not get to play head-to-head, nor were they even near each other on the course. Hogan was teeing off a full one hour ahead of Snead in both the morning and afternoon rounds. Such is the quirkiness of U.S. Open golf here in 1953. The top players are not paired together.

3rd Round

Teeing off at 8am, George Fazio made par on the first 5 holes. Then he bogeyed both the par 3 6th and par 3 8th holes to make the turn in 39. When he bogeyed the 10th and double bogeyed the 15th it effectively dropped him out of contention. He finished the round with a 5 over par 77.

Teeing off at 9am, Ben Hogan, birdied the 1st hole for the 3rd day in a row. Immediately his lead was now 3 shots on Sam Snead and George Fazio. But Hogan then bogeyed the 3rd and 5th holes on his way to a 38 on the front 9.

Lloyd Mangrum, playing 30 minutes behind Hogan, was 1 under for his round when Hogan made the turn, thus pulling within 2 of Hogan.

Sam Snead, playing an hour behind Hogan teed it up on the 1st hole at 10am. He proceeded to have a dream start. Snead birdied the 1st, 2nd and the 4th holes and passed Hogan and went into the lead at about the time Hogan had finished his front 9.

Scores when Hogan reached the middle of the round 3

-6 Sam Snead (1 hour behind Hogan on the course)

-4 Ben Hogan

-2 Lloyd Mangrum (30 minutes behind Hogan)

+1 George Fazio (1 hour ahead of Hogan)

Snead's Scare

Now in the lead, although he may not have known it at the time, Sam Snead bogeyed the 6th.

And then came a fateful hole.

As Snead lined up a birdie putt at 8 he heard the crowd roar. Hogan had just drained a 20 footer for birdie at 12. This seemingly unnerved Snead who proceeded to 3 putt and bogey the hole.

Snead had suddenly lost his lead and was tied with Hogan.

Scores when Snead reached the middle of the round 3

-5 Sam Snead (1 hour behind Hogan on the course)

-5 Ben Hogan

-2 Lloyd Mangrum (30 minutes behind Hogan)

Mangrum's Move

When Lloyd Mangrum birdied the 12th, there was a magic moment for him. Ben Hogan suffered a double bogey at 15 at about the same time. And Sam Snead bogeyed the 10th.

Suddenly there was a bona fide 3 man race in the U.S. Open.

Scores after Mangrum's 12th hole of the 3rd round

-4 Sam Snead (1 hour behind Hogan on the course)

-3 Ben Hogan

-3 Lloyd Mangrum (30 minutes behind Hogan)

But Mangrum's move was short lived as he bogeyed 14, double bogeyed 15 and bogeyed 17.

Hogan meanwhile picked up a stroke with a birdie on 17. And at just about the same time, Snead bogeyed 13.

Even though Snead parred in the rest of the way he had lost the lead.

Scores after 3 rounds

-4 Ben Hogan
-3 Sam Snead
+1 Lloyd Mangrum

4th Round

After a short break the players were back out for the final round. Hogan was still playing 1 hour in front of Snead.

Hogan birdied the 1st hole for the 4th consecutive round.

He now led the tournament by 2 shots over Snead.

Then Hogan promptly bogeyed 7 and 8. But Snead had given back a shot at the 3rd hole so Hogan still led by 1 when he reached the turn with 9 holes to play.

Scores when Hogan started the back 9 in round 4

-3 Ben Hogan
-2 Sam Snead

Hogan's Steely Back 9

It was a close 2 man race. The tournament was up for grabs at this point.

And when Ben Hogan needed it most, his game was rock solid. Hogan parred 10, 11 and 12 and birdied 13.

Meanwhile Snead's putter became totally unreliable. He missed 4 putts of under 8 feet on the front 9 of the final round. If he had made 2 of those 4 putts the tournament would have been tied at this point.

Scores when Snead started the back 9 in round 4

-4 Ben Hogan (5 holes to play)
-2 Sam Snead (9 holes to play)

Hogan's Under Pressure

Hogan then lost a shot at 15, reducing his lead to just 1 shot again.

When he came to the 292 yard par 4 17th hole, Hogan hit his driver *"with all his power"* according to Lincoln Werden of the New York Times. Hogan's ball landed 35 feet from the pin. His eagle putt narrowly missed and he tapped in for birdie.

On the 462 yard par 4 18th, Hogan hit driver and 5 iron to less than 10 feet from the hole and sank the putt for another birdie.

His sensational birdie-birdie finish gave him a back 9 score of 33. And a total of 283 (5 under par) for the tournament.

It was the clutch performance of a champion.

Snead Finds Out Hogan's Final Score

Snead lost a shot at 12 and then word reached Sam Snead while he was on the 13th hole that Ben Hogan had finished the tournament with a 5 under par score of 283. At this time Snead was 4 shots behind.

Scores when Snead Found Out Hogan Had Finished the Tournament

-5 Ben Hogan (finished)
-1 Sam Snead (6 holes to play)

Snead's Slim Chance

Behind by 4 with 6 to play, Snead must have known his chances were slim. The birdies at 17 and 18 had effectively sealed the tournament for Ben Hogan.

Snead parred 13 and 14 and remained 4 shots back with 4 to play.

Then Snead bogeyed 15 and 16 to fall 6 shots back. And that's how it remained.

Hogan finished as the only player under par for the tournament.

Only 2 players, Snead and Mangrum, were within 10 shots of Ben Hogan.

FINAL SCORES of the 1953 U.S. Open

-5   **Ben Hogan**
+1   **Sam Snead**
+4   **Lloyd Mangrum**
+6   **Jimmy Demaret, Pete Cooper and George Fazio**

Hogan's 6 shot victory looked larger than it was. When he stood on the 17th tee he had to assume the tournament was in doubt with Snead an hour behind him. His final 2 hole birdies, in spectacular fashion, had won him his 4th U.S. Open.

Sam Snead Speaks to the Press

Snead was quoted in the Pittsburgh Sun Telegraph saying, ***"Every open is won on the greens. I had plenty of opportunities but took 36 or 37 putts. I***

3-putted from 6 feet on number 8 in the morning. And 3-putted both 12 and 13 in the afternoon."

In his defense, Snead is bothered by an injured left wrist and indicated he is going to Johns Hopkins to have it examined after the tournament.

Sam Snead now has 4 runner up finishes in the U.S. Open.

While Ben Hogan tied the all-time record with 4 U.S. Open victories.

Hogan to Compete in the British Open

Ben Hogan told the press after the tournament that he felt good. His legs had held up for the grueling 36 holes. Although he said he was, *"more tired in the morning than the afternoon."*

He also announced that he plans to play in the British Open for the 1st time. Hogan plans to leave for Scotland in 10 days to prepare for the British Open that begins on July 8th at Carnoustie.

NOTE From The Sports Time Traveler™

Ben Hogan has now won both the Masters and the U.S. Open in 1953 and is heading to Scotland for the British Open. The Sports Time Traveler™ is very excited about the virtual trip across the Atlantic next month to see if Hogan can make it 3 majors in one year.

POSTSCRIPT

Hogan's 67 in the 1st round remained the best round in U.S. Open competition at Oakmont until 1973.

CHAPTER SEVEN

Ben Hogan Battles the British and His Own Body

1953 BRITISH OPEN

INTRODUCTION From The Sports Time Traveler™

Ben Hogan, the greatest golfer of his time, was at his height in the summer of 1953, despite the fact that he was 40 years old and playing an extremely limited schedule of only about a half dozen tournaments a year.

Hogan struggled to walk a golf course due to his near fatal auto accident in 1949 that disrupted his career when he was at his peak. Prior to the accident Hogan had won 30 times in the first 3 post-war years from 1946 - 1948, including the 1948 U.S. Open. The accident wiped out the 1949 season for Hogan and there was concern he would never walk, let alone play golf again.

But Hogan epitomized the word determination. The amount of practice he put in is legendary. The great golfer Gary Player believes Hogan practiced more than anyone in history. And so Hogan willed himself back to competitive golf.

While he could practice endlessly, his body could only endure walking the course for a few tournaments a year, and this put a severe limit on the number of tournaments he could play.

Despite his handicap, in April 1953, Hogan won the Masters for the 2nd time. And he followed that up in June with his 4th U.S. Open title.

Ben Hogan then decided to do something he had yet to do in his storied career - travel across the Atlantic to Scotland to compete in the British Open.

He had started to consider making the trip prior to the U.S. Open. In early June, newspapers ran stories that Hogan had filed his entry papers and that he would go to Scotland if he could get hotel reservations. This seemed like a half-hearted commitment. On June 9th the London Daily Telegraph reported that Hogan had booked a hotel and the paper indicated they believed he would make the trip.

But it is likely that Hogan didn't fully make up his mind to trek across the Atlantic until after he won the U.S. Open. Prior to the U.S. Open, the Fort Worth Star-Telegram had reported that Hogan was intent on capturing his 4th U.S. Open before taking his first shot at the British Open.

Once he had the U.S. Open title a week later, and had victories in the first 2 majors of the year, he had encouragement from golf officials on both sides of the Atlantic to try and go for a 3rd major.

In the June 17th Leicester Evening Mail in England Hogan said he was primarily going to make the trip, *"because so many people want me to."*

Naturally, I just had to make the virtual trip to Carnoustie in the Scottish Highlands to follow Ben Hogan's one and only British Open, and experience the famous golf links there that have hosted the British Open 8 times.

Here is the story from my virtual trip to Scotland in July, 1953.

CARNOUSTIE, SCOTLAND – Tuesday June 23, 1953

Ben Hogan arrived at Glasgow's Prestwick Airport today to prepare for next month's British Open here in Carnoustie, Scotland. He traveled here with his wife Valerie, and American amateur player, Frank Stranahan, who will also be playing in the Open.

The Nottingham Evening Post reported that Hogan was asked if he had any special reason why he wanted to win the British Open. Hogan replied, *"No, it doesn't feel any different to me than any other tournament. I always go out to win. It's pretty silly to enter a tournament and not try."*

Hogan explained why he arrived so early, 2 weeks before the start of the tournament. *"I don't know how different conditions here will affect me. I have come over early so that if there is a transition period I can give myself a chance to get over it."*

The Nottingham Evening Post also noted that the only golf course Hogan will play during his entire stay here in Scotland is Carnoustie.

FIRST PRACTICE ROUND – Thursday June 25, 1953

Morris Peden of the London Daily Herald reported that Ben Hogan played his first practice round at Carnoustie yesterday and shot a 69 on the 7,200 yard course. Peden noted that no one has ever broken 70 during British Open play at Carnoustie in the past and it was all the more astonishing given he just arrived from another country where there are vastly different conditions and a larger ball is used. As a result, Peden announced that it should be no surprise he is picking Hogan to win the British Open. He wrote, *"As far as I'm concerned* (he) *clinched that position finally on his performance yesterday."*

Practice Rounds – Saturday June 27, 1953

The Fort Worth Star-Telegram is keeping close tabs on Hogan's trip for his local supporters in Texas. In an article today it was noted in his 2nd practice round he shot a 70. But yesterday he struggled to finish his round that he played with Frank Stranahan and Robert De Vicenzo and Antonio Cerda of Argentina. After shooting 36 on the front 9, he started *"lifting his ball out of bunkers and failing to hole out on the greens. At the end of the round he walked off the last green while the others still were putting."*

Today Hogan took a day off. He told local reporters, *"It's tiring me out. It's different from what I'm used to."*

Burnside Course – Monday June 29, 1953

For the first time since he arrived in Scotland Hogan played a course other than Carnoustie on Sunday. He played the Burnside Course which will be the sight of one of the qualifying rounds that must be played prior to the start of the British Open.

The Fort Worth Star-Telegram reported that Hogan's popularity in Scotland his hindering his practice at Carnoustie. *"Crowds swarm all over the little Texan wherever he goes. A crowd of 3,000 showed up Sunday and prevented Hogan and his partners, Lloyd Mangrum, Frank Stranahan and Roberto De Vicenzo from putting."*

Carnoustie – Wednesday July 1, 1953

Hogan was back at Carnoustie yesterday for a practice round in which he played with Lloyd Mangrum and two Brits, Dai Rees and Max Faulkner. Rees shot 70, Mangrum 73 and Hogan and Faulkner 74. Hogan told an AP reporter that Carnoustie, *"requires a whole bag full of shots."*

The article noted that Carnoustie doesn't have a formal par score for the course because it is built right on the coast and is subject to variable winds. But a 74 is regarded as, *"a normal score."*

Carnoustie – Thursday July 2, 1953

Hogan rested again yesterday. An AP article noted, *"His absence disappointed several thousand local fans who turned out early hoping to see the U.S. Open champion."*

Predictions – Friday July 3, 1953

George Harley writing in The London Daily Mirror today shared the bookmakers odds for the tournament. Hogan is of course the favorite. Harley wrote, *"There is nothing open about this year's Open championship according to the folk that have been dazzled by the brilliance of the great Ben Hogan. They will tell you that the first prize check of 500 pounds could be paid into Hogan's handsome bank account even before the first stroke at Carnoustie on Monday."*

LONDON BOOKMAKERS ODDS TO WIN

7 – 4   **Ben Hogan**

5 – 1   **Bobby Locke, South Africa (the defending champion)**

8 – 1   **Robert De Vicenzo, Argentina**

9 – 1   **Lloyd Mangrum, USA**

20 – 1   **Eric Brown, Scotland**

25 – 1   **Peter Thomson, Australia (the 1952 runner-up)**

Harley also predicted that Hogan will have a record round of 68 during one of the early rounds of the tournament, but that, *"the course will take its revenge for this cavalier treatment on the last day. A mild error on an ordinary course can become a calamity at Carnoustie. And not even the great Ben is immune from error."*

As a result of this bold prediction, Harley is picking Scotland's Eric Brown to win the tournament. He is going with the Scot because he won the Scottish Amateur at Carnoustie in 1946 and the fact that a Scot is due to win. No Scot has won the British Open since 1931.

Hogan's Fitness – Saturday, July 4, 1953

James Goodfellow of the London Evening Standard interviewed Ben Hogan yesterday. He asked Hogan how he had mastered the smaller British Ball. Hogan replied, *"I don't think a player has ever mastered any ball."*

Goodfellow also reported on a positive indication regarding Hogan's fitness. He played 2 practice rounds; the first time he had done that since his 1949 car accident. But Goodfellow said Hogan's chances to win will be dependent on the weather. Hogan has said that he can't play well in the cold. The practice rounds have all been played in warm weather. But Goodfellow noted, *"All assessments of Hogan's chances will be valueless if the cold wind – and it can be very bitter – sweeps in from the sea next week."*

Pre-tournament Preparations - Sunday July 5, 1953

An AP article in the Fort Worth Star-Telegram described Scotland's overwhelming positive reception to Ben Hogan over the past 2 weeks, *"They call him the 'wee ice mon' and have begun openly to compare him with an old hero of theirs – Bobby Jones."*

Scots are also grateful just for the fact that Ben Hogan is in Carnoustie. *"Hogan's presence here has made the British Open once again the major international golf event of the year."*

In the London Sunday Mirror, humorous sports columnist Jack Peart described the hoopla surrounding Hogan, *"It's been 'Ben this — Hogan that,' ever since America's Mr. Golf sent in his entry form. Damned if I know why the rest of the field don't stick to poker and pints. Not only is Hogan the world's greatest golfer, but I'm convinced he has the greatest publicity agent."*

Peart finished his article on Hogan with this cute little joke, *"What a pity though that Hogan and Mangrum didn't get Bing Crosby and Bob Hope to caddie for them. Where there's Crosby there's always Hope."*

The Qualifying - Monday July 6, 1953

Today begins the 2 days of qualifying for what is called the "competition proper."

Only 8 Americans are here for the qualifying rounds which will take place today and Tuesday.

There are several drawbacks for why most top American pros do not make the trip to the British Open back here in 1953. In addition to the expense and time to travel, the cold, rainy and windy conditions and the requirement to play with the smaller British golf ball, there are several major issues:

THE LACK OF MONEY

There is also the lack of money to be won. If you come in 6th place, for example, you earn only 30 pounds or about $150. The entire purse is only $7,000. The funds are just not there as the British economy is still ravaged from World War II.

THE SCHEDULE CONFLICT

The final 2 days of the PGA Championship in the USA overlap with the qualifying rounds of the British Open. The PGA conflict didn't impact Hogan's decision however, for Hogan never played in the PGA Championship in the

1950s, as it required 36 holes to be played on each of the final 4 days in the match play format at that time.

Hogan's damaged legs simply could not physically handle the demands of the PGA Championship until it was changed to a stroke play event many years later.

THE QUALIFYING CONUNDRUM

On top of all the other issues keeping the Americans away, was the prospect that if you fail to qualify for the "competition proper" in the 2 days of qualifying rounds, your entire trip to Scotland earns you nothing.

The Americans

As a result of all the aforementioned issues, only 8 Americans entered the 1953 British Open, and 2 of the 8 Americans were amateurs. The professionals included Hogan, Mangrum, D.W. Fairfield, George Wise, Glenn Peeples and Tony Longo. The amateurs were U.S. army lieutenant J.S. Meiklejohn, and an interesting character named Frank Stranahan.

FRANK STRANAHAN - The "Professional" Amateur

Stranahan, 30, is the son of Robert Stranahan, the founder of the Champion Spark Plug company and a multi-millionaire. Frank's father's fortune has enabled him to live a life of ease and he has chosen to focus his time on golf. He is one of the leading amateurs in the world and has won the British Amateur twice.

He is a regular player in all the majors and finished 2nd in the 1947 Masters.

Tee times were in the newspapers this morning for the 2 days of qualifying. Hogan is scheduled to tee off at 2:09pm today at the Burnside course and at 10:24am on Tuesday at Carnoustie.

Each player must play one round at the 6,400 yard Burnside course and one at 7,200 yard Carnoustie during the 36 holes of qualifying. A maximum of 100 golfers out of the field of 170 will qualify for what is known as "the competition proper" that begins on Wednesday.

Qualifying round 1 - Tuesday July 7, 1953

Yesterday was the first of the 2 days of qualifying rounds.

The London Daily Telegraph's Leonard Crawley reported, *"From early morning it was clear that a large number of people had decided to take Monday off."* They went to the Burnside course where Hogan and defending champion Bobby Locke were playing. The Telegraph described the scene when Hogan teed off for 1st day of qualifying, *"an excited seething mob endeavored to follow the great man round this narrow course. Some were pushed into the burn at intervals and the more cautious gave up to watch less famous men."*

Crawley did manage to follow Hogan around. Ben quickly got to 4 under par and finished with a 70.

Locke meanwhile was sensational, shooting 65 to break the course record by 2 strokes. He was the low scorer on the Burnside course for the day by 3 shots over Max Faulkner. Hogan's 70 was tied for the 4th best score of the day on the easier, shorter Burnside layout. Dai Rees also shot 70.

Over at Carnoustie, John Panton scored a 3 on the 401 yard opening hole, the rest of his round was *"faultless, except for one indifferent stroke to the ninth,"* according to Pat Ward-Thomas of the London Guardian. Panton shot a 69. That put him 3 shots ahead of Antonio Cerda's 72. Frank Stranahan was in a group of 6 that shot 73. No one else at Carnoustie scored better than 75. Lloyd Mangrum could only manage a 78 putting him in jeopardy of not qualifying for the competition proper.

Qualifying round 2 - Wednesday July 8, 1953

Playing in his 1st competitive round at Carnoustie, Ben Hogan was not happy. He shot a 41 on the front 9 and although he came back in just 34, he had posted a 75 for the day. After he finished, George Harley of the London Daily Mirror wrote that Hogan snarled about the greens, *"You can't play on putty. I'll send them over a lawn mower to cut those greens when I get back home.* Then a grumpy Hogan, *"waved aside albums and pencils with a curt, 'no autographs.'"* Just then Hogan saw a face that made him smile and mellow out. It was Sydney Lanfield, the man who had directed the movie, "Follow the Sun," about Hogan's life up to 1950, when he returned from his horrific car accident to play in the Los Angeles Open. Hogan then told Harley, *"I played terrible. I just haven't learned how to judge distances with the British ball."*

The 75 was more than enough however for Hogan to qualify for the competition proper. The cut line came in at 154 with 91 players earning their spot in the competition proper that begins today.

Bobby Locke shot 71 at Carnoustie to be the qualifying medalist (the low score) at 136. That earned him 15 pounds (about $75). Locke was 5 shots clear of John Panton, who could only muster a 72 at Burnside after his brilliant 69 at Carnoustie.

Frank Stranahan shot a 71 at Burnside for a 2-day total of 144, which was actually a shot better than Hogan.

Lloyd Mangrum tore up the Burnside course with the lowest score of the day, a 67, and that got him into a tie with Hogan at 145 as well.

While Bobby Locke was 9 shots ahead of Hogan and Mangrum it meant nothing for the competition proper. When the tournament starts today everybody's scoring starts over again.

Besides Hogan, Mangrum and Stranahan, the only other American to make the qualifying cut was D.W. Fairfield with a 149.

1st ROUND of the British Open - Thursday July 9, 1953

The New York Times described the conditions faced by the 91 players that began the competition proper yesterday, *"wind, hail and cold that beset the ancient Carnoustie layout."*

But that didn't deter an estimated 10,000 fans from coming out to follow Ben Hogan. This consisted of nearly all the fans in attendance on the entire course in the 1st official round of the tournament. Hogan treated them to, *"a flawless exhibition against the wind to the turn* (the end of the 9th hole),*"* according to Leonard Crawley in the London Daily Telegraph. Crawley marveled at how the steely Hogan played despite the conditions, *"Caught in a violent hailstorm at the 6th, he hit the ball just like an arrow to the green."*

Hogan "parred" 14 of the 1st 15 holes according to the New York Times which published a chart of the suggested pars for each hole. However, "bogeys" down the stretch left him with a 1st round score of 73, still good enough for a tie for 7th place.

Hogan was not satisfied. The Times reported him saying, *"I don't mind scoring high. But I hate to do stupid things."*

Compared to the crowd following Hogan, Frank Stranahan, *"played in comparative privacy,"* according to the Times. He equaled the course record with a 33 on the back 9. That gave him a 70 and the lead after 1 round.

Lloyd Mangrum shot a 75 to put him in a tie for 15th. And the 4th American D.W. Fairfield was well back with an 82.

LEADING SCORERS AFTER ROUND 1

70   **Frank Stranahan, USA**

71   **Eric Brown, Britain**

72   **Bobby Locke, South Africa, Roberto De Vicenzo, Argentina and Dai Rees, Britain**

73   **Ben Hogan, USA and Fred Daly, Ireland**

2nd ROUND 2 - Friday July 10, 1953

Ben Hogan got off to a great start to round 2. The London Daily Telegraph reported, *"Those who saw his first five holes roundly declared that they ought to have been five threes... It is not until one has seen the amazing accuracy of his iron play that one can appreciate the full stature of this astounding golfer."*

But his great iron play was offset by his struggles on the green and he had to settle for a 71 and a 2 day score of 144. The New York Times quoted Hogan after the round, *"I'd feel real good about it if I was just putting a little better."*

Hogan's 144 put him 2 shots off the lead at the halfway mark of the tournament. The leaders were 2 Britain's, Dai Rees and Eric Brown at 142.

Stranahan started the day well with a 36 on the front 9, but he had to scramble on several holes on the back 9 and came in with a 38 for a score of 74 on the day, and a 144 after 2 rounds, to put him in a tie with Hogan.

Mangrum shot a 76 to give him a 2 day total of 151, putting him well back, but inside the cut line of 154.

LEADING SCORERS AFTER ROUND 2

142   **Eric Brown, Scotland and Dai Rees, Wales**

143   **Roberto De Vicenzo, Argentina**

144   **Ben Hogan, USA, Frank Stranahan, USA and Peter Thomson, Australia**

145   **Bobby Locke, South Africa, Max Faulkner, England and T.H.T. Fairbairn, England**

FINAL ROUNDS - Saturday, July 11, 1953

The final day of the British Open is a 36 hole affair. This made it exceedingly difficult for the damaged hero Hogan. Coming after 4 days of playing 18 holes each day, this was the biggest test yet for Ben Hogan.

3rd ROUND

Leonard Crawley covered the action in the London Daily Telegraph. He described Hogan's start in round 3, *"Hogan, followed by a crowd the like of which I have never seen on any golf course, began 4, 3, 4."*

Hogan was striking the ball well, but Crawley noted, *"the nightmare of three putts,"* kept him from scoring better.

At the 250 yard par 3 16th hole, Hogan managed a 3 with what Crawley described as *"the finest spoon* (3 wood) *I ever saw."*

Hogan was the equivalent of "3 under" for his round coming into the 454 yard 17th hole. He was in the sand trap in 2, blasted out and 3-putted for a 6. But he got a shot back when he only needed 4 strokes at the 503 yard 18th hole to finish with a round of 70.

That put Hogan into a tie for the lead with De Vicenzo of Argentina at the lunch break.

Hogan's 3 rounds had been successively better at 73, 71 and 70.

The low round of the morning was posted by Antonio Cerda with a 69. That boosted him from 10th place to a tie for 3rd.

Stranahan had a difficult round, but a 3 at 18 gave him a 73 and kept him at 3 strokes off the pace.

LEADING SCORERS AFTER ROUND 3

214   Ben Hogan, USA and Roberto De Vicenzo, Argentina

215   Antonio Cerda, Argentina, Dai Rees, Wales and Peter Thomson, Australia

217   Eric Brown, Scotland and Frank Stranahan, USA

4th Round

After lunch the sun came out. Hogan would now begin the difficult test of playing another round of 18 on his wrapped up legs.

Crawley wrote, *"He went off with four perfectly played fours and then at the fifth had a break. His tee shot finished in a vile spot. He played a grand second but his ball spun back to the lip of the bunker. After infinite study he decided to chip with a straight faced club and holed out. That made and inspired him once again."*

The New York Times described the 50 foot birdie chip shot as *"one of the most dramatic shots of the tournament."*

Hogan then followed that up by reaching the green in 2 on the 567 yard 6th hole. He 2-putted for a 4 on his way to a front 9 score of 34.

De Vicenzo, meanwhile had a 37 on the front 9. He finished with a 73, well off the lead.

Stranahan also had a 37 on the front 9 keeping him well back. But he came back with a course record 32 on the back 9, including another 3 on the long 18th hole for a 69 to finish the tournament. Still he was far behind Hogan.

Rees, who started the final round just 1 back, was having a good afternoon. But after a 5 on the 457 yard 15th, he could not keep pace with Hogan.

Cerda, *"finished gallantly in 71,"* according to Crawley, but it left him too far back.

Hogan played rock steady on the final 9 holes. He had a 2 on the 168 yard 13th hole, and never scored higher than the 5 he had on the 473 yard 14th hole.

Hogan had shot a stunning 68. The same score that George Harley of the London Daily Mirror had predicted Hogan might score in one of the early rounds. Except Hogan did it in the final round and never faltered.

In fact Hogan had set an Open championship record for a final round.

Ben Hogan had improved his score in each round of the competition proper, ending the championship with a 282 to capture the British Open title by 4 shots.

FINAL SCORES

282   Ben Hogan, USA

286   Frank Stranahan, USA, Antonio Cerda, Argentina, Dai Rees, Britain and Peter Thomson, Australia

287   Roberto De Vicenzo

Leonard Crawley called Ben the, *"unbeatable Hogan,"* which was his headline in the London Daily Telegraph. And he followed that up writing, *"who shall say he is not the best of all time?"*

Morris Peden of the London Daily Herald started his article with this, *"Hail the greatest golfer of our time - Ben Hogan of the United States - the man who staked his reputation on a bid to win the British Open championship and succeeded late last night in the most memorable finish in the history of the event."*

George Harley in the London Daily Mirror wrote, *"Hogan has proved himself the greatest golfer in the world. His final round was a picture of sustained accuracy, splashed with brilliance."*

Hogan, exhausted after the final 36 holes, announced that he plans to rest and not compete again until the 1954 Masters.

VIDEO

There is a very short 77 second highlight video of the 1953 British Open.

You can access it at this link on Kindle or by searching for "82nd Open - Carnoustie (1953)":

https://www.youtube.com/watch?v=tUKmsdDMA00

At the 30 second mark you can see Hogan teeing off.

At the 1 minute mark you can see Hogan holing his final short putt on the last hole of the tournament.

POSTSCRIPT From The Sports Time Traveler™

No one besides Ben Hogan has ever won the Masters, U.S. Open and the British Open in the same year.

If the PGA Championship would have been a stroke play event, held in the month after the British Open, as was the case for most of the 6 decades starting in the mid-1960s, it is very possible that Ben Hogan could have won the grand slam in 1953.

Regardless of the possibilities, Hogan's 1953 season is one of the all-time greatest in professional golf. And this from a man who was reduced to playing in constant pain in just a few tournaments a year.

NEW YORK CITY - July 22, 1953

Yesterday, there was a spectacle that has never been again seen in the world of golf - a ticker tape parade for a golfer.

Ben Hogan arrived back in America yesterday, with the claret jug for winning the British Open.

The ocean liner that carried him home was named the United States. When it passed the Statue of Liberty, on its way into New York, fire and police boats saluted Hogan. Then *"newspaper reporters, photographers, newsreel cameramen and television people boarded the liner,"* according to the New York Times.

And when the United States docked at pier 86 at 8:15am, there was a crowd on hand and giant signs that read, *"Welcome Hogan."*

4 hours later, Hogan got into the back of a convertible in lower Manhattan to begin the best automobile ride of his life.

Ben Hogan was having a New York City ticker tape parade in his honor.

4 years earlier, Hogan had the worst automobile ride of his life, when he was involved in a near fatal accident. He missed almost an entire year of golf, and he is still a physical wreck here in 1953. He has to wrap his legs to walk a golf course and he can only do it sparingly, playing just a half dozen tournaments a year.

And yet, Hogan captured the Masters, the U.S. Open and the British Open in this 1953 season.

He became the 1st man to ever win all 3 of those tournaments in the same year.

And no one else has done it since.

150,000 people lined the parade route, and tons of paper rained out of office building windows along the way.

The parade ended at City Hall where New York Mayor, Vincent Impelliterri, told Hogan, *"Here you are, the greatest golfer in the world, being introduced by the worst one."*

Hogan told the crowd, *"Only in America could such a thing happen to a little guy like me... I have tough skin, but I have a soft spot in my heart, and this tips anything that has ever happened to me... you just want to cry."*

He then received a telegram from President Eisenhower. Mayor Impellitterri read it out loud, *"Millions of Americans would like to participate with the New Yorkers today, who are extending their traditional welcome upon your return from your magnificent victory. We are proud of you."*

Today Ben Hogan's picture appeared on the front page of both the New York Times and the New York Daily News. The Daily News wrote in the caption, *"Ben's Approach is Perfect."*

You can watch a short news reel video of Hogan's arrival in New York and the ticker tape parade here:

https://www.youtube.com/watch?v=XXPQ7Zxyvhk

Or you can find it by searching YouTube for, "Ben Hogan Returns To USA (1953)."

CHAPTER EIGHT

Arnie's Open

THE 1962 U.S. OPEN AT OAKMONT

The Sports Time Traveler has now jumped ahead 9 years to 1962 to the U.S. Open. I wanted to see Arnold Palmer, at the top of his game, play a major on his "home course" at Oakmont.

OAKMONT – Tuesday June 12, 1962

The 1962 U.S. Open golf tournament starts in 2 days. Arnold Palmer is at the height of his career. He has already won 6 tournaments "this season" including the prestigious Colonial, the Tournament of Champions and his 3rd Masters. The Open is the 2nd major of the season and is being played at Oakmont, just a 45 minute drive from Palmer's home in Latrobe, Pennsylvania.

Palmer has substantial course knowledge at Oakmont. He won the West Penn Amateur at Oakmont in 1949 and competed in the U.S. Open at Oakmont in 1953. Palmer is the prohibitive favorite to win the U.S. Open at Oakmont which would set up a chance for the grand slam. But when asked who he thought was going to win, Palmer picked young Jack Nicklaus. Sportswriters aren't having any of that. Palmer is the clear pick to win the U.S. Open in the Pittsburgh Post Gazette.

Jack Nicklaus is just a 22 years old rookie. And he has never won a PGA Tour event. How could Palmer pick the young rookie to win? One reason is that as an amateur Nicklaus finished 2nd to Palmer in the 1960 U.S. Open and took 4th in the 1961 U.S. Open finishing well ahead of Palmer. Nicklaus also finished 2nd in the PGA Tour event last weekend in Montclair, NJ. And he is 4th on the money list for the season having netted $28,198 in 17 tournaments including 6 top 5 finishes.

Palmer leads the money list with more than double Nicklaus's winnings at $60,331. So again, why is Palmer picking Nicklaus? Perhaps its best summed up by Tour pro Ed Kroll who had this to say after missing the cut in Montclair, *"Nicklaus is simply unbelievable. If anyone ever had the power to bust a golf ball in two it is he. Watching Jack play is a thrill in itself. Guys like Palmer and Snead are almost as long off the tee. But where their low bullets occasionally hit a bunker 280 yards out, Nicklaus hits them so high they fall beyond the trouble spots. I think Jack has a real good chance of winning the Open."*

On Thursday, Arnold Palmer and Jack Nicklaus are scheduled to tee off together in the 1st and 2nd rounds. It's going to be an interesting couple of days.

Opening Rounds – Saturday June 16, 1962

Arnold Palmer is tied for the lead after 36 holes with Bob Rosburg at 3 under par. Palmer's playing partner the first two days has been rookie Jack Nicklaus. Jack is 3 back at even par. The final 36 holes will be played today (the U.S. Open didn't adopt the more standard 4 day / 18 hole format until 1965).

Record crowds have come out to Oakmont Country Club and they're almost entirely following Palmer who lives in nearby Latrobe, PA. Kenneth Eskey of the Pittsburgh Press wrote about yesterday's 2nd round, *"Arnold Palmer drew more fans on the practice tee early today than other contenders attracted in action on the course."*

Although more than 100 golfers teed off before Palmer hit his opening drive of the tournament at 1:42pm on Thursday, Al Abrams, sports editor of the Pittsburgh Post-Gazette wrote, *"nothing really began until King Palmer started the festivities. The crowd then waited politely for the chunky blond Nicklaus to follow him. They weren't so polite after that."*

Post-Gazette reporter Alvin Rosensweet followed the Palmer crowd all day Friday. He described *"Palmer's army"* as *"the hardiest breed of spectator in all sports - the 18 hole walking watcher."* After the round, Rosensweet *"walked up to an attractive young redhead"* and asked, *"Did you follow Palmer around for 18 holes?"*

"Well I walked for 18 holes, but I wasn't following Palmer," replied Barbara Nicklaus, wife of Jack Nicklaus.

When a spectator made a derogatory remark about Jack, his wife Barbara told him to, *"shut up."*

Even Palmer himself had to scold the crowd for bad behavior. When Palmer holed out first on several holes the crowd began to stampede to the next hole while Nicklaus was putting.

Regarding the actual play, Dave Ailes, of the Latrobe Bulletin, wrote, *"If Arnold Palmer doesn't win the 1962 U.S. Open it won't be because he didn't play two of the greatest opening rounds of golf in his 7 year star studded professional career."* Palmer has been 1st or 2nd in 6 of the last 9 majors and has won 4 of them.

Jack Nicklaus also had strong praise for Arnold Palmer after completing his second round with him on Friday. Speaking to Joe Greenday, of the Philadelphia Inquirer, Nicklaus said, *"I've never seen Arnie drive any better than he has the past two days. There is a big premium on drives on this course and he's driving well and playing super golf."*

The Sports Time Traveler is headed back to Oakmont "tomorrow" for the grueling final 36 holes.

OAKMONT, PA - Sunday June 17, 1962

On page 1 of the Pittsburgh Press today a large picture of Arnold Palmer dominated the top middle of the page. Just to the right of the picture was the lead story with the headline that began, *"Arnie's Open."*

This is Arnold Palmer country and his rabid fans came out yesterday to watch him win a U.S. Open on his "home course."

At the start of play "today" the leaderboard looked this:

-3   Arnold Palmer & Bob Rosburg

-1   Billy Maxwell

EVEN   Bobby Nichols, Jack Nicklaus and Gary Player

3rd Round

The crowd on the final day was thought to be the largest to ever witness a golf event. Shirley Uhl, who penned one of two stories about Palmer on the front page of the Pittsburgh Press reported that 10,000 fans followed Palmer. Uhl reported, *"Arnold Palmer's admirers - labeled 'Arnie's Army' by the Marshals — continued to dominate the scene."* Jack McNamara, who wrote the lead article in the paper described the scene on the course yesterday, *"The gallery following Arnold Palmer was a cheering section that lined each fairway from tee to green."*

Early on the final day, Gary Player took the lead as Palmer, with a flurry of 3-putt greens, took 38 strokes on the front nine. But Palmer surged on the back nine of the 3rd round capped by a brilliant eagle on the short par 4 dogleg 17th hole. Playing just 292 yards, Palmer drove the green to within 18 feet of the pin. Jack McNamara described the fans reaction, *"when he rammed the putt home for an eagle, they gave him an ear splitting ovation that lasted 2 minutes."*

After 54 holes Palmer was back in a tie for the lead:

-1   Arnold Palmer and Bobby Nichols

EVEN   Bob Rosburg and Phil Rodgers

+1   Jack Nicklaus & Gary Player

4th Round

In the last round Palmer started with birdies on 2 of the first 4 holes to reach 3 under for the tournament.

Nicklaus, playing with Billy Maxwell, who he regularly outdrove by 40 yards, got off to a slow start with a bogey on the 1st hole, and after Palmer made his two early birdies Nicklaus was 5 shots behind Palmer with 12 holes to play.

But Nicklaus birdied 7, 9 and 11. While Palmer bogeyed 9 and 13, putting the two players in a tie at 1 under when Arnie had 5 holes to play. It was actually a three way tie as Bobby Nichols had also managed to reach 1 under par at this point. But when Nichols bogeyed 15, it was just Palmer and Nicklaus alone in a tie.

Several others that had been contending fell off the pace. Palmer's playing partner Bob Rosburg had faded badly, going on to shoot a 79 in his final round. Gary Player could only manage a round of 74. And Billy Maxwell, the 1951 U.S. Amateur champion, also carded a 74.

As Palmer and Nicklaus made pars on 14, 15, 16 and 17, it set up the potential for one of them to win the tournament with a birdie on 18.

Nicklaus was playing in the group ahead of Palmer. On the final hole Nicklaus had a 12 foot putt to take the lead. He missed it one inch to the left. Tapping in for a score of 1 under par, 283 for the tournament, the "freshman" was tied for the lead as he waited for Palmer to finish.

Palmer playing in the last group of the day, with Bob Rosburg, fired his 2nd shot on the par 4 18th hole to 10 feet from the pin. Arnold Palmer now had a putt to win the U.S. Open at Oakmont. He also missed by an inch to the left.

Arnold Palmer, the King of golf, and Jack Nicklaus, a rookie who has never won on the PGA Tour, each missed putts on the 72nd hole of competition in the U.S. Open yesterday and now will face each other head-to-head for the third time this week in an 18 hole playoff today.

For Palmer it had been a woeful day on the greens. He started with 3 putts on 4 of the first 9 holes. New York Daily News writer, Dana Mozley, best captured the impact of the missed opportunities with this line, *"Because he is putting no better than your Auntie Mame, Arnold Palmer is going to have to work overtime."*

Palmer himself made light of his putting problems in the post round press conference joking, *"Any putters in the crowd that want to give me a lesson tonight?"*

Nicklaus sitting next to Palmer in the press conference shot back, *"I'd hate to see him when he's putting good."*

Palmer had another misfortune that cost him a stroke in the middle of the day when he was disturbed by a low flying plane that carried one of the TV cameras. The plane gunned its engine right as he was hitting an 18 inch putt causing him to miss.

It was a long day for Palmer, and not just because of all the missed putts. The golfers played 36 holes on this final day of the tournament as is the custom of the U.S. Open here in 1962.

Asked about the playoff during the press conference, Palmer joked again saying, *"I wish it was against someone else other than this big strong dude. I thought I was through with him yesterday."*

Nicklaus said, *"I feel wonderful and hope I feel better tomorrow night."*

The playoff starts at 1:45pm today at Oakmont Country Club. The Sports Time Traveler will be there.

OAKMONT PA - June 18, 1962

Arnold Palmer had the home course advantage in yesterday's 18 hole playoff for the U.S. Open Championship. Oakmont Country Club is just 45 minutes from his home. The 10,000 fans that came out to follow the 2 golfers were solidly behind Palmer. Dana Mozley estimated four-fifths of the gallery were *"members of Arnie's Army - many of them loyal rooters from Palmer's home in nearby Latrobe."*

The playoff began with Palmer bogeying the first hole. Nicklaus birdied the 4th hole to go up by 2. And then on the 6th hole Nicklaus birdied while Palmer bogeyed putting Jack up by 4.

Phil Gundlefinger, of the Pittsburgh Post-Gazette, wrote that, *"Jack out-drove, outputted and for most of the way outslowed Palmer."* Nicklaus' slow play irritated Palmer and drew a warning from USGA officials who told him to play faster halfway through the round. Afterward Palmer said, *"I like to play faster."* Nicklaus defended his pace saying he is usually in a hurry and misses strokes and didn't want that to happen.

But Palmer is the ultimate competitor, and he managed to rally with birdies on 9, 11 and 12 to cut Nicklaus's lead to one. Then on the par 3, 161 yard, 13th hole. Palmer made a mental error. Dana Mozley quoted Palmer, *"I made a stupid mistake. I thought I'd get smart and hit an easy 4 iron. The pin was so far back. At the last minute I decided on the 5 iron and flubbed the shot."* Palmer's tee shot left him 65 feet from the hole and he three-putted for a bogey which put him 2 behind with 5 to play.

Each man parred the next 4 holes leaving Palmer still down by 2 entering the final hole. Nicklaus's tee shot on the 462 yard par 4 final hole missed the fairway by just a couple of feet, and found high rough. Palmer then drove his ball into the middle of the fairway, although not as far as Nicklaus. On his second shot,

Palmer hit *"a 3 iron so fat it didn't even reach the trap fronting the green"* according to Dana Mozley. Nicklaus then hit a *"safety shot"* out of the rough, setting up a 9 iron 3rd shot that landed 15 feet from the hole. Palmer then chipped his 3rd shot to 12 feet from the hole.

Both men were now on the 18th green in 3 shots, there was still a small opportunity for Palmer to possibly tie the match up. If he could sink his 12 footer and by some chance Nicklaus 3-putted there would be a tie. Nicklaus was away and went first. He left his putt 3 feet from the hole. No gimme. Now the pressure was on Palmer. If he made his 12 footer all he needed was Nicklaus to miss his 3 footer and the match would be tied.

But Palmer missed his putt. He then half-heartedly tried to tap the ball into the hole and missed again and wound up with a double bogey 6. At that point, Palmer picked up Nicklaus's mark to concede the match and congratulate Nicklaus. But the playoff was based on stroke play, not match play, and USGA officials quickly intervened. They placed Nicklaus's ball on the green and required him to putt out. Nicklaus made the 3 foot putt to officially win the U.S. Open.

Despite the rabid crowds favoring Arnold Palmer, a rookie, Jack Nicklaus, had kept his cool, and in defeating Palmer by 3 shots, he captured the 1962 U.S Open. He also gave evidence that at just 22 years old, he might be a major championship contender for years to come.

Dana Mozley, of the New York Daily News, described the outcome, *"young in years but old in know-how of the game, Jack Nicklaus today sprung one of golf's major surprises."*

And Nicklaus grew great praise from Dave Ailes in Palmer's hometown newspaper, The Latrobe Bulletin, *"Nicklaus is particularly impressive in that he makes so few mistakes despite his tender years. His tee shots look like they come out of a cannon and he seldom hits anywhere but down the middle."*

This was Nicklaus's first professional win, but he had previously won two U.S Amateur titles in 1959 and 1961. As an amateur, Nicklaus also had previously come in 2nd in the 1960 U.S. Open and 4th in the 1961 U.S. Open. In winning this year's U.S. Open Nicklaus now has the best score in U.S. Open golf over the past 3 championships.

Phil Gundelfinger, writing in a front page story in the Pittsburgh Post-Gazette said, *"The defeat was a bitter one for Palmer, who saw his dream of winning the pro grand slam shattered."* Palmer had won the Masters in April for the 3rd time.

Phil Grose of the Charlotte Observer wrote that Palmer said, *"I guess this was the greatest disappointment of my golfing career. I'd still like to have the British Open and the PGA. But I guess I'll have to wait till next year for the grand slam."*

Palmer struggled with his putter all day as he had the day before. He 3-putted 3 times. Arnold described his putting this way, *"I was stroking a wet noodle."* Palmer clearly lost this tournament on the greens. Over the 90 holes of tournament play, Palmer 3-putted 12 times while Nicklaus 3-putted just once. Palmer said, *"I've used this putter for 5 years and I guess it's time for a change."*

Palmer had great praise for Nicklaus after the match, *"He's the finest young player in the game today. He has everything to become a truly outstanding player."*

CHAPTER NINE

The Best He Ever Played

THE 1962 BRITISH OPEN

TROON, SCOTLAND - Saturday July 14, 1962

Arnold Palmer, the king of golf, came to Scotland last week on a mission to win the British Open and avenge his gut wrenching playoff loss last month in the U.S. Open to the upstart rookie Jack Nicklaus.

But quite remarkably the defending champion found himself in a position to miss qualifying for the Open Championship. This past Monday was the first of 2 days of qualifying rounds. Here in 1962, all of the 355 entered players still have to qualify to play in the British Open once they are here, even the defending champion, Arnold Palmer.

Each player traversed both the 18 holes at Troon and 18 holes at nearby Loch Green on Monday and Tuesday. Palmer played the longer and more difficult Troon course on Monday and shot just 76. That put him in danger of missing the top 120 that would qualify for the beginning of the 72 hole tournament on Wednesday. The cut off at that time was projected to be a score of 150. Palmer explained later that his stomach was upset from something he ate in the morning.

He said, *"I took something that made me feel drunk when I went out to the first tee."*

On Tuesday, Palmer was on the shorter Loch Green course. He needed to shoot par or better to be assured of a qualifying spot. He did better. He shot a 67 which enabled him to easily qualify with a 2 day score of 143.

But Palmer revealed his physical struggles were continuing as he said immediately after the round, *"Now I'm off for some heat treatment to this back, it's been killing me. That's why a lot of my drives drifted off to the right."*

The first round of the tournament was on Wednesday. Palmer said his back *"is still troubling me a little, but it's better than it was yesterday."* He shot an opening round 71 to put him in 3rd place, two shots behind the leader Keith MacDonald.

On Thursday, in the 2nd round, Palmer said he felt only slight hip soreness and fired a 69 to take a 2 shot lead over Nagle.

Here were the leading scorers after 2 rounds:

-4   **Arnold Palmer**

-2   **Kel Nagle**

+1   **Bob Charles, Jimmy Martin, Ralph Moffit, Phil Rodgers**

Jack Nicklaus, who shot 80 on the first day was at +8, and 12 shots back of Arnold. Regarding his 80 in the 1st round, Nicklaus had told a reporter, *"How do you shoot an 80? I couldn't shoot an 80 if I tried."*

Friday was the final day and the golfers had to play 18 holes in the morning and another 18 in the afternoon. Palmer was paired with Nagle who birdied 1 and 2. And when Palmer hooked a shot into the bunker and bogeyed the 4th, he was suddenly a shot behind Nagle.

Arnie is legendary for his come from behind victories and perhaps this was the stimulus he needed. On the 210 yard par 3 fifth hole, Palmer hit his tee shot to

10 feet and sank the birdie putt. Nagle bogeyed the hole and just like that Palmer was back in the lead.

On the back 9 of the 3rd round Palmer *"went wild"* according to Fred Tupper in a special to the New York Times. He birdied 12 and 13 and then at 15 he *"deliberately hooked an iron shot that swung into the green and fetched up 6 feet from the cup."* He made the birdie putt and yet another at 16. He finished up with a course record 67 and was up by 5 shots on Nagle and 8 shots on 3rd place, held by Bob Charles, as the players took their short lunch break.

The final 18 holes in the afternoon were somewhat chaotic. Palmer's play was steady but the 30,000 fans were *"running amok on the course now, ignoring the stewards' signals, yelling when the players were striking the ball and knocking each other down in wild scrambles,"* according to Tupper. The AP article in the Los Angeles Times indicated that *"the fans swirled all over the fairways, moved at times as the players lined up their putts and talked at other vital shot making times."*

Palmer was heard saying, *"Please stay - please,"* and Nagle urged the crowd, *"please be quiet."* Palmer said afterwards, *"I don't think I've ever experienced crowds like this one. We had to wrestle with them the whole way."*

Palmer however never came unhinged. Pat Ward-Thomas of the London Guardian wrote, *"The early afternoon was a marvellous exhibition of Palmer's immense power and control, crushing power and technique."*

In the final round he had 6 birdies and missed several other birdie opportunities in firing a 69 for the easy win.

Arnold Palmer didn't just win the British Open "yesterday" at Troon. He crushed the field and set the Open Championship record. Palmer played so well that young Jack Nicklaus said he played *"unbelievable on a course that is the toughest I've ever seen."*

The magnitude of the victory was so stunning that some sportswriters were moved to share heartfelt pieces about what they had witnessed. Writing in the Birmingham Post in England, Maurice Woodbine started his front page article with this, *"There are some sporting occasions which linger in the memory after more important matters have faded. This one, I am quite certain, will stay with me for the rest of my days."*

Other writers shared in emphatic terms how extraordinary Palmer's performance was. Jimmy Stevenson of the London Daily Mirror wrote, *"It was the conquest of the century."*

Palmer even impressed himself saying, *"I've never played four rounds of golf like these in my whole life."*

No one is surprised that Palmer won The Open Championship. He was the favorite coming in. The fashion he did it in is what is so remarkable. Perhaps Palmer was driven to avenge his playoff loss last month to Jack Nicklaus at the U.S. Open. If that was the case then Palmer most emphatically proved who is the better golfer many times over. Palmer's 72 hole score of 276, the new Open Championship record, was an astounding 29 shots better than Nicklaus's total of 305 which put him in a tie for 32nd place.

Palmer also tied a record for the largest margin of victory in Open Championship history, finishing 6 shots ahead of the 2nd place finisher, 1960 champion, Kel Nagle. Another mind boggling statistic is that 3rd place was another 7 shots behind Nagle. Never before had an Open champion been 13 shots ahead of 3rd place.

And Palmer and Nagle were the only 2 players to break par for the Open.

In addition to having his name etched on the Claret Jug, Palmer won $3,920 (8000 pounds) for 1st place.

Pat Ward-Thomas summed up Palmer's performance as, *"the greatest exhibition of golf supremacy that Britain has seen in modern times. It was a rout without parallel."* Thomas also praised Palmer for his participation in the tournament, *"Palmer's presence these past 3 years has brought greatness once more to the Open Championship."*

FINAL SCORES of the 1962 British Open

-12	Arnold Palmer
-6	Kel Nagle
+1	Phil Rodgers and Brian Huggett
+2	Bob Charles
+4	Sam Snead and Peter Thomson

THE SPORTS TIME TRAVELER wishes to add a note to the article that was not revealed in any of the newspapers stories from July 14, 1962.

A quick look at Palmer's record in major championships reveals that in the 11 majors starting with the 1960 Masters through the 1962 British Open, Palmer won 5 times and took 2nd three more times. He was 1st or 2nd in 8 of 11 majors. And in the other three all he did was finish 5th, 7th and 14th. This was one of the most remarkable stretches of play in major championships in golf history.

In addition, it is also worth noting that Palmer was one stroke away from winning the 1962 U.S. Open which he had lost in a playoff to Nicklaus. Thus, Palmer was very close to being only the 2nd man to win the first 3 majors of the season (Ben Hogan did that in 1953).

CHAPTER TEN

The Masterpiece

THE 1964 MASTERS

INTRODUCTION from The Sports Time Traveler

The early 1960s was the era of the Big Three in golf - Gary Player, Arnold Palmer and Jack Nicklaus.

Coming into the 1964 Masters, every Masters title of the decade so far had been won by one of the Big Three - Palmer (1960 and 1962), Player (1961) and Nicklaus (1963).

Of the first 22 majors in the 1960s, the Big Three won 13 of them.

But those major titles weren't evenly distributed.

Gary Player won 3, Jack Nicklaus won 4 and Arnold Palmer, "The King," won 6.

Arnold Palmer began the decade of the 1960s with a run that has never been duplicated, not by Jack in his prime, and not even by Tiger Woods.

Palmer finished in 1st or 2nd in 8 of the first 11 majors of the 1960s. In the 3 that he didn't place in the top 2, he finished 5th, 7th and 14th.

In addition, Palmer won 29 PGA tournaments in the first 4 years of the 1960s. While Player and Nicklaus each won less than 10.

Palmer's dominance in that 4 year stretch from 1960 - 1963 is even greater than Tiger Woods best 4 years in terms of PGA TOUR victories, as Woods never won more than 27 events in any 4 year span.

Palmer's success spawned the formation of Arnie's Army, his legion of fanatical followers on the golf course.

But in the beginning of 1964, Palmer was in a drought and there were many doubts about whether he was still on top of his game.

For the first time since early in his pro career in 1956, Palmer had not won a tournament prior to the Masters.

He also had not won a major in 1963, his first year in the 1960s without a major title.

Arnold Palmer had a lot to prove coming into the 1964 Masters, to himself and to his army of fans.

Naturally The Sports Time Traveler™ just had to go back to see if Arnold Palmer, or one of the other members of the Big Three, could win another Masters.

AUGUSTA, GA - April 13, 1964

I'm here in Augusta, virtually, where yesterday the 1964 Masters concluded.

Arnold Palmer was so determined to end his drought on tour and in the majors that he was the first of the Big Three to fit in a practice round at Augusta back on March 15th.

While Jack Nicklaus has already won earlier this season in Phoenix, and Gary Player in Pensacola, Arnie has not won on tour since last October. And he hasn't taken a major since the 1962 British Open.

With questions lingering around Palmer's prowess, a UPI article, by Oscar Fraley, was bullish on Arnie, Fraley opened his pre-tournament article stating, *"This week's Masters golf tournament could be the one in which Arnold Palmer proves "The King" is not dead."*

Oddsmakers were also having none of the talk that Palmer is past his prime. They set the defending champ, Nicklaus, and Palmer as 3 - 1 co-favorites to win the Masters. While fellow Big Three member, Gary Player was next at 6 - 1.

You can experience the 1964 Masters via this 45 minute YouTube video:

The 1964 Masters Video on YouTube

You can find the video by searching on YouTube for "1964 Arnold Palmer."

Here's my recap of the key highlights with the time stamps on the video:

4:45 - See Jack and Arnie in brief interviews just before the start of the tournament. Nicklaus notes that Palmer always plays well at The Masters and is eager for a win. Palmer said that he's had trouble with his putting and he hopes it's just temporary.

OPENING ROUND

7:15 - Watch the honorary starters tee off - Jock Hutchison, age 79, winner of the 1921 British Open and Fred Mcleod, age 81, winner of the 1908 U.S. Open.

14:00 - The Masters scoreboard at the end of the 1st round appears in the unique style used at Augusta which shows the hole by hole over/under par totals for the tournament. The system is fantastic for seeing at a glance how the leaderboard changed throughout the round.

At the end of the round 1 here were the top scorers:

-3 Arnold Palmer, Gary Player, Bob Goalby, Kel Nagle Dr. and Davis Love

-2 Don January, Gene Littler, Dave Marr and an amateur, Billy Joe Patton

-1 Jack Nicklaus, Bob Charles, Gary Cowan (amateur), Jim Ferrier, Dow Finsterwald and Chi-Chi Rodriguez

It is notable that Gary Player is playing the Masters with infected tonsils and will require a tonsillectomy immediately following the tournament. This makes it all the more remarkable that Player shares the lead.

SECOND ROUND

18:20 - Palmer sinks a 35 foot birdie putt on the 15th hole and moves into a commanding lead. Bobby Jones, seated by the 15th green gives Palmer a pat on the back. Then Palmer sinks another birdie at 16.

19:15 - The round 2 leaderboard shows Palmer birdied 3 of the final 4 holes to take a 4 shot lead.

At the end of the round 2 here were the top scorers:

-7 Arnold Palmer

-3 Gary Player

-2 Don January and Gene Littler

-1 Bob Charles, Dow Finsterwald, Tony Lema and Dave Marr

Jack Nicklaus is a shot further back at even par with a group of 11 golfers including 3-time winner 53 year old Jimmy Demaret.

THE THIRD ROUND

In the 3rd round, the Master's pairings did not have the leader tee off in the last group as is customary for all PGA TOUR events back in the present time.

Palmer teed off in the 7th to last group on Saturday.

Palmer was spurred on by his loyal fans now famously referred to as "Arnie's Army," as their hero was clearly on a track that could take him to victory.

Jim Becker of the AP shared this quip about the army, *"It was a little awesome to behold. Sherman who had some experience with marching in these parts, would have run for cover at the sight of this army."*

The army's rank and file identify with Arnie's everyday man approach to the game. Becker's article continued with this:

"'Go get 'em, Arnie,' they growled, as Palmer stalked to the first tee like an angry panther, tugged at his yellow shirt, tugged at his white visor cap and tugged at his low-slung trousers."

Becker then provided this description of Arnie's Army's antics:

"Loyal to a fault, hardy as a pack of Death Valley mules, strong, agile, loud, kind, obedient, reverent and clean, Arnie's Army charged, rolled, swept, cluttered and straggled around the Augusta National Golf Course behind their hero Saturday."

Never before has the game of golf witnessed such a rabid fan base for one player.

27:30 - Watch 51 year old Ben Hogan birdie the 13th hole to go 3 under on his round (but still 1 over for the tournament). Then see the camera pan to capture the enormous crowd following the twosome of Hogan and Demaret, winners of 5 Masters between them.

28:15 - See the 3rd round leaderboard at the midway mark for the final groups of the day. Palmer teeing off earlier, and now thru 14 holes, has stretched his lead to 5 shots over Dave Marr. Player is 6 shots back and Nicklaus 7 shots behind.

At the end of the 3rd round the scores were as follows:

-10 Arnold Palmer

-5 Bruce Devlin

-4 Dave Marr

-3 Gary Player, Peter Butler and Jim Ferrier

-2 Bo Wininger

-1 Jack Nicklaus, Ben Hogan, Deane Beman (amateur), Billy Maxwell, Dan Sikes and Johnny Pott

Palmer finished his round with a stretch of 3 straight birdies at 14, 15 and 16 to become the only player in the field to shoot 3 consecutive rounds in the 60s.

And even though he had a 4 stroke lead coming into the round he played as aggressively as ever. The Greenville News (in South Carolina) quoted Arnie about his lead, *"I went out to make it bigger if I could."*

He explained his great scoring to the Atlanta Constitution after Saturday's round, *"I've never seen this course playing so easy."*

Australian Bruce Devlin, who won his 1st PGA tournament last month in St. Petersburg, Florida, vaulted into 2nd place by going 5 under par from the 12th thru 16th holes on his way to a 67.

Ben Hogan also shot 67 on Saturday, equaling the low round of the tournament so far. What is quite amazing is that Hogan is playing in his first competitive tournament of the year, and only plans to play in one more in 1964, The Colonial, in his home state of Texas.

Defending champion Jack Nicklaus, suffering from poor putting in the first 2 rounds, was mounting a small charge with birdies on 8 and 11 in the 3rd round when he suffered a ghastly tee shot on the par 3 12th that disrupted his play.

25:15 - Back up to the 25:15 mark on the tape to see Nicklaus's errant shot on the 12th hole in round 3. Announcer Chris Schenkel said, *"It must be years since he cold shanked a shot like that."*

The AP wrote, *"Nicklaus shanked his 8 iron far to the right bringing an astonished gasp from the gallery."*

Nicklaus described the shot humorously after the round, *"I nearly hit the boys coming up on the 13th tee."*

Although he finished with a 71 on the round, Nicklaus lost any momentum with the shank at 12, and was hopelessly behind Palmer at 9 shots back going into Sunday.

Gary Player, despite the raging soreness in his throat, birdied 13, 15 and 16 on Saturday to reach 5 under late in his round before carding bogeys at 17 and 18 to fall back to minus 3. At 7 shots back he had no realistic chance to catch the King.

With his 5 shot lead, newspapers were ready to hand the green jacket to Arnie a day early, especially since Devlin, his nearest pursuer, had only made the cut in the Masters for the first time this week.

Headlines in Sunday's papers focused on the opportunity for Palmer to better Ben Hogan's record 14 under score in 1953. The Macon Telegraph ran a headline, *"Palmer Nears New Record."* The Asheville Citizen had a headline that read, *"Palmer Aware Record Possible."*

THE FINAL ROUND

32:35 - Watch the great swing of Ben Hogan as he tees off in the final round. Hogan will shoot a final round of 72 to finish the Masters at -1, good for 9th place. Not bad for a guy over 50 playing in just 2 tournaments all year.

35:00 - On the leaderboard you can see Bruce Devlin has birdied the opening two holes to pull within 3 strokes to go to minus 7, while Palmer making pars remains at minus 10. But Devlin then misses a par putt at 4 and on the video he misses a par putt at 5 and falls back to 5 shots behind Palmer. Devlin will not contend any further.

37:20 - We can see the leaderboard again at the turn. Palmer has gone out 1 under for the day to reach minus 11 for the tournament. Devlin is still minus 5, but now Dave Marr has reached minus 7. He's within 4 strokes of Arnie.

Palmer then bogeys the 10th hole to fall back to minus 10 and suddenly Dave Marr is only 3 shots back.

37:45 - Palmer tees off at the par 3 12th and puts his ball 18 feet from the pin. Now Marr tees off. It's possibly the biggest moment in Marr's young golf career. At 30 years old, he has never contended for a major.

A birdie could bring Marr within 2 shots. But instead Marr hits the ball in the water and loses a shot. Palmer's lead is now back to 4 shots with 6 to play.

38:55 - Now Jack Nicklaus is making a charge, as Jack frequently does in the final rounds of majors. His 2nd shot on the par 5 13th hole hits the pin and stops less than 3 feet from the hole. Nicklaus makes the short putt for an eagle 3 and is now 4 under on his round.

Nicklaus then birdies 15 to go to 5 under on the round and 6 under for the tournament.

Jack Nicklaus has vaulted into 2nd place and is just 4 shots behind Arnie.

39:33 - Nicklaus tees off at the par 3 16th. A birdie here could put real pressure on Palmer. Nicklaus fires right at the pin which is tucked on the left side of the green close to the water. It's a gamble. And it works. Nicklaus's shot lands 10 feet short of the hole. His birdie putt to pull within 3 strokes stops inches from the left side of the cup. Nicklaus sinks to his knees as the missed putt all but sinks the possibility of a miracle come from behind finish.

Nicklaus pars out to finish with a sensational 67, the low round of the day and tied with Ben Hogan and Bruce Devlin for the low 18 hole score of the 1964 Masters.

40:05 - Staying aggressive, Palmer is hole high on the par 5 13th hole in 2, and has an eagle putt from the fringe. Watch the antics of Palmer and his caddy as the eagle bid just misses.

40:20 - See the leaderboard with Palmer through 14 holes at 11 under. Palmer has just 4 holes to play and he leads Nicklaus by 5 shots.

40:30 - Palmer is still not playing it safe. On the par 5 15th hole he elects to go for the green in 2, risking the water hazards in front of and behind the green. He perfectly executes the shot that lands on the right side of the green and rolls towards the center. He has a makeable eagle putt. And he receives a standing ovation from his army as he walks up to the 15th green.

41:20 - Palmer two putts 15 for a birdie to move to 12 under, 2 shy of Hogan's record of 14 under with 3 holes remaining. He's now 6 shots in front of Nicklaus.

Palmer pars 16, but bogeys 17. The record is now out of reach.

Palmer has a 5 shot lead going into the final hole.

42:25 - Dave Marr sinks a long birdie putt to go to 6 under for the tournament to tie Jack Nicklaus for 2nd place.

42:45 - Arnold Palmer sinks his 20 foot birdie putt on 18 to get back to 12 under par and he wins the Masters by 6 strokes.

Arnold Palmer is now the first man to ever win 4 Masters titles. He's also recorded a top 10 finish for the 8th straight year.

But Ben Hogan's record of 14 under remains intact.

43:15 - See the final leaderboard. Chris Schenkel mentions that Palmer only had a single 3-putt green in the 72 holes.

43:40 - Watch a magical moment take place. One year earlier, Palmer had placed the Green jacket on Nicklaus in what seemed to be a formal changing of the guard at the top of golf world. Now on the video, Jack Nicklaus puts the Green Jacket on "The King," Arnold Palmer.

For Arnie's Army the golf world order is back to the way it should be.

Palmer has surged back to the top of professional golf with his convincing 6 stroke victory.

The New York Times quoted Palmer today saying his Masters victory was, *"the most exciting single tournament of my life. I really won this one. This time there was no doubt in my mind or anyone else's mind. Sure, I won the Masters 3 times before, but I never was certain before that I really had won it. It was always an assist from the weather, or from somebody else shooting a bad round to eliminate themselves.*

This one I won. I won it all by myself."

Jesse Lamar, the sports editor of the Atlanta Constitution wrote today, *"Some skeptics had said, and others intimated, that Palmer was past his prime. In one pulsating four-day blitz at Augusta, the General had routed his critics and the field and reclaimed his Masters throne."*

POSTSCRIPT

The 1964 Masters was Arnold Palmer's masterpiece.

It was also the only time that Jack Nicklaus ever put the Green Jacket on Arnold Palmer.

CHAPTER ELEVEN

Chi Chi Rodriguez – The Grand Showman of Golf

THE 1964 WESTERN OPEN

INTRODUCTION from The Sports Time Traveler

In 2024, when I learned that Chi Chi Rodriguez had passed away, I knew I had to make the virtual trip back precisely 60 years to experience one of Chi Chi's choicest moments.

CHICAGO - August 14, 1964

About 10 miles northwest of Wrigley Field lies The Tam O'Shanter Country Club. This past weekend it was host to the Greatest Golf Show on Earth.

Officially, the event being held was the Western Open, one of the oldest and most important tournaments on the PGA TOUR. Not long ago the Western Open was considered by some to be a "major."

But the 61st rendition of the tournament might as well have been called, "The Chi Chi Show," because Juan "Chi Chi" Rodriguez made it the most entertaining golf tournament of the year as he delighted the record crowd.

Many came to see Chi Chi last weekend because he was featured in the current, August 10, 1964, issue of Sports Illustrated which hit newsstands just before the Western Open got underway.

SI writer, Dan Jenkins, described Chi Chi, in the sub-heading of the article, as, *"the brash song-and-dance man who delights galleries (and annoys fellow pros) with his japes off the tee and his jigs on the green."*

Jenkins explained that Chi Chi, who is presently 9th on the 1964 money list, is developing a following in his 5th year on tour as he delights the crowds both with his antics and his mammoth drives, totally unexpected from someone who stands just 5'7" and weights not much over 120.

Jenkins noted that, *"His Bandidos sometimes outnumber Arnie's Army, his tee shots sometimes outdistance Jack Nicklaus's."*

The SI article also described how many of his fellow touring pros are not thrilled with his on course antics, although The King, Arnold Palmer told Dan Jenkins, *"Personally, I like him... I think a little of his clowning around goes a long way."*

Jack Nicklaus also had kind words for Chi Chi in the magazine, *"I do think his cutting up has a tendency to bother some of the players who have trouble concentrating, but I realize we need Chi Chi's kind of color in the game."*

Jenkins also devoted a large portion of the article to describing a serious side of Chi Chi, his struggles growing up poor in Puerto Rico and his reflections on the touring pros who are not appreciative of his constant interactions with the gallery.

Overall it was a highly flattering piece.

And now my daily reports on the 1964 Western Open.

THE FIRST ROUND - August 6, 1964

The Sports Illustrated article must have been a real confidence builder for Chi Chi. On his opening 9 holes he birdied the 3rd, 4th, 5th, 6th and 7th holes.

5 consecutive birdies.

Chi Chi nearly made it 6 straight birds, as his 20 foot putt on the 8th hole was, *"dead center inches short,"* according to Charles Bartlett of the Chicago Tribune.

After the round, Chi Chi said, *"It hurt me to miss that birdie putt on No. 8, because I wanted seven birdies in a row. I knew I'd birdie No. 9."*

He did birdie the 9th.

Chi Chi went out in 30, 6 under par.

He came home in 34, including a birdie on the final hole, for an 18 hole score of 64 and good for a tie for the lead with Billy Casper.

Bill Jaus of the Chicago Daily News described Chi Chi on the course, *"He is a naturally engaging little guy, and the working folk who pluck down a fin apiece to see tourney golf realize this.*

"They pull for him. He hams it up too for the fans' benefit. They love it."

"I've always been like that," Chi Chi told Jaus. *"Money's not everything... Oh sure I want a little spending money... but I'd rather make friends."*

Always joking, Chi Chi provided some great lines for the press corps here in Chicago after the round. Apparently, Chi Chi had gone to see a White Sox game last night before the tournament began. His old semi-pro teammate from Puerto Rico, Juan Pizzaro, was pitching and threw a 13-inning complete game 3 - 1 loss to the Tigers. Chi Chi told the press after his opening 64, *"I was a baseball pitcher, too. In golf the last three weeks I have been in a slump, like your White Sox. I'm little, but I can throw fast. Maybe I could sign with the Mets?"*

Chi Chi was making light of the fact that the Mets, here in 1964, are among the worst teams in baseball history.

THE SECOND ROUND - August 7, 1964

On a day when only 29 of the 150 golfers could break par, Chi Chi followed up his spectacular opening round with a 2 under 69. While Thursday co-leader Casper, could only manage an even par 71.

However, the defending champion, Arnold Palmer, hit 17 of 18 greens, and had 6 one-putt greens, including a 65-foot birdie putt at no. 6. Palmer carded a 66 to give him a 2-round total of 134, placing him 1 behind Chi Chi.

At the end of the day, Chi Chi was leading the Western Open.

But Chi Chi was self-critical of his round. He told Bill Jauss of the Chicago Daily News, *"I played it too commercial."* Jauss explained that Chi Chi meant he was playing for pars.

THE THIRD ROUND - August 8, 1964

Chi Chi and Arnie both had great finishes on Saturday.

Palmer birdied 2 of the final 4 holes to cap off a 67.

Chi Chi put his approach shot at 18 just 3 feet from the pin and sank the birdie putt for a 68.

The pair were tied for the lead at 201 after 3 rounds.

Hammond, Indiana sports columnist Gary Galloway wrote in the Sunday morning paper on August 9th a piece about how Chi Chi doesn't stop entertaining when the round is over. After the 3rd round, Chi Chi spent a long time talking to the press.

Hammond wrote, *"Chi Chi will sit in on a golf bull session as long as there's anybody around to listen. This one took place in an unlikely corner of the Tam locker room. Unglamorous perhaps to be sitting on a concrete floor, legs sprawled under a bench."*

Chi Chi told a story that when he worked as a caddie, the only time he could get onto a course to play was after the course closed. *"I learned to play a round of golf in 45 minutes. I had to. The course shut down at 6:30... I only had 45 minutes till dark and most of the time the pro was chasing me."*

Then Chi Chi told stories of playing baseball in Puerto Rico.

"One-time I strike out 18 in a no hit, no run game against some pros, and they didn't want to play when they saw me warming up. Just a skinny kid they thought. I showed them."

THE FINAL ROUND - August 9, 1964

Going into Sunday, Chi Chi seemed to have found the perfect balance between clowning and contending. The 28 year old, 5th year pro, who has only won 2 PGA events on tour, was tied for the 54 hole lead with Arnold Palmer at 11 under par.

Arnold Palmer, the winner of this year's Masters, is also the defending Western Open champion.

The pair were 4 shots clear of 3rd place, Don Massengale, and the rest of the field. And what a field it was.

Lurking 5 shots behind, in 4th place, was Billy Casper, winner of 22 PGA tournaments including the 1959 U.S. Open.

In a tie for 5th, 6 shots behind, was reigning U.S. Open champion Ken Venturi.

And 7 shots back was the always dangerous Jack Nicklaus. The 24-year-old phenom, has already won 3 majors (5 if you include his 2 U.S. Amateur victories). Nicklaus has been in the top 3 in 8 of the past 11 majors. And while he didn't win one this year, he came in 2nd in the Masters, the British Open and the PGA. Nicklaus shot a 6 under par 65 yesterday. Another 65 could win the tournament. And you know that's what Jack must have been thinking.

Nicklaus started hot, with birdies on 2, 3 and 4 to pull to 7 under par just 4 shots off the lead.

And Massengale, who was paired with Palmer, birdied the first 3 holes to get to 10 under par.

That made it interesting.

However, neither of them got any closer. Massengale shot a 70 and Jack shot a 67. They both finished tied for 3rd, 7 shots behind the ultimate winner.

Arnold Palmer was determined to be that winner. He went 3 under par on the first 7 holes to reach minus 14.

Chi Chi who was playing ahead of Palmer's group, was 1 under on his first 7 holes, and fell 2 strokes back of Palmer.

Then Palmer bogeyed the 8th and his lead on Chi Chi was down to a single stroke.

Both players parred the 9th and 10th.

Palmer still held a 1 shot lead with 8 to play.

At the 159 yard par 3 11th hole, Chi Chi hit his 6 iron tee shot to 2 and a half feet from the hole. He sank the putt to tie Palmer for the lead.

Then at the 433 yard par 4 12th hole, Chi Chi hit his 2nd shot, an 8 iron, to 12 feet from the hole. Again he made the birdie putt. Chi Chi now had a 1 shot lead over The King.

Palmer tied it back up at minus 14, when he also birdied the 12th.

On the 13th hole, a 434 yard par 4, Chi Chi's 2nd shot was another beautiful 8 iron that landed 15 feet from the pin. He then sank his 3rd consecutive birdie putt to go to minus 15 and re-take a 1 shot lead over Arnie.

This time Palmer couldn't match Chi Chi, and the 5'7" player from Puerto Rico held a 1 shot advantage over the King with 4 holes remaining.

On the par 5 15th, Chi Chi reached the green in 2 and then 2 putted from 40 feet.

That took Chi Chi to minus 16, and it gave him a 2 shot lead.

But Arnie also reached the 15th in 2 and he was only 25 feet from the hole. His eagle putt *"grazed the cup,"* according to Charles Bartlett in the Chicago Tribune.

Arnie tapped in for a birdie and that put him just a stroke behind Chi Chi with 3 holes to play.

Chi Chi then carded a 3 at the par 3 16th.

Several minutes later Palmer hit his tee shot at 16 to just 10 feet from the hole. Barlett wrote that Palmer, *"just missed a 10 foot chance for a deuce."*

Chi Chi was still in front by 1 shot with 2 holes to play.

Chi Chi parred the 367 yard par 4 17th. But Palmer overshot the green at 17 and left himself 25 feet from the hole on his 3rd shot. He missed that putt and bogeyed the hole.

Chi Chi was again up by 2.

On 18, Chi Chi hit into the right trap on his 9 iron approach shot. As he hit out of the sand he was trying to hole the shot. It landed 4 feet past. He made the putt for the par.

On that 4 foot putt Chi Chi put on a show for the crowd as he covered the hole with his hat and then picked up the hat to peek at the hole where his ball resided.

Chi Chi was now in the clubhouse with a course record 268 (minus 16).

He had carded a brilliant 31 on the par 35 back 9, with 4 birdies on the final 8 holes. Chi Chi's 268 bested the prior record of 269 by Byron Nelson in 1945.

However Arnold Palmer still had a chance. His tee shot at 18 landed about 25 yards away from the plaque in the fairway that denotes the spot where 11 years earlier Lew Worsham had holed a 104 yard wedge shot that won the first ever golf tournament to be broadcast nationally on television.

Palmer's shot settled 18 feet from the cup. Then he drained the birdie.

But Chi Chi had won the Western Open by one stroke.

The Monday, August 10, 1964 Chicago Tribune sports section had a banner headline celebrating Chi Chi's victory.

The article also included an innovative golf box score that described the performances of the top golfers.

You can see for example that Chi Chi hit 16 greens in regulation, what the Tribune called "Php. - putting areas hit in par," during the final round. None of the other leaders had more than 15.

With the win, Chi Chi earned a $11,000 check, boosting his earnings for the year to over $46,000. He is now 6th on the PGA money list for 1964.

The National Media Embrace Chi-Chi Following his Victory

What has happened in the past several days since Chi Chi's win over Arnold Palmer in this "near major" event has been quite incredible.

Sportswriters around the country have taken the opportunity to introduce Chi Chi Rodriguez to casual golf fans in the most flattering way.

In the August 10, 1964, Atlanta Constitution, sports editor Jesse Outlar, wrote a long piece about Chi Chi that included this:

"For the first time Rodriguez's Band of Bandidos outnumbered Arnie's Army."

"Sportswriters seldom applaud a winner in the press room, but Rodriguez was given a rousing round of applause as he strolled into the clubhouse."

"A man wanted to know if he was aware that he was breaking Byron Nelson's course record... 'No,' said Chi Chi... 'But if my father were still living and heard about it he would say, 'You broke it, you pay for it.'"

Jim Murray of the Los Angeles Times, who writes a nationally syndicated column, decided it was time to showcase the *"Happy Fella,"* as he titled his article on August 11, 1964.

Murray's description of Chi Chi included these classic passages:

"Chi Chi Rodriguez plays golf as if it were a New Year's Eve party. When he holes a putt, he does a little South American dance... His name, they suggest, should be "Cha Cha" Rodriguez."

"When he birdies a hole, he waves his arms in the air as if he has just liberated Paris..."

"...Chi Chi plays the game as if it were meant to be fun."

"You probably saw Chi Chi on TV sweetly lift his first major golf tournament, the Western Open, from Arnold Palmer...

"...Chi Chi strolled around as if he were another spectator... dropped his hat over sunk putts, and had the time of his life. He LOOKED around for TV cameras and patiently waited till they could get his good side..."

"...The golf tour may be a lot of fun from here on out with Chi Chi around."

Bill Carter, wrote a story on Chi Chi that appeared on August 12, 1964, in the Alexandria, Louisiana Town Talk. Here's what Carter had to say about Chi Chi:

"Palmer, Tony Lema, Gary Player, Jack Nicklaus, Ken Venturi and other top golfers have their special following... All of them, however, may soon switch over to a little guy named Chi Chi Rodriguez... If the fans want to noise it up a bit, Chi Chi will join them.

"Chi Chi, who could diet over the weekend and qualify for a mount in the Kentucky Derby, likes to ham it up, himself. He enjoys kidding with the spectators. In fact, he seems capable of adding some refreshing color to a now-popular sport.

"Cheers to Chi Chi. Whether he wins or loses, and whether the pros like it or not, I hope he continues to add color...

"If he wins over the other supporters, all the pros may have to turn comic."

My favorite article on Chi Chi Rodriguez came out this morning, August 14th, in the Lansing State Journal. Lad Slingerlend devoted his sports column to Chi Chi's victory at the Western Open. Here are the excerpts that caught my attention.

"Chi Chi has arrived... always a crowd pleaser... he won the Western Open golf championship and now must be considered a top performer by his fellow pros."

"Chi Chi is a showman from the word go and entertains the gallery with his antics from the first tee to the 18th green to say nothing of the practice area. Now that he has won a major tournament, his Bandidos will double in number."

Slingerlend also described something I never knew before - how Chi Chi got his nickname:

"As a youngster he leaned towards baseball and idolized a player named Chi Chi Flores. Hence Juan became Chi Chi."

CLOSING NOTE from The Sports Time Traveler

When I first wrote this chapter back in 2024, I was surprised that none of the coverage of Chi Chi in 1964 mentioned his now-famous sword dance that long-time golf fans probably most vividly recall when conjuring up visions of Chi Chi Rodriguez.

The best version of it that I have found is in this short YouTube video from the 1984 Heritage Classic when Chi Chi was 48.

Chi Chi's sword dance in 1984

You can find it on YouTube by searching on "Classic Chi Chi Rodriguez Sword Dance (1984) PGA Heritage Classic"

There may never be another golfer that entertains on the course quite like Chi Chi Rodriguez. But it would be nice if some of the top golfers today could find a way to emulate a little bit of Chi Chi to keep his spirit alive.

POSTSCRIPT

I recently had an interesting encounter with a United Airlines gate agent in the Denver airport. He told me he was from Puerto Rico. So I asked him on a whim if he had ever met Chi Chi Rodriguez. His face lit up as he told me he had indeed had one encounter with Chi Chi. I then asked him what was Chi Chi like. And he told me that Chi Chi was as friendly and funny as could be. I wasn't surprised. Chi Chi was the real deal, a genuine kind soul. We will all miss the goodness he shared with everyone.

CHAPTER TWELVE

The Big Three Foursome

THE 1964 CANADA CUP

INTRODUCTION from The Sports Time Traveler

In my sports time travels, the stories that get me most excited are the ones I never knew about, and that seemingly no one else does either. These are the forgotten stories. They made the newspapers at the time they took place, 50 – 100 years ago. But they didn't make it into the pantheon of sports history.

I found one such story recently and I'm very excited to share it with you. It takes place in 1964.

It's the only time that the Big 3 of golf, Arnold Palmer, Gary Player and Jack Nicklaus ever played in the same group on the final day of an important golf tournament.

It happened in the final round of the Canada Cup. And oddly, the Canada Cup that year took place in Kaanapali, Hawaii. It was called the Canada Cup because the tournament was founded by Canadian businessman, John Jay Hopkins, who sought to promote international goodwill through this annual event that featured both a national team golf competition as well as an individual championship. The tournament was initiated in 1953. The name of the event was changed to the **World Cup** in 1967 and was played every year until 2018, attracting the top players in the game.

Perhaps the most captivating Canada Cup was the 1964 edition.

Now I take you back in time to experience it.

Kaanapali, Hawaii - December 7, 1964

I'm here virtually at Kaanapali Golf Resort on the island of Maui, where the final round of the Canada Cup concluded yesterday.

The Canada Cup is both a national team and individual golf tournament.

This year, 34 "national" teams are represented. I put national in quotes because one of the national teams is Hawaii! And another is Puerto Rico!

Each national team has 2 players. Hawaii is represented by Ted Makalena and Paul Scodeller.

Hawaii has strong competition. The USA is represented by Arnold Palmer and Jack Nicklaus. Puerto Rico's team includes Chi Chi Rodriguez. And South Africa's team has Gary Player.

Player, Palmer and Nicklaus are considered the "Big 3" in golf.

In every year of the 1960s thus far, one of the Big 3 has been the leading money winner.

In every year of the 1960s thus far, one of the Big 3 has won the Masters.

And the Big 3 have collectively won 11 of the 20 major titles thus far in the 1960s.

Perhaps even more impressive is thus far in the decade, one of the Big 3 has finished either 1st or 2nd in 15 of the 20 majors played.

The Standings Going Into the Final Round of the 1964 Canada Cup

The final day on the 7,215 yard par 72 course began with the United States team of Arnold Palmer and Jack Nicklaus holding a 9 shot lead over South Africa.

The national leaderboard looked like this to start the round, with Hawaii in a surprising 5th place:

-26 USA

-17 South Africa

-11 Argentina

-3 Spain

-1 Hawaii

Individually, the Big 3 were running 1st, 2nd and 3rd. Arnold Palmer had been brilliant shooting rounds of 66, 67 and 67 to take a 3 shot lead after 54 holes.

-16 Arnold Palmer (USA)

-13 Gary Player (South Africa)

-10 Jack Nicklaus (USA)

-9 Ted Makalena (Hawaii)

-8 Robert De Vicenzo (Argentina)

-4 Denis Hutchinson (South Africa)

Ted Makalena of Hawaii was a surprising 4th, just a shot behind the Golden Bear and 1 shot ahead of De Vicenzo of Argentina. De Vicenzo was one of the top international players in the world and had finished 3rd at the British Open just a few months earlier. While somewhat of an unknown, Ted Makalena had qualified to play in this year's U.S. Open and finished 23rd.

Only 6 of the other 56 players were under par. Chi Chi was one of them at -1.

With the USA and South Africa running 1st and 2nd in the team competition, this set up an incredible final day with the Big 3 all playing in the same foursome.

Final Round Play Begins

Palmer was intent on winning the individual honors in this tournament that he had failed to capture in 3 previous tries.

But Jack, beginning the day 6 shots behind in the individual play, started fast with birdies on the opening 2 holes to pull within 4 shots of the King early on. Nicklaus then birdied the 5th and the 8th, before a bogey at 9 gave him a 3 under 33 for the front 9.

Player also birdied number 2, to put him just 2 shots back of Arnie. But Player gave that shot right back when he bogeyed the 3rd hole. He finished the front 9 with an even par 36.

Palmer started steady. He parred the first 4 holes. Then he bogeyed the 5th hole and 7th holes and carded a 38 on the front 9.

The Hawaiian surprise, Ted Makalena, got off to a great start playing 2 groups ahead of the Big 3. He parred the opening 5 holes and then birdied the 6th. A bogey at 9 gave him a front 9 score of 36.

INDIVIDUAL SCORES with 9 holes to play

-14 Palmer

-13 Player

-13 Nicklaus

-9 Makalena

The Big 3 were all within one shot of each other entering the back 9 and 4 shots clear of the field. It was setting up to be a classic finish.

On the 10th hole both Nicklaus and Palmer hit their drives into bunkers and bogeyed, this pulled Gary Player into a tie for the lead with Arnie at 13 under, while Jack slipped to minus 12.

But on the 11th, Nicklaus got his 4th birdie of the day and the Big 3 were all tied!

A hole ahead, Ted Makalena parred the 12th, but a few minutes earlier he had eagled the par 5 11th hole.

Ted Makalena was now just 2 shots behind the Big 3!

What a finish this was turning out to be!

INDIVIDUAL SCORES with 7 holes to play

-13 Palmer

-13 Player

-13 Nicklaus

-11 Makalena (6 holes to play)

At the 13th, Nicklaus birdied while Palmer and Player bogeyed. Nicklaus now had the lead for the first time.

A hole ahead, Makalena hit into the water on his approach shot on 14 and double bogeyed. It was a 3 shot swing for Makalena in the wrong direction.

INDIVIDUAL SCORES with 5 holes to play

-14 Nicklaus

-12 Player

-12 Palmer

-9 Makalena (4 holes to play)

Gary Player followed his bogey on 13 with 2 more on 14 and 15. Jack also bogeyed 15. With 3 holes to go Nicklaus led by 1 shot over Palmer. While Makalena picked up a shot with a birdie on the par 5 15th. When Ted parred the 16th he pulled even with Gary Player.

INDIVIDUAL SCORES with 3 holes to play

-13 Nicklaus

-12 Palmer

-10 Player

-10 Makalena (2 holes to play)

Nicklaus then bogeyed 16 and suddenly it was all tied again between the King and the Golden Bear. Player however, suffered his 4th consecutive bogey on 16, to fall 3 shots off the lead. He remained tied for 3rd with Makalena who bogeyed 17 up ahead.

INDIVIDUAL SCORES with 2 holes to play

-12 Nicklaus

-12 Palmer

- 9 Player

- 9 Makalena (1 hole to play)

At 17, Palmer 3-putted from 20 feet for a bogey to fall 1 back of Jack. While Makalena parred his final hole for an even par 72 for the day.

INDIVIDUAL SCORES with 1 hole to play

-12 Nicklaus

-11 Palmer

- 9 Player

- 9 Makalena (completed the round)

On the par 4 18th hole, Palmer needed a birdie. The Honolulu Star-Bulletin described what happened, *"Palmer made a great attempt to gain a tie on the last hole but overshot the green. He chipped to within four feet and two-putted."*

Meanwhile on the last hole on Nicklaus's 2nd shot, *"a wedge from the rough stopped four feet from the pin. He two-putted for a par and victory."*

Arnie bogeyed 18. And Jack Nicklaus parred to win the individual scoring by 2 shots.

For 1st place in the individual competition Nicklaus won $1,000.

FINAL INDIVIDUAL SCORES

-12 Nicklaus

-10 Palmer

- 9 Player

- 9 Makalena

- 7 De Vicenzo

Jack had shot a final round 70, while Palmer had ballooned to 78 and Player had shot 76.

Team Competition

The Palmer-Nicklaus USA squad took the team event by 11 shots over Argentina in what was somewhat of a forgone conclusion for the fans amidst the competitive individual scoring race between the Big 3 and the great showing by the local hero Makalena.

The prize for winning the team event was $2,000 that Palmer and Nicklaus split.

FINAL TEAM SCORES – Top 10 Teams

-22 USA

-11 Argentina

-8 South Africa

-4 Spain

+2 England

+3 Hawaii

+8 Canada

+9 Japan

+11 Brazil

+12 Belgium

What Happened to the King

How did Arnie go from shooting 66, 67, 67 to a 78 on the final day?

The final round was the hottest it got all week with the temperature hitting 90. In addition, the round took 6 hours to play.

Palmer refused to make any excuses. He told the AP, *"I just couldn't get myself together. I played unbelievably bad. It was all my fault. But the team won. That's the important thing."*

And he told Bill Gee of the Honolulu Star-Bulletin, *"I was never able to get back into the groove. I was just disgusted."*

The London Evening Star had a better explanation, *"Nicklaus consistently outdrove the other three and his accurate iron shots to the green eased his task greatly. Palmer was often in difficulties in the rough and usually left with long putts after his approaches."*

The Players Desire to See the Individual Competition Abolished

Both Jack Nicklaus and Arnold Palmer spent their time in the post round press conference promoting a change in the tournament format. They want the Canada Cup to be just a team event, with no individual competition.

An AP reporter quoted Palmer, *"Our objective from the start of the week was to win the Canada Cup for the United States. But then it turned out we were fighting each other. This doesn't make sense. All week we were comparing notes on clubs, positions and such as a team."*

Nicklaus agreed completely. He told Tom Hopkins of the Honolulu Star-Bulletin, *"We are rooting for each other and at the same time competing against one another in this type of tournament."*

Palmer was careful to point out how important he felt this tournament was while also suggesting the format change. He told Hopkins, *"This is a great tournament. One of the greatest in golf. I'd like to see it perpetuated."*

POSTSCRIPT

The 1964 Canada Cup was not on TV. And only 20,000 fans saw the tournament over the 4 days according to the Honolulu Star-Bulletin.

So it's likely that less than 10,000 people got to witness this bit of sports history - the only time the big 3 ever played head-to-head-to-head in the final round of an important tournament.

Not only did they play head-to-head-to-head, but the Big 3 also finished 1-2-3. This was also a rarity. Golfcompendium.com has only identified 3 times that ever happened. And it's interesting to note that Golfcompendium.com didn't recognize the Canada Cup as one of the three.

It seems this incredible tournament has been somewhat forgotten in golf history.

By the way, the suggested change to eliminate the individual competition in the Canada Cup was not implemented.

CHAPTER THIRTEEN

The Old Man and the Snead

THE 1965 GREATER GREENSBORO OPEN

Similar to the old man Santiago, of Hemingway's creation, Sam Snead was consumed by the thrill of the big catch in the deep blue. The Slammer also enjoyed holing long putts for money on a green.

When Sam Snead, the old man of the PGA TOUR, was a month shy of 53, he arrived at Greensboro, NC, where the annual Greater Greensboro Open was played on the PGA TOUR.

Slammin' Sammy was slated to be celebrated by the city that had witnessed some of his greatest links success. It was to officially be Sam Snead week. He was also set to compete in the tournament for the 25th time, teeing off against nearly all the best golfers in the world.

No one had performed better than Snead in the history of this PGA event. Sam Snead had won the GGO 7 times, including the inaugural edition back in 1938. He had finished 2nd three times and had ended up in 3rd place another six times. He had competed in every one of the Greater Greensboro Opens ever staged, with the sole exception of the 1947 tournament. In his prior 24 tries at the event, he had been in the top three 16 times.

Sam Snead also came into the week with a career record **81 PGA** victories, the most ever by a large margin.

In addition, Snead held the record for the longest span of years between victories at **25**.

Here was the all-time top 10 PGA TOUR win list as of the last week in March, 1965*:

PGA TOUR WINS and the span of years between wins

81 Sam Snead 1936 - 1961

64 Ben Hogan 1938 - 1959

52 Byron Nelson 1935 - 1951

45 Walter Hagen 1914 - 1936

44 Arnold Palmer 1955 - 1964

39 Cary Middlecoff 1945 - 1961

38 Gene Sarazen 1922 - 1941

36 Lloyd Mangrum 1940 - 1956

31 Jimmy Demaret 1938 - 1957

30 Harry Cooper 1923 - 1939

30 Horton Smith 1928 - 1941

* the count of PGA TOUR wins represents the modified official count in 1987

But Sam Snead had not won a **PGA TOUR** event in nearly 4 years, not since he was in his late 40s. The celebration being scheduled for him by the city of Greensboro was not one for a conquering hero. It was a nostalgic tribute to an old man's past accomplishments. Snead, however, knew he still had some fight left in him.

This raised the question, was he the old man? Or was he was still the Slammer, the man with the smoothest swing - "the Snead?"

The Sports Time Traveler just had to go on a virtual trip back in time, to experience Sam Snead's welcoming and his play in the 1965 Greater Greensboro Open.

Greensboro, NC - April 5, 1965

The Sports Time Traveler has been here in Greensboro virtually for the past week. Yesterday was the final round of the Greater Greensboro Open. What a round it was! And what a week it was here in the heart of tobacco country in central North Carolina.

What follows are my daily reports from this incredible week

The datelines are of those of the newspapers that carried the stories.

PRE-TOURNAMENT COVERAGE - Sunday, March 28, 1965

The Greensboro News and Record ran a full page of stories on Sam Snead in today's Sunday paper on page 28.

On page 31, it was announced that Ed Sullivan would be coming to the Sam Snead celebration to take place prior to the tournament this coming week.

On the Ed Sullivan show tonight Gary Player was Ed's guest. You can watch the 2 minute segment by typing in the words below in the search engine on YouTube. You'll see Gary show off his legendary strength. Near the end of the segment, Ed Sullivan mentions, *"Gary and I are flying down to Greensboro, North Carolina to play in the Sam Snead tournament."*

Gary Player on The Ed Sullivan Show - March 28, 1965

Despite what Ed Sullivan called it, the tournament is still officially called the Greater Greensboro Open, but it might as well be re-named for Sam Snead since The Slammer has completely dominated it through the years. And Snead has been in the top 10 each of the last 16 years.

PRE-TOURNAMENT COVERAGE - Monday, March 29, 1965

The Rocky Mount Telegram ran a picture of Sam Snead, last year, fishing between rounds of the 1964 Greater Greensboro Open.

It was also announced that 800 people are expected for a "Testimonial Dinner" to honor Sam Snead on Tuesday night in Greensboro.

PRE-TOURNAMENT COVERAGE - Tuesday, March 30, 1965

The Greensboro News and Record ran a large article about the Testimonial Dinner at the Plantation Club. The article included pictures of Sam Snead and the featured speaker, Ed Sullivan.

PRE-TOURNAMENT COVERAGE - Wednesday, March 31, 1965

The Durham Herald-Sun featured a rare photo of Sam Snead without a hat, and Ed Sullivan, at the Testimonial Dinner.

The paper reported, *"after his introduction by television's Ed Sullivan, Snead entertained the crowd with some of his choice stories. He closed with the comment, 'The only reason I play golf now is so that I can fish and hunt. I don't expect to win here, but those boys better watch out.'"*

PRE-TOURNAMENT COVERAGE - Thursday, April 1, 1965

Irwin Smallwood, writing for The Greensboro News and Record, noted that the field for the Greater Greensboro Open was set to include, *"almost every top name in the game... perhaps 40 players fully capable of winning. There are approximately three dozen who have won regulation PGA Tour events before."*

In fact, the field included Arnold Palmer, Gary Player, Billy Casper and every one of the top players in the world with the exception of Jack Nicklaus. As the last tournament prior to the Masters, Nicklaus opted to practice at Augusta rather than tune up in Greensboro.

PRO-AM RESULTS

Wednesday's PRO-AM was played in frigid conditions. There had actually been snow and sleet in the early morning.

Sam Snead played with the tournament chairman, and with UNC football coach Jim Hickey. Snead managed a 74 in what the Greensboro Record called, *"bone-chilling"* weather. After the round Snead told reporters, *"I shot better than I scored."* Snead blamed his 3 over par score on several 3-putt greens.

Arnold Palmer, had one of the best rounds of the day with a 69. Palmer, is familiar with this part of the country as he went to college at nearby Wake Forest University.

Ed Sullivan played with Gary Player who shot a 70. The Greensboro Record reported, *"Sullivan, besieged by autograph seekers from the first tee to the finish line and beyond said, 'I feel like I had been playing football.'"*

The low score of the day was a 67 posted by Rod Funseth who took away $500 for the effort.

Also scoring well was Billy Casper, winner of 4 events last year in 1964, who tied Palmer with 69.

FIRST ROUND - Friday, April 2, 1965

The temperatures for yesterday's first round started out in the low 40s and only made it up to 57 degrees in the afternoon.

In Carlton Byrd's column in the Winston-Salem Sentinel he wrote, *"When Snead walked into the warm pressroom and somebody remarked that it didn't look like he was dressed for the cloudy and 42-degree weather, he pulled up one pants leg and quipped, 'Look, I got on my long thermal underwear, a heavy short and sweater with a lot of wool in it... I was colder out there today than I was way back in 1940. Remember when it snowed us out on Easter Sunday that year? I hit my ball onto the second green and there was so much snow on it I couldn't find the ball. I told the Jaycees to call the thing off or get me a pair of skis. They postponed it.'"*

Despite the conditions The Slammer scored 3 straight birdies on holes 4, 5 and 6, sinking 10 to 12 foot putts on each. And that powered Snead to an opening round of 68. That put Snead in a tie for 4th.

Snead remarked, *"My putting was wonderful today for an old man like me."*

Here were the leading scorers after the 1st round:

66 - Tommie Aaron

67 - Bernard Hunt

67 - Bill Martindale

68 - Sam Snead

68 - Duff Lawrence

All the big names were farther back:

70 - Billy Casper

71 - Tony Lema

71 - Dow Finsterwald

72 - Arnold Palmer

73 - Gary Player

SECOND ROUND - Saturday, April 3, 1965

Friday's temperature reached 62 in the afternoon after another chilly start. Despite the warmer weather, only 6 players broke 70. One of them was Sam Snead who shot a 69.

That was good for a 2 day total of 137 and a share of the lead with Billy Casper. Casper is one of the winningest players on the PGA TOUR in the last 5 years bagging 15 victories since 1960.

Irwin Smallwood, writing in the Greensboro News and Record, asserted that Snead, *"putted superbly for the second straight day though he felt his tee-to-green performance left something to be desired."*

Smith Barrier, also of the Greensboro News and Record, was even more emphatic about Snead's putting. He penned an article with a headline that read, *"Snead's Putter Talking... It Means Watch Out."* He quoted Snead saying, *"Anytime I three-putt only once in 36 holes, which I have done, none Thursday, one Friday it's wonderful."*

Here were the leading scorers after the 2nd round:

- 7 Sam Snead and Billy Casper

- 6 Howie Johnson and Tommie Aaron

- 4 Seven players including Phil Rodgers

Some of the biggest names were farther back, but within the cut line of +4:

+1 Gary Player, Julius Boros & Tony Lema
+2 Arnold Palmer

THIRD ROUND - Sunday, April 4, 1965

Bob Hampton of the Winston-Salem Journal opened his article on the 3rd round this morning with this line, *"Two bugs of different varieties reshaped the looks of the $65,000 Greater Greensboro Open golf tournament yesterday. They attacked 36 hole leaders Billy Casper and Sam Snead."*

Hampton went on to describe how a stomach bug had hit Billy Casper hard. So hard that Casper told the Charlotte Observer, *"I felt like I was going to die."* Casper did manage to shoot a 1 over par 72 for the day. That dropped him into a tie for 3rd place, 4 shots off the lead, but still very much in the tournament if he can recover for today's final round.

The other bug Hampton described was the one that hit Sam Snead on Saturday. Hampton wrote, *"The other (bug) might be termed the No. 8 bug because Snead apparently has the "bug" to win his eighth GGO title."*

Hampton's assertion was based on the fact that the old man of the field fired a 68 on Saturday to give him a 2 stroke lead going into the final round this afternoon.

Snead thus became the only player in the field to shoot in the 60s all 3 days.

In 2nd place is Labron Harris Jr. who was not even born when Snead won his first GGO title in 1938. One month ago, Harris' father, Labron Harris Sr., was in a similar position at the PGA Seniors Championship at Palm Beach Gardens in

Florida. After 54 holes Harris Sr. was in 2nd place behind Sam Snead. He didn't catch him and Sam Snead captured his 2nd PGA Seniors title since turning 50.

Snead had a fantastic round on Saturday. He missed only one green. He rolled in putts of 12, 18 and 25 feet and he had just one 3-putt green. That came at the 17th hole in which Snead's approach shot left him far from the pin. Snead described to Smith Barrier what happened with his 7-iron shot on 17, *"Couple of fellows back of me were rattling the coins in their pockets, and that's all I could hear. I got my mind on all that money and forgot golf."*

The game's current stars were all well back of Snead. Arnold Palmer shot a 1 under 70 on Saturday, but was still 11 strokes behind Snead through 3 rounds.

The defending champion Julius Boros, and South African sensation Gary Player are 12 shots behind.

Champagne Tony Lema, winner of last year's British Open at St. Andrews is 8 shots back after firing a 68 on Saturday.

Being on top of this stellar field had Snead in a jovial mood after the round. The Charlotte Observer reported on the post round press conference in which Snead was the man of the hour with his 2 shot lead. Snead told the reporters, *"I just hope somebody wants to talk to me Sunday - after the tournament is over."*

Here were the leading scorers after the 3rd round:

-8 Sam Snead

-6 Labron Harris Jr.

-4 Billy Casper & Phil Rodgers

-3 Jay Dolan

-2 Miller Barber, Jack McGowan, Bruce Devlin, Gordon Jones

Some of the biggest names were farther back and out of contention:

E Tony Lema

+3 Arnold Palmer

+4 Gary Player & Julius Boros

FINAL ROUND - Monday, April 5, 1965

Yesterday, Sam Snead teed off at 1pm. His threesome included Phil Rodgers who was 4 shots behind and Jay Dolan who was 5 shots back.

Labron Harris Jr., who was in 2nd place, just 2 shots behind Snead was playing ahead of Snead in the 12:50pm group along with Billy Casper (4 shots back) and Gordon Jones (6 shots back).

This is the way PGA TOUR final day groupings are set up back here in 1965.

Harris Pulls Within One!

After 6 holes Labron Harris Jr. pulled to within 1 shot of the Slammer. But when Snead birdied the par 5 6th hole and Harris bogeyed the 8th, he was suddenly 3 shots behind, and he effectively lost another stroke on the par 5 9th when his tee shot landed behind a tree. Harris made par, but the 9th was a hole that most players (including Snead) birdied.

Hot Rodgers!

While Harris dropped back, Phil Rodgers, who began the day 4 shots behind Snead, was heating up. Rodgers, playing head-to-head with Snead, opened the round birdie-birdie to Snead's par-par to instantly pull within 2 shots. One of the birdie putts was from 70 feet according to Don Shea in the Durham Morning Herald. Rodgers then birdied 6, chipped in for a birdie at 8 and birdied 9 for a spectacular 31 on the front 9. Rodgers ended the front 9 just a shot behind The Slammer.

Rodgers a winner of 3 prior PGA TOUR events, just missed out last week on his 4th victory when he lost a playoff at the Azalea Open.

Rodgers famously lost another playoff back in 1963 for the British Open, when he was crushed in the grueling 36-hole playoff by Bob Charles, falling to the New Zealander by 8 shots at the Royal Lytham & St Annes Golf Club.

Now Rodgers had a real chance at redemption if he could just outlast the old man on the back 9.

Going for Pars

Sam Snead started the day with a strategy of going for pars. And he did just that on all the par 3's and 4's on the front 9. In addition, he played the par 5s as if they were par 4s, and birdied both of them on the opening side. The Slammer played the front 9 like a champion with a 2 under 34.

Feeling Fantastic!

Also playing like the champion he has been on many Sundays, was the always dangerous Billy Casper. Casper. who had been violently ill just the day before. He told the Charlotte Observer on Sunday, *"I felt I was going to die on Friday."* But on the final day, Casper said, *"I feel fantastic."*

Billy birdied the opening hole to get within 3 shots before Snead had teed off, and finished his front 9 with a cool 33 that included 3 more birdies on the 5th, 6th and 9th.

McGowan's Move

Another player giving himself a chance in the final round was Jack McGowan, who hadn't joined the PGA TOUR until he was 30 in 1960, and had won just a single PGA TOUR event. McGowan eagled the 6th hole when he put his 2nd shot to just 10 inches from the hole. Playing 2 groups in front of Snead, the eagle pulled McGowan to just 4 shots off the lead at that point.

Dolan's Opportunity

One more golfer who was just barely in contention was Jay Dolan, a 26 year old, 5th year player, who has yet to win a tournament. Dolan found himself in the unusual position of playing in the final group with the legendary Sam Snead. And early on he made the best of it shooting a 34 on the front 9 to keep even pace with Snead, although still 5 shots back for the tournament.

Here were the scores of the leaders after the front 9:

-10 Sam Snead

- 9 Phil Rodgers

- 7 Billy Casper

- 6 Labron Harris Jr.

- 5 Jay Dolan

- 4 Jack McGowan

THE BACK 9 - A Chance to Make History

Sam Snead, age 52 and 10 months, entered the back 9 in the lead. A victory would make him the oldest man ever to win a PGA TOUR event, surpassing John Barnum who had won the Cajun Classic in 1962 at age 51. But Barnum had not played against a field with all the top stars, as are in the field this week. When Barnum won his last event, it was being played opposite the Canada Cup, which siphoned off many of the world's top players including Gary Player, Arnold Palmer and of course, Sam Snead.

The Big Names Finish

Shortly after Snead teed off on 10, Gary Player, a member of the big three of golf, who had teed off at 10:50am, finished with a spectacular 66. It was the South African's only round under par as he wound up -1 for the tournament. The Durham Sun amusingly reported that Player has earned so much money playing golf that he owns a game farm near his home that has lions, tigers and zebras.

Arnold Palmer finished soon after Player with a typical Arnie's Army charge. Mel Derrick of the Charlotte Observer, reported Palmer had, *"one of his fearsome stretch drives going Sunday. He was six under par for his round going into the wicked No. 16."*

But a 3-putt bogey at 16, followed by another bogey at 17 left him 4 under for the day and tied at -1 for the tournament with fellow big three member Gary Player, and 9 shots behind the leader on the course - Sam Snead.

The 10th

Phil Rodgers, playing in almost a match play type set up now with Sam Snead, as they were both in the final group, with just a shot separating them, bogeyed the 10th hole to fall back to -8.

But Snead also bogeyed the 10th with a 3-putt, dropping to -9 for the tournament. This brought Billy Casper, in the group ahead, back into serious contention since he made pars at 10 and 11 and held steady at -7, just 2 shots off Snead's lead.

Leaderboard after the final group finished the 10th:

- 9 Sam Snead

- 8 Phil Rodgers

- 7 Billy Casper

- 6 Labron Harris Jr.

- 4 Jack McGowan

- 4 Jay Dolan

The 11th

Snead then made another 3-putt at the 11th, his second in a row. With Rodgers making par at 11, there was now a tie on top at -8.

Was Snead getting the yips? Was his putting, the weakest part of his game, about to do him in down the stretch? Snead had been putting near perfectly all week. He had just a single three-putt in the opening 36 holes, and just one more on Saturday when a 2-foot putt hit a cleat mark.

Snead explained what happened on the 11th green to Smith Barrier, *"I misjudged a big break in that green and rolled my putt eight feet past."* It sounded like Snead had not lost his confidence in his putting, he just needed to read the greens better. He later told Bob Hampton, *"I guess some of 'em were saying, 'well, there goes ole Sam.' But I wasn't disturbed."*

Leaderboard after the final group finished the 11th:

- 8 Sam Snead
- 8 Phil Rodgers
- 7 Billy Casper
- 6 Labron Harris Jr.
- 4 Jack McGowan
- 4 Jay Dolan

The 12th hole

At the 12th, Rodgers, playing alongside Snead, missed a short par putt. Casper, playing in the group ahead had earlier bogeyed the 12th. And Harris, playing with Casper bogeyed the 13th while Snead and Rodgers were on 12.

This put Snead back in the lead by himself and opened up breathing room ahead of Casper and Harris Jr.

Leaderboard after the final group finished the 12th:

- 8 Sam Snead
- 7 Phil Rodgers
- 6 Billy Casper
- 5 Labron Harris Jr
- 4 Jack McGowan
- 4 Jay Dolan

Lucky and Unlucky 13

The 13th hole was unlucky for Rodgers. His tee shot hooked badly. But then he caught an even worse break. In one account the ball hit a spectator's camera. In another story the ball bounded off the foot of a marshal. The end result was the same. The ball went out of bounds leading to a double bogey 6 on the par 4.

Snead meanwhile had a challenge on 13 as well. He was on the green in two, but he had left himself far from the hole. The potential existed for yet another three-putt hole.

Snead told Smith Barrier later about the 13th green, *"I'm about as far from the pin as you could get... oh, from China to Japan, 60 feet at least. I just wanted to get up close. I just wanted to get down in two. Three-putt again? Not me. I whacked that thing. And when it went in I just said, 'holy cow.'"*

Snead's incredible putt had blown the tournament wide open from his perspective. He told Smith Barrier that he thought, *"That was it. This won the tournament."*

It was a natural reaction to a 3-shot swing over Rodgers, who had been tied with Snead just 2 holes earlier.

But what Snead didn't know at the time was that Billy Casper had birdied 13 just a little while earlier and was now in 2nd place just 2 shots back. Casper had amazing luck on the 13th hole. His 2nd shot was heading into the woods. Casper described what happened next to Smith Barrier, *"The ball hit a spectator and bounced on the green. I sank a 30 foot putt for bird, then went over to the fan and asked him to go on down the next fairway and stay in front. I needed the help."*

Also of note was that Labron Harris Jr. bogeyed 13, effectively ending his chances.

Leaderboard after the final group finished the 13th:

- 9 Sam Snead

- 7 Billy Casper

- 5 Phil Rodgers

- 4 Jack McGowan

- 4 Labron Harris Jr

- 4 Jay Dolan

The par 5 14th

The first two par 5s on the front side had been playing like par 4s. Now the leaders came to the only par 5 on the back 9. There was opportunity to be had.

McGowan was the first of the leaders to reach the hole. And he made the most of it. Carding his 2nd eagle of the day, McGowan vaulted himself to -6, just 3 shots back of Snead.

Next was Casper, playing in the group ahead of Snead. Billy couldn't make birdie and held steady at - 7.

Then came the group with Snead, Rodgers and Dolan. Dolan bogeyed 14, putting him well out of contention.

Rodgers eagled to put him back to -7 and tied for 2nd with Casper.

The ageless Snead didn't falter. He birdied the hole.

Sam Snead now had a 3 shot lead with just 4 to play.

Leaderboard after the final group finished the 14th:

- 10 Sam Snead

- 7 Billy Casper

- 7 Phil Rodgers

- 6 Jack McGowan

The 15th

McGowan followed up his eagle on 14 with a birdie on 15, to move into a tie for 2nd at -7, just 3 shots back of Snead, but with only 3 to play.

Casper reached 15 next and he bogeyed the par 4, dropping him back to -6 and 4 shots off of Snead's pace.

Rodgers parred 15 playing alongside Snead.

But the old man came up with yet another birdie.

Sam Snead now led the tournament by 4 shots with just 3 holes to play.

Leaderboard after the final group finished the 15th:

- 11 Sam Snead

- 7 Phil Rodgers

- 7 Jack McGowan

- 6 Billy Casper

The 16th Hole

Last year, in 1964, Sam Snead triple bogeyed the 16th hole, and that cost him getting into a playoff. But this year, Snead parred the 16th, while McGowan hit in the water and had a double bogey, and Casper carded a bogey up ahead.

Sam Snead now led by 4 shots with just 2 holes remaining.

Leaderboard after the final group finished the 16th:

- 11 Sam Snead
- 7 Phil Rodgers
- 5 Jack McGowan
- 5 Billy Casper

The 17th and 18th

The 17th was not so kind to Jay Dolan. His tee shot landed in a creek and he took a double bogey 6. That dropped him all the way to -1 for the tournament. It was an educational day for Dolan playing alongside Sam Snead and Phil Rodgers.

Snead made par on 17. When Rodgers made bogey it gave Sam Snead a 5 shot lead just 1 hole left. The celebration could begin.

McGowan and Casper made birdie on 18 to pull into a tie for 2nd place, 5 shots back of Snead.

Snead and Rodgers both made par on 18. And the tournament was done.

FINAL LEADERBOARD

- 11 Sam Snead

- 6 Phil Rodgers

- 6 Jack McGowan

- 6 Billy Casper

- 5 Labron Harris Jr.

Finishing far back were some of the biggest names in golf:

-4 Tony Lema

-2 Bobby Nichols

-1 Gary Player

-1 Arnold Palmer

+2 Julius Boros

The Record Books for Sam Snead

The victory was celebrated wildly in Greensboro. It was an astonishing achievement for the old man. To win the tournament on the week which had already been proclaimed, "Sam Snead Week," was befitting of a fairy tale.

Bob Hampton titled his article today in the Winston-Salem Journal, ***"273 Total Climaxes Storybook Finish."*** His opening line was precious, ***"It reads like fiction, but Sam Snead won Sam Snead's golf tournament yesterday as if by design."***

Snead had set numerous records with the victory:

- Oldest player to win a PGA TOUR event at 52 years and 10 months old

- First player to win a single PGA TOUR event 8 times

- Longest span between victories on the PGA TOUR at 29 years (1936 - 1965)

And while not a record, it was certainly notable, that against this loaded field of golfers, only Sam Snead shot all 4 rounds in the 60s.

Sam Snead had a great time joking with the press after the tournament. He said, *"I don't believe these youngsters are ready yet."* And he followed up with his assessment of his chances next week in the Masters, *"This ought to drive the odds down on the Masters from 20-to-1 to about 19-to-1."*

On a serious note Snead shared, *"This gives me as big a thrill as anything I've ever won, except maybe The Masters."*

In the Durham Morning-Herald this morning, Don Shea wrote that Snead said during the press conference, *"Oh, what's the difference, anyway. Fifty years from now none of us will remember anything about it."*

POSTSCRIPT

It's been 60 years now since Sam Snead won his final PGA TOUR event.

And Sam, we still remember it!

Sam Snead remains the oldest man to win a PGA TOUR event.

Little did anyone know it at the time, but in the official counting of PGA TOUR events that was developed two decades later, the Greater Greensboro Open was Snead's 82nd PGA TOUR victory.

And that put Snead in first place on the all-time list until he was tied by Tiger Woods in 2019.

This pairing, Sam Snead and Tiger Woods, remain tied to this day as the co-leaders in all-time PGA TOUR wins.

Here is current the all-time top 10 PGA TOUR win list as of April, 2025*:

WINS		SPAN of YEARS between WINS
82	Sam Snead	1936 - 1965
82	Tiger Woods	1996 - 2019
73	Jack Nicklaus	1962 - 1986
64	Ben Hogan	1938 - 1959
62	Arnold Palmer	1955 - 1973
52	Byron Nelson	1935 - 1951
51	Billy Casper	1956 - 1975
45	Walter Hagen	1914 - 1936
45	Phil Mickelson	1991 - 2021
39	Cary Middlecoff	1945 - 1961
39	Tom Watson	1974 - 1998
38	Gene Sarazen	1922 - 1941
36	Lloyd Mangrum	1940 - 1956
34	Vijay Singh	1993 - 2008
31	Jimmy Demaret	1938 - 1957
30	Harry Cooper	1923 - 1939
30	Horton Smith	1928 - 1941

* the count of PGA TOUR wins represents the modified official count in 1987

CHAPTER FOURTEEN

Big Three Thrills

A BRIEF NOTE ON THE 1965 MASTERS AND THE 1974 WESTCHESTER CLASSIC

APRIL 12, 1965 - Augusta, Georgia

This past weekend in 1965, the Big Three were in all good form at The Masters.

Arnold Palmer, Gary Player and Jack Nicklaus came into this year's Masters as the only 3 players that have won this tournament so far in this decade.

The winners' list of the last 5 Masters looked like this:

1960 – Arnold Palmer

1961 – Gary Player

1962 – Arnold Palmer

1963 – Jack Nicklaus

1964 – Arnold Palmer

Gary Player took the lead in the 1st round with a 65. Jack was 2 shots back at 67 and Arnie, the defending champ had a 70.

In the 2nd round, Palmer began with 3 straight birdies on his way to a 68, while Player slipped to a 73 and Jack managed a 71. That put the Big Three into a 3 way tie at the top going into the weekend. That was really something to see when I looked at the April 10, 1965 New York Times.

In the 3rd round Jack took over, firing a 64. Lincoln Werden of the New York Times wrote, ***"Nicklaus's long hitting reduced the four par 5's of the course to 4's... he did it with such apparent ease that gasps came from the stunned spectators."***

Nicklaus set a 54 hole Masters record with his score of 202. He was now 5 shots ahead of Player and 8 ahead of Palmer.

In the final round, Jack must have played more conservatively as he made par on all 4 of the par 5's. He shot a 69. Player had a 73 and Palmer a 70. Jack Nicklaus won the Masters in a record 271. The Golden Bear was an incredible 9 shots clear of the field.

Tied for 2nd place were fellow Big 3 members Arnold Palmer and Gary Player at 280. And that pair was another 3 shots clear of anyone else.

The Big 3 dominated the tournament and Jack dominated the Big 3.

What is interesting to note is that this is the only time the Big 3 went 1 – 2 – 3 in a major.

Here was the final leaderboard:

-17   Jack Nicklaus

-9   Gary Player and Arnold Palmer

-5   Mason Rudolph

-3   Dan Sikes

-2   Gene Littler and Ramon Sota

-1   Frank Beard and Tommy Bolt

Only 9 players had broken par, and yet Nicklaus was 17 under par.

NOTE from the present

Nicklaus's record score stood for 32 years until Tiger Woods won by a record 12 shots with an 18 under score of 270. In that year, 16 golfers broke par.

Sam Snead, who won the prior week at the Greater Greensboro Open, by 5 shots, to become the oldest player ever to win a PGA TOUR event (a distinction he still holds), finished one shot outside the cut line.

You can watch highlights from the 1965 Masters in this video: https://www.youtube.com/watch?v=gRIdjDC5p-k

You can find the short video on YouTube by typing in the search "Jack Nicklaus Wins Masters Golf (1965)."

At the end of the video watch as Arnold Palmer, the 1964 Masters champion, puts the green jacket on Jack Nicklaus. It was the 2nd and last time that Palmer put the green jacket on Jack.

The Sports Time Traveler and The Big Three in Real Life

WESTCHESTER COUNTRY CLUB – August 22, 1974

I actually got to see the Big 3 play live, one time, in an important PGA TOUR event. It was on August 22, 1974, at the Westchester Classic.

Two of the Big 3 were very much in their prime at the time. Player had won 2 of the 4 majors that year. Jack was shut out from the majors in 1974, but he won 6 of his majors after that year. And while Palmer was on the backside of his career, he was still very competitive, finishing 5th in the U.S. Open 2 months earlier.

The Westchester Classic was played at Westchester Country Club a little outside of New York City. It had the largest purse on the PGA TOUR at that time at $250,000 with $50,000 going to the winner.

I was just 10 years old at that time when my dad took me to see my first ever PGA TOUR event in person. It was an incredible day. The grounds of the golf club were the most stunning I have ever seen.

I got my first ever PGA TOUR player autograph when Jim Dent came off the driving range.

I remember Palmer teeing off on the drivable par 4 304 yard 10th hole. The crowd around him was so deep that we could barely see the King at all.

We saw Nicklaus on the reachable par 5 12th hole. The Golden Bear had nearly as large a crowd following him as Palmer.

And we saw Gary Player hit his approach shot on the dogleg par 4 7th hole. I remember he was decked out in a matching baby blue shirt and slacks. Player had a much smaller crowd.

I also remember feeling a little sad that the legendary Sam Snead, age 62, had almost no one watching him. We saw him putt on the 8th green using his croquet style in which he stood facing the hole and used a short putter that was on his right side. It's a style of putting I've never seen anywhere else.

On that day, both Palmer and Nicklaus shot 68s to finish the opening round just 1 shot off the lead. Arnie played the final 10 holes in 6 under par, proving he still had a lot of competitive firepower.

Player shot a 71 and Snead had a 73.

Johnny Miller shot 69 in that first round and then followed that up with rounds of 68, 65 and 67 to win the tournament by 2 shots for one of his 8 victories in his best year. Nicklaus finished the tournament 6 back. Player was 14 behind. Sam Snead was 16 behind. And Arnie ballooned to an 80 on the final day and finished 23 shots back of Miller.

Going to see the 1974 Westchester Classic was one of the great father-son experiences of my childhood. And it was a foundational experience in my love of the game. Thanks Dad!

CHAPTER FIFTEEN

Jack's Thinking Grand Slam

THE 1972 BRITISH OPEN

INTRODUCTION from The Sports Time Traveler

In late June, 1972, the British Open was all Jack Nicklaus was thinking after he had bagged both the 1972 Masters and U.S. Open.

Naturally, The Sports Time Traveler had to go back in time to follow the run-up to the 1972 British Open and see if Jack Nicklaus can take the 3rd leg of the Grand Slam.

NORTH PALM BEACH, FL - June 21, 1972

Yesterday Jack Nicklaus, the number one golfer in the world, invited some sports-writers to his North Palm Beach office for a little press conference that started at 1:15pm. The Sports Time Traveler has it covered for you thanks to Pete Jeff of the Miami Herald who was there.

The 32 year old Nicklaus has now won both the 1972 Masters and the 1972 U.S. Open, the first time anyone has captured the opening two majors of the year since Arnold Palmer in 1960. Nicklaus didn't just win the U.S. Open this year at Pebble Beach; he dominated in a wire-to-wire victory by 3 shots over Bruce Crampton and 4 shots over Palmer.

Nicklaus however is not content as was made clear in "yesterday's" press conference. The Grand Slam is on his mind. No golfer has ever won the four professional majors in the same calendar year (Masters, U.S. Open, British Open and PGA Championship). *"All I'm thinking about now is the British Open"*, said Nicklaus. *"I'm going to take a 10 day vacation with my family to the Bahamas and then be set for the British Open."* The 1972 British Open is at Muirfield (where Jack won in 1966) and takes place July 12 - 15 and the 1972 PGA Championship will be at Oakland Hills from August 3 - 6.

Nicklaus also sees room for improvement in his game. *"I had the entire five and a half hours of the U.S. Open taped for me so I could see what I was doing wrong. I found out why I wasn't putting. I wasn't in any position to putt comfortably. That's why I could never get the darn club back right."* Jack also allowed the reporters into his mind, discussing his mental preparation and specifically the importance of controlling his emotions related to the desire to win. *"If you get that tense, so tense that you've got to win, then you can't win. When I came to Pebble Beach, I didn't come with that 'have to win' attitude. I was more relaxed. Sure I wanted to win. But I didn't let it affect my game."*

Nicklaus is not the only one thinking about the Grand Slam as he noted, *"You know the Saturday night press conference at Pebble Beach* (after the 3rd round of the U.S. Open) *was the first time that I can recall since I won the Masters that the Grand Slam wasn't brought up."*

And sportswriters are also not the only ones thinking about the Grand Slam. The Fort Lauderdale News reported today that Jimmy "The Greek" Snyder has laid odds against Jack winning the modern Grand Slam this year. Snyder said, *"I see where Jack Nicklaus took a stab at the odds of his chances and he said, 'maybe 50 to 1 or a 100 to 1'. Well it's better than that... right now 24 to 1. He's got to go in* (to the British Open) *as the favorite at odds of 4 to*

1, no matter how many Americans cross the Atlantic to compete. And if he's still alive he'll be 6 to 1 in the PGA."

The Sports Time Traveler also hopes to cross the Atlantic (virtually) to cover the 1972 British Open next month.

Muirfield, Scotland - Friday July 7, 1972

The London Guardian published the odds to win the British Open which starts next week.

JACK NICKLAUS (9 to 4)

Jack Nicklaus loves Muirfield, Scotland. He won the British Open here in 1966. And he arrived here a week early to practice for the 1972 British Open. The 32 year old has not played a competitive round since he captured the U.S. Open at Pebble Beach 3 weeks ago. It's all part of the strategy for Nicklaus who focuses on the majors like no one else. Nicklaus has won 4 of the last 8 majors. And he finished in the top 6 in all 8 of those majors. This year he has won the first 2 majors of the year, the Masters and the U.S. Open. And in those 2 majors he dominated, leading after each round. He came to Scotland determined to win the third leg of the grand slam and the bookies have made him the 9 to 4 favorite to win.

LEE TREVINO (6 to 1)

Lee Trevino likes to make money and have fun on the golf course. He enjoys playing lots of tournaments and talking non-stop to anyone who will listen as he walks the course. The 32 year old was quoted saying, *"I'm going to play as much as I can, as hard as I can,* (and) *win all I can by the time I'm 40."* He's 2nd on the money list this year to Nicklaus having already won $129,147 this year alone. He won the 1971 U.S. Open last year in a playoff over Nicklaus and he also was victorious in the British Open in 1971. Last week he played in the Canadian Open finishing 10th, before flying on a red eye flight to Scotland and playing his Monday practice round on no sleep. The London bookies give the defending champ a 6 to 1 chance of repeating.

TONY JACKLIN (16 to 1)

Tony Jacklin is the UK's hope. He won the British Open in 1969 and the U.S. Open in 1970. He's also won on the PGA Tour this year, taking the Jacksonville Open.

Together these three golfers, Nicklaus, Trevino and Jacklin have won 8 of the past 12 majors.

Odds on additional golfers:

12 to 1   **Gary Player**

20 to 1   **Billy Casper**

20 to 1   **Jerry Heard**

25 to 1   **Arnold Palmer**

1st ROUND - Thursday July 13, 1972

In the first round on Wednesday, the favorites found themselves behind a virtually unknown 22 year old, Peter Tupling, a 2nd year pro, who has won only $750 this year, but managed to post a 3 under par 68.

Jacklin carded a 69 to finish a shot back. Nicklaus missed 7 fairways and said, *"I didn't think I was swinging well. I know I can play a lot better."* He was on his way to a 1 under par 70 and a tie for 3rd. Trevino finished his first round one shot further back at even par 71.

The most noteworthy item about the first round was that when it was over it was the first time this year that Nicklaus was not in the lead in a major at the end of a round.

2nd ROUND – Friday July 14, 1972

In Thursday's second round, Tupling toppled to a 3 over par 74 for a two day score of even par 142. This was good enough however to place him in a tie for 3rd and just one behind the leaders, Jacklin, who shot 72 and Trevino who shot a 70.

Nicklaus said, *"I didn't play well. I like to think I still have plenty of good shots ahead because I certainly haven't used many good shots so far."* This was how he described his 2nd round score of 72, which placed him 1 shot off the lead in a tie with Tupling and 5 others including Gary Player and the low scorer of the day, Johnny Miller, who shot a 66.

Miller's 66 was a course record and was highlighted by an extremely rare double eagle. Miller made the albatross on the 558 yard par 5 fifth hole. Hitting a 3 wood from 280 yards, Miller's ball landed on the front of the green and ran into the cup. Miller said, *"I knew it was a good shot, but there were no cheers like when Arnie* (Palmer) *belts one. It was only when I got to the hole that I realized what had happened."* It was the first double eagle in a British Open in 102 years since it was done by Young Tom Morris in 1870.

3rd ROUND - Saturday, July 15, 1972

The 3rd round belonged to Trevino. He tied Miller's course record to take sole possession of the lead by 1 shot over Jacklin, who posted a 67. He did it with what the Los Angeles Times described as *"swaggering and laughing his way around the course."* Included in the merry round was an amazing stretch that started with birdies on 14 and 15.

On the 16th hole Trevino hit his tee shot on the par 3 into a greenside bunker. Fred Tupper in the New York Times reported, *"It was a bad lie against the lip... He swung. The ball cleared the trap going like an express train, and it hit the pin on a fly and dropped into the cup."* Trevino said, *"If it hadn't gone in the hole, it would have gone all the way across the green."* Trevino had holed out from the bunker for his 3rd straight birdie.

Trevino then had a routine birdie on 17 for his 4th in a row. On 18, his 2nd shot landed in the right rough about 30 feet from the pin. Tupper described Trevino's next shot, *"He chipped and the ball bounced onto the green and rolled right into the hole."*

Trevino had birdied the final 5 holes in a row.

Nicklaus meanwhile had a lackluster day. On the first hole he had a bogey when he missed a two footer. He finished with an even par 71 that dropped him to 5th place and 6 shots behind Trevino. Michael Williams in the London Daily Telegraph wrote, *"It seems safe to assume that Nicklaus's dream of the world's four major championships in one season - the grand slam - is now over."* Nicklaus himself lamented, *"I just haven't played well all week."* But then Nicklaus let it be known he wasn't throwing in the towel, *"There's one more round. Maybe I'll find something out there tomorrow. You never know."*

Leading scores after 3 rounds:

– 6   **Lee Trevino**

– 5   **Tony Jacklin**

– 2   **Doug Sanders**

– 1   **Brian Barnes**

Even Jack Nicklaus

FINAL Round - Sunday July 16, 1972

Entering the final day of the 1972 British Open Jack Nicklaus was 6 shots back and had his grand slam dream was on the line. Jack Nicklaus set a target of 65 for the round. And in the first 9 holes he was on fire. On the par 4 349 yard 2nd hole, Nicklaus drove the ball just shy of the front edge of the green. He pitched up and made the birdie putt. On the next hole he hit his approach shot to 6 feet from the pin and registered his 2nd birdie.

When Trevino bogeyed the 5th hole the leaderboard showed that Jack was just 2 shots back at 3 under par through 7 holes. Nicklaus had 11 holes to play.

Nicklaus continued to charge. When he birdied the 9th to go out in a 32, he moved a stroke ahead of Jacklin and was now just one behind Trevino.

At this moment a very strange event occurred. Trevino was putting for par on the 7th when a large hare darted around the green breaking Trevino's concentration in the middle of his stroke. He missed the putt and slammed his putter down on the green as the hare dashed off the green and down the fairway. Trevino gave a dejected look as he watched the hare race off before tapping in his bogey. Suddenly Nicklaus and Trevino were tied at 4 under par.

On the 10th hole, Nicklaus hit a brilliant 2nd shot from the rough to within 5 feet and got his 5th birdie of the day. This moved him into the lead by one shot with 8 holes to go.

Trevino and Jacklin both played the 9th hole sensationally. Each was on the green in 2 on the par 5. Trevino was 20 feet from the pin and sank his eagle putt. This drew a loud roar from the crowd as it put him back in the lead by a shot at 6 under.

Meanwhile Jack Nicklaus was on the 11th green preparing for a birdie putt also from about 5 feet. It is almost a certainty that Nicklaus heard the roar for Trevino as he was lining up his putt. But what he could not know was that Jacklin was now putting for an eagle from just 5 feet away. As Jack was crouched over and about to putt, Jacklin sank his eagle for another loud roar. This one Nicklaus definitely heard. He stood up and backed off and started his putting routine again. The Golden Bear was not fazed however. He drained the birdie putt, his 3rd in a row and 6th for the day. Nicklaus was 6 under for the tournament and tied again with Trevino with 7 holes to play.

Nicklaus shot par on the 12th and when Trevino bogeyed 10, it was Jack back in front again by a shot.

Trevino then gained a shot back on 11 with a birdie, while Jack had par again on 13 and once more the two golfers were in a tie at 6 under par for the tournament.

Another break in concentration happened for Nicklaus as he was preparing to drive on 15. Jacklin at the 12th hole had a 15 foot putt for birdie. When he ran it into the cup and gave a fist pump the crowd went crazy. Jacklin, the British hope, was tied for the lead with Nicklaus and Trevino at 6 under. Nicklaus heard the roar and backed out of his stance on the tee.

As Nicklaus began his driving routine again and addressed the ball there was yet another distant roar. Trevino, also putting from about 15 feet on number 12 just barely missed a birdie putt and settled for par to retain the three way tie. Nicklaus hearing the sudden crowd noise gave a frustrated look and backed out of his stance a second time. But the winner of 13 majors (including his U.S. Amateur titles) is not easily disturbed. He hit two great shots on 15 to set up a 5 foot birdie putt. The putt, to put him back in the lead, just lipped out.

Jacklin and Trevino both took par on the 13th and 14th holes.

Thus, Nicklaus arrived at the par 3 16th hole in a three way tie for first place with Trevino and Jacklin. Nicklaus hit his tee shot in the rough to the left of the green. His chip shot rolled to just 3 feet from the pin. He aimed the putt outside of the cup on to the right. It broke left and missed the cup on the left side. His bogey dropped him to a shot off the lead at 5 under.

Nicklaus got his par on 17. On 18, Nicklaus narrowly missed a birdie putt from 35 feet and closed at 5 under for the tournament. He had shot a final round 66 to tie the course record. It could have easily been a 65.

Nicklaus was the leader in the clubhouse. His hopes for a grand slam were still alive, but two golfers on the course were still one shot ahead of him.

Jacklin and Trevino were coming to the par 5 17th hole when Nicklaus finished. Trevino hooked his drive into a bunker and threw his club to the ground in disgust. Jacklin hit his tee shot straight down the middle. On his 2nd shot Trevino had to blast out of a deep fairway bunker. He was so far from the green on his 3rd shot that he still needed to hit a wood. He hit his ball left and short of the green into the foot high rough. At this point Trevino said to Jacklin, ***"I'm through it's all yours."***

Now hitting from deep rough Trevino bounced his 4th shot through the green and into the rough again about 30 feet beyond the pin. Double bogey seemed possible and bogey was just about a certainty.

Jacklin was just short of the green in the shallow rough in two shots. His eagle chip however landed 18 feet short of the pin.

Next up was Trevino. He was chipping for par. He hit a bump and run and as it rolled in a steady line Trevino could see hit heading straight for the cup and he started a dance even before it landed in the cup. He had saved par on 17 without ever hitting a ball in the fairway. And he was still in front of Jack Nicklaus by one shot.

Jacklin however had a putt for birdie to take the lead. He hit a putt with the right pace but it broke too far left and edged 2 feet past the hole. He then missed on the two footer. In a stunning reversal of fortune, Jacklin, who seemed certain to take the lead, had dropped a shot behind.

Trevino came to the 18th tee with a one shot lead. When Jacklin got in trouble on the hole all Trevino needed was a par to win the Open for the 2nd straight year. His drive was perfect and his iron shot to the green looked routine as the ball landed just short of the pin and rolled 6 feet past. He two putted to win the Claret Jug.

For Nicklaus the dream of the grand slam was officially over. Afterwards Nicklaus said that, ***"I felt a 65 would do it. I had a 65 and let it get away."*** But Nicklaus had proven himself once again to be a ferocious competitor who is almost always in contention to win a major.

Trevino gave an entertaining winning speech as always. And he thanked Jack Nicklaus for all of his encouragement.

Finally, in case you were wondering, Peter Tupling shot an 81 on the final day and finished 18 shots behind Trevino. His $346 (dollar equivalent) check put him over $1,000 for the year.

FINAL LEADERBOARD

– 6   Lee Trevino

– 5   Jack Nicklaus

– 4   Tony Jacklin

– 3   Doug Sanders

– 1   Brian Barnes

+1   Gary Player

+2   **Arnold Palmer, Guy Hunt, Davi Vaughan and Tom Weiskopf**

You can watch the highlights from the 1972 British Open in a fantastic 50 minute video produced by the Royal & Ancient Golf Club of St. Andrews. Here is the link: https://www.youtube.com/watch?v=8Hz4N79gZtk

You can find it on YouTube by searching on "1972 British Open Official Film."

To save you time here is a listing of the time stamps for the key moments:

16:26 - Nicklaus misses a 2 footer on the opening hole of the 3rd round

23:05 - Trevino chips in on the 16th hole in the 3rd round

25:45 - Trevino chips in on the 18th hole in the 3rd round

32:00 - The dashing hare causes Trevino to miss a putt on the 7th in the final round

34:40 - Jacklin makes eagle and Jack has to back off his putt when he hears the roar

36:00 - Nicklaus has to back off his tee shot twice as the crowd roars on the 12th green

43:30 - Trevino chips in on 17 for par to take a one shot lead with a hole to play

47:50 - Trevino receives the Claret Jug and gives a short and entertaining speech

CHAPTER SIXTEEN

A 60 Year Old Contends for a Major

THE 1972 PGA CHAMPIONSHIP

INTRODUCTION from The Sports Time Traveler

On Sunday August 6, 1972, something remarkable was taking place. 60 year old Sam Snead was contending in the final round of PGA Championship on the same course where he nearly won the U.S. Open in 1937

OAKLAND HILLS COUNTRY CLUB, BLOOMFIELD, MI - August 7, 1972

At the end of the third round of play on Saturday the leader in the PGA Championship by 1 stroke was Gary Player. At this time, he is one of just 4 golfers in history to win all 4 of golf's professional major championships, a feat known as the Grand Slam (the other three are Gene Sarazen, Ben Hogan and Jack Nicklaus).

6 shots back in a tie for 15th place was a man who is still gunning for the final piece of the Grand Slam, 60 year old Sam Snead. Snead has won 7 majors. He's won this event, the PGA Championship 3 times, the first time 30 years ago in

1942. He's won the Masters 3 times and he won the British Open once. But he never won the U.S. Open.

Snead had nearly won the U.S. Open several times. He finished in 2nd place on 4 separate occasions. And one of those 2nd place finishes was on this course, Oakland Hills, 35 years ago in 1937.

A Family Affair

Something unique in the annals of golf's major championships took place when Sam Snead teed it up on the 1st hole yesterday to begin his final round. His playing partner was another Snead, Sam's 31 year old nephew, J.C. Snead. Both Snead's just happened to have finished the 3rd round in a tie for 15th place, 6 shots back of Gary Player.

Early in his final round Sam was playing like he remembered his 1937 round. He recorded 3 birdies and posted a 9 hole score of 32. This put him just 2 shots off the lead with 9 holes to play.

Snead is the Leader in the Clubhouse

Sam wasn't able to keep up his torrid pace on the back 9. Shooting a 37, he had a final round of 69. That was 6 shots better than his nephew. And that score gave him a total of 4 over par 284 for the week. At this point Sam Snead, at age 60, was the leader in the clubhouse in the PGA Championship.

Player is Shaky

Meanwhile Gary Player, well behind Snead on the course had started very shaky. Posting a 37 on the front 9, Player was at 1 over for the tournament at the turn. Jim Jamieson, a man who had never won a major tournament, birdied the 9th and 11th holes and pulled ahead by a shot at even par.

Jamieson Stumbles

Down the stretch however, Jamieson bogeyed the last 3 holes and finished with a 3 over par 283. This was enough however to unseat Snead as the new leader in the clubhouse.

A Miraculous Shot

Jamieson's string of bogeys opened the door for Gary Player. Coming to the 16th tee, Player was clinging to a one shot lead. Then he sliced his drive into deep rough on the par 4 and couldn't see the green. His next shot he later called, *"one of the best shots I've ever hit."* He landed the blind strike just 4 feet from the pin. His birdie putt gave him a 2 shot lead which he maintained on the final 2 holes to win his 2nd PGA Championship and 6th major title of his career. His final 72 hole score was a 1 over par 281.

Snead Finishes in 4th Place in a Major at Age 60

Snead's 284 was good for 4th place, just 3 shots behind the winner, an almost incomprehensible feat at age 60. His score was only 1 shot worse than he had scored 35 years earlier, when he finished 2nd in the 1937 U.S. Open.

And Snead's 284 was actually 3 shots better than Ben Hogan's winning score on this same course in the 1951 U.S. Open.

Snead had beaten British Open champion Lee Trevino (286), Masters and U.S. Open champion Jack Nicklaus (287), and the ever popular Arnold Palmer (289), who is still a top player on tour.

Snead's final round of 69 was also tied for the lowest round of the day.

FINAL LEADERBOARD

+1   Gary Player

+3   Jim Jamieson and Tommy Aaron

+4   Sam Snead, Ray Floyd and Billy Casper

+5   Gay Brewer, Jerry Heard, Phil Rodgers and Doug Sanders

Snead speaks to the Press

Snead had plenty to say in the clubhouse afterwards. *"I guess I'm too dumb to quit"*, he joked. *"But I like to play with these fellas and see what the kids are doing. I thought if I could get a couple more under par on the back 9, I might throw a scare into them. I figured if I could get in with a 65 or 66 it might do the trick. That would have been a helluva turnaround to lose the Open here (in 1937) and then win the PGA about 40 years later."*

POSTSCRIPT

If Sam Snead would have shot the same score of 69 that he did in the final round of the 1972 PGA, back in the 1937 U.S. Open, held on this same course, he would have tied for 1st place, and quite possibly could have won the U.S. Open title that eluded him in his career.

CHAPTER SEVENTEEN

The Newcomer vs. The Kings

THE 1972 SAHARA INVITATIONAL

INTRODUCTION from The Sports Time Traveler

Arnold Palmer has been the king of golf since his spectacular year in 1960 in which he won the Masters, the U.S. Open and the hearts of a new wave of golf fans.

In a late October, 1972 piece, Jim Murray, of the Los Angeles Times wrote, *"Palmer was the first player a guy carrying a lunch pail could identify with."* Palmer at his best was exciting to watch because he didn't just play a golf course. He attacked it. As Murray wrote, *"He was a one-round fighter. He flattened the course or missed the cut."*

The 43 year old Palmer at this time had won 60 PGA tournaments. And he was still near the top of his game. He won over $200,000 the prior year, in 1971, to be the 3rd leading money winner. But coming into the Sahara Invitational in Las Vegas in October, 1972, he was hungry as ever for number 61. He had not won a tournament all season and this could be his last chance of the year.

Jack Nicklaus, is recognized as the best player in the world here in 1972. The Golden Bear won both the Masters and the U.S. Open this year. Coming into the Sahara Invitational, Nicklaus had won $284,429 on the season to lead all golfers. He has 2 more chances this year to become golf's first $300,000 winner.

Lee Trevino is the 3rd man in the current big three of golf. He won this tournament last year. And he has won 3 of the last 8 majors.

Also in the field this week is a 22 year old rookie, Lanny Wadkins. Not a single newspaper in the country ran a story on Lanny the morning of the first day of the tournament on Thursday. Wadkins has not won a tournament in his rookie year. But an AP story in January said Wadkins was one of two rookies with "can't miss labels."

Sahara Invitational - ROUND 1 - Friday October 27, 1972

Lanny Wadkins got off to a great start in the first round on Thursday. His 65 put him in the lead early in the day. By the end of the day however, Arnold Palmer and three others had caught him for a five way tie at the top of the leaderboard.

Jack Nicklaus was just 1 shot back. Last year's winner, Lee Trevino, bothered by the slow play of his fellow Tour professionals, was 5 shots back at 70.

After the round, Palmer said, *"It looks as if I'm off to another start. I just hope I don't choke the last 2 rounds."* Palmer was no doubt referring to his performance the prior week, at the Kaiser Invitational, in which he had opened with rounds of 66 and 67 for the halfway lead. And then fired 75 and 74 over the weekend to finish 12th.

No interviews of Wadkins could be found in any newspapers after the 1st round.

Sahara Invitational - ROUND 2 - Saturday October 28, 1972

Palmer shot 69 on Friday as did Wadkins. They shared the 2nd round lead at 134 with John Mahaffey whose 66 was the low round of the day.

After the round Palmer said, *"This time I just hope I can keep it going for 2 more days."*

Nicklaus, who also shot 69, was again just 1 shot back at 135, tied for 4th place with George Knudson and Art Wall. Knudson won last week's Kaiser Invitational and was now in contention to win back-to-back tournaments.

Defending champ Trevino shot 72 to stand 8 shots back at 142. He sounded off about the slow play after the round. *"Yesterday I almost quit because of the slow play. It took 5 hours for a round. We're going to be out here to watch the Johnny Carson show in a few years if this keeps up. Something's got to be done.* (In Mexico) *they take a siesta after 9 holes and they still play faster than we do."*

Sahara Invitational - ROUND 3 - Sunday, October 29, 1972

The 3rd round belonged to George Knudson who shot a bogey free 65 on a day when the other leaders all shot over 70. As a result, Knudson found himself with a 3 shot lead at the end of play.

But Knudson appeared exhausted after Saturday's round and said, *"I think it's the tension doing it. I'm not used to being in the lead so often."*

Wadkins shot 70 to stand alone in 2nd place 3 shots behind.

Palmer shot 71 which left him in 3rd place and 4 shots behind. Nicklaus could only manage a 73 and was now 7 shots back.

Again, there were no published comments from Wadkins after the round. But this was because most of the media attention surrounded Lee Trevino.

Trevino, who started the round 8 shots back, was 4 over par on his 1st 6 holes on Saturday and then simply left the course after 9 holes without telling any officials.

One of Trevino's playing partners, Chuck Courtney, said that Trevino remarked, *"I'll see you guys later."*

People near Trevino on the 9th hole heard him say, *"I've had it."*

PGA Tournament supervisor Wade Cagle said, *"As far as I know he didn't talk to anyone. I'll make a report to the commissioner and then the matter will be in his hands."*

Sahara Invitational - ROUND 4 - Monday, October 30, 1972

In the final round yesterday, Wadkins started shaky. On the par 5 opening hole he put his 2nd shot in the water. But he *"got a big lift by sinking a par putt."*

Knudson, who started with a 3 shot lead could only manage a 37 on the front 9. And with Wadkins going out in 33, suddenly the 22 year old had a 1 shot lead over Knudson and 3 over Palmer going into the back 9.

Knudson continued to slide, finishing with a 76 which dropped him all the way back to a 7th place tie.

But Palmer, playing in the same group with Wadkins and Knudson, was starting to charge. And a couple of holes in front, Jack Nicklaus was also making a big move.

When Wadkins reached the par 3 16th tee, he was 2 strokes ahead of Palmer and Nicklaus. Wadkins hit a 4 iron which he thought was perfect. But the ball rolled off the back of the green into thick rough and he carded a bogey.

Now Nicklaus, up ahead on the 18th, was just 1 back. The Los Angeles Times writer quipped, *"Nicklaus was about as interested in finishing 2nd as Russia."* Trying to reach the par 5 in 2, Nicklaus tried too hard on his drive and sent the ball out of bounds. Then Nicklaus put another ball in the water. He ended up with a 7. Suddenly Jack Nicklaus was out of contention.

A hole back on 17, Wadkins and Palmer both got pars. Thus, Wadkins had a 1 shot lead on Palmer as they started play on the 72nd and final hole of the tournament.

If he was nervous he didn't show it. Wadkins *"split the fairway with his drive,"* according to Cal Soto in the Arizona Republic. And then he hit a wood shot just short of the green on the par 5. His chip went 18 feet past the pin. He missed the birdie putt and tapped in for a closing round of 69.

Now Palmer, was left to putt for a chance to tie. Palmer had also come just short of the green in 2 and had chipped even closer, to just 12 feet shy of the pin. He needed to sink the putt to send the tournament to a playoff. *"His many fans held their breath,"* wrote Soto.

The putt slid past the hole. And with that, young Lanny Wadkins had won his first PGA Tour event in spectacular fashion holding off the kings of golf.

After the tournament, Wadkins was asked about the presence of Palmer and Nicklaus looming over him. *"Pleasing rather than disturbing,"* said Wadkins, prompting the Los Angeles Times writer to proclaim, *"apparently he'd rather get run over by the Titanic than a row boat."*

FINAL LEADERBOARD
- − 11   **Lanny Wadkins**
- − 10   **Arnold Palmer**
- − 9   **Gay Brewer and Hale Irwin**
- − 8   **Jack Nicklaus and Bob Eastwood**
- − 7   **John Mahaffey, George Knudson and Lionel Hebert**

POSTSCRIPT from The Sports Time Traveler™

Lanny Wadkins went on to win 21 PGA Tour events and 1 major, the 1977 PGA Championship. In 2009, he was inducted into the World Golf Hall of Fame. He is presently a commentator on The Golf Channel.

CHAPTER EIGHTEEN

Jack Nicklaus Goes to Disney World

THE 1972 WALT DISNEY WORLD CLASSIC

INTRODUCTION from The Sports Time Traveler

I've traveled virtually back to the first week in December, 1972 to catch two big events in central Florida. The Golden Bear and Apollo 17 were both in central Florida and primed for out of this world performances.

Jack Nicklaus is playing in the 2nd annual Walt Disney World Golf Classic. And the last of the Apollo missions to the moon is about to launch.

Jack Nicklaus came here to Disney World with his family, after a month off, to defend his title that he won in the inaugural event one year ago, and to enable his family to visit the Magic Kingdom.

Nicklaus Enjoying His Best Year

Nicklaus comes into this final event of the 1972 season on top of the money list with a record $290,542 in winnings for the season. He has a chance to become the first golfer ever to earn over $300,000 in a single year.

Jack has had a sensational season. He's only played 20 tournaments, but he's won 6 of them and finished 2nd in 4 others. He's been in the top 2 in 50% of the tournaments he's entered.

He won the first 2 majors of the year, the Masters and the U.S. Open. And then he nearly won the 3rd major, the British Open.

And now here's my report on the 1972 Walt Disney World Classic.

1st Round - December 1, 1972

There are 2 golf courses in Disney World - the 6,900 yard Palm and the 7,200 yard Magnolia. The golfers play one of them in each of the first 2 rounds.

The colorful Chi Chi Rodriguez played his best round of the year on the longer Magnolia course in the opening round. Despite sometimes heavy rain he shot a tournament record 65 for a 1 stroke lead. His round included a 148 yard 7-iron shot that he holed out for an eagle.

Jim Warters of the Orlando Sentinel referred to Chi Chi as *"the clown prince of the pro golf tour."* But noted that Chi Chi is *"discarding his crowd pleasing capers of the past."* In an interview Chi Chi told him, *"It's the 3 D's now. Determination, dedication and desire,"* as he explained he has 13 relatives that he's now supporting in Puerto Rico.

Warters noted that Chi Chi's new approach means, *"no more putter wielding acts of sword simulation."* Chi Chi elaborated, *"Lee Trevino has taken my place. When Trevino came on the tour my jokes didn't seem funny anymore."*

Chi Chi's more serious approach is working for him as he's 11th on the money list with $112,608 and one victory this season.

Nicklaus, also playing the longer Magnolia course shot 68 to put himself in a tie for 6th place, 3 shots back.

Arnold Palmer, playing the shorter Palm course, shot a 69 to put himself in good position to contend for what would be his first and only victory of the season. Coming into this season, Palmer had won at least one tour event each year he's been on the PGA TOUR.

2nd Round - December 2, 1972

Nicklaus, playing the shorter Palm course shot another 68 and finished the day with a 1 shot lead over George Archer. Asked if it's hard to maintain focus in this end of year event, after a month layoff, Jack said, *"If I'm in contention after the first 2 rounds, there's no difference in my desire. I'm just as excited as if it was the National Open."*

Chi Chi, also playing the Palm course, shot a 73 on day 2 to fall 2 shots behind Nicklaus and into 3rd place. He attributed his drop off to the water hazards on the course. *"There's too much water out there. I'm allergic to water. I'm glad the last 2 days of the tournament are on the Magnolia."*

Arnold Palmer, playing the more difficult Magnolia course shot 77 and missed the cut. This was a monumental moment. For Palmer it marked the end of a remarkable professional streak. He had won at least one tournament every year since his rookie year in 1955. A streak of 17 consecutive seasons with a victory. That streak is a PGA TOUR record. Now the streak was over. Palmer said, *"I just played awful. It was one of those days."*

NOTE from The Sports Time Traveler

I interrupt this chapter for a quick note. Arnold Palmer's streak of 17 consecutive years with a PGA TOUR victory remains the record. But Jack Nicklaus tied the record in 1978. There really has never been another pair of competitors like Arnie & Jack.

3rd Round – December 3, 1972

Great weather led to low scores. Starting the day 4 shots back, Jim Dent fired a bogey free 65. Dent, who has only won $7,101 on tour the entire year, and has never won a PGA TOUR event, put himself in contention to win with a 3 round total of 205. Dent, who is 6-foot-3 and built like an NFL linebacker, credited the soft touch on his putter for his great round. *"I only had 23 putts today and when you putt that well you can hang in there."*

George Archer birdied the 3rd, 4th and 5th holes and pulled even with Nicklaus early in the round. And when Nicklaus bogeyed the 7th, Archer took the lead. But Archer then double bogeyed 8 and bogeyed 17 and finished with a 69 for a 3 round total of 206.

Nicklaus managed a 67 for a 54 hole score of 203 and a 2 shot lead over Dent.

Dave Marr, who shot 65, pulled to within 4 shots of Nicklaus. But Marr has no ideas about beating Jack on Sunday. He remarked about Nicklaus, *"Par for him on this course is about a 68. He'd have to play really bad and think bad for anyone to catch him."*

Chi Chi, playing with an upset stomach, could only manage a 75 and fell out of contention at 10 shots back.

Leading scores after 3 rounds

− 13 **Jack Nicklaus**

− 11 **Jim Dent**

− 10 **George Archer**

− 9   **Dave Marr and Bob Goalby**

Final Round – Monday December 4, 1972

Nicklaus started the final round with a 2 shot lead over Dent. The Golden Bear birdied the 1st hole, but bogeyed the 2nd.

Then Dent, playing in the group ahead of Nicklaus, birdied the 3rd and eagled the 4th.

Suddenly Jim Dent had a 1 shot lead over Jack Nicklaus with 14 holes to play.

The lead lasted for approximately 2 minutes.

Nicklaus promptly birdied the 4th hole to tie Dent. Then Dent, a hole ahead, missed a 2-foot par putt. Nicklaus was back in front by a stroke.

Then Nicklaus made a 6 foot putt for birdie at the 6th and a 22 foot putt for birdie at 7 and the lead was up to 3 shots. Nicklaus was out in 33.

On the back 9 Nicklaus turned into a birdie machine. On the par 5 526 yard 10th, Nicklaus was 20 feet from the pin in 2 shots and 2 putted for another birdie. Then came 3 more birdies in a row at 13, 14 and 15.

Finally, on the 468 yard 18th hole, Nicklaus' 5-iron 2nd shot stopped 24 feet from the cup. He 2-putted for his 5th birdie of the back 9. That gave him a back 9 total of 31 and a record-tying 64 for the round.

No one else got close again after Dent's brief moment in the lead early in the round.

Dave Marr, who started 4 back, never contended in shooting 71. George Archer, who started 3 back could only manage a 73.

Jim Dent finished very respectably with a 1 under par 71 to tie for 2nd place which earned him $11,600. That's 50% more money than he had earned in the entire year up to this tournament.

Jim had no qualms about his finish. ***"You don't give Jack Nicklaus a 2 stroke lead on the final day of the tournament and beat him. All I was trying to do was grab onto Jack's back pocket and hang on for 2nd place money."***

Jack set a new 72 hole tournament record of 267, 6 shots better than Jack scored in his 1971 victory here.

A Stunning Margin of Victory

Nicklaus won the tournament by 9 shots. It was the largest margin of victory and the lowest under par score in a PGA TOUR event in 1972.

No one had won a tournament by a larger margin since Arnold Palmer mauled the field by 12 strokes at the 1964 Phoenix Open.

It was also Jack's 7th win of 1972.

And Jack's $30,000 winner's check blasted him past the $300,000 barrier, the first golf professional to exceed that amount in one year.

Jim Warters, in the Orlando Sentinel, likened Nicklaus' performance to a lopsided boxing match, *"Most of the world's premier golfers took an unmerciful beating from Jack Nicklaus... officials should have stopped it after 10 holes."*

Nicklaus demolished the field and the course. He was the only player to shoot in the 60s all 4 rounds. Walt Disney World president, Card Walker, said that after the inaugural tournament last year, *"We tried to toughen up the course, but it didn't work... Next year we're going to let Jack play 3 extra holes to even things up."*

Jack attributed some of his performance to the relaxed atmosphere at Disney World. *"I walked in the park with my kids every night. Strolled Main Street. My feet are sore. I know that."* Then he went on to add something that would probably make the other touring pros cringe, *"I certainly hope to be better next year. I'm still a young man (32) and I feel I can improve."*

And then he added a few more words of wisdom that everyone can benefit from thinking about. *"Winning breeds winning. Every time you win, you learn something. You learn something when you lose too."*

Here was the final leaderboard:

— 21   **Jack Nicklaus**
— 12   **Jim Dent, Larry Wood and Bobby Mitchell**
— 11   **Bert Yancey, Bob Goalby and Frank Beard**
— 10   **Sam Snead, Ed Sneed, Len Thompson, Dave Marr and Tommy Aaron**

The Grandest Fireworks in History

The stellar finish by Nicklaus in the Walt Disney World Golf Classic and his proclamation that he's reaching for the stars, was the perfect entree for me to scroll over to the cape to catch the largest display of manmade pyrotechnics the world as ever seen, the launch of Apollo 17.

Not only is Apollo 17 the last of the manned missions to the moon. It's also the first and only Saturn V launch to take place at night. Originally scheduled for the evening of Tuesday, December 6th, the countdown was delayed until after midnight, thus the launch was taking place on December 7th. You can watch the Apollo 17 launch on YouTube video via this search, "APOLLO 17 - Night Launch."

Pondering Nicklaus' Place in History

Before finishing my virtual trip back in time, I picked up the December 8th Tampa Tribune. Sports editor, Tom McEwen, was compelled by Nicklaus's 1972 season accomplishments, to write these words, ***"Is Jack Nicklaus just the best now, or is he the best of them all, ever?"***

The answer to the question is not what's important. It's that some sportswriters are now asking the question.

CHAPTER NINETEEN

The King Attempts to Regain His Crown

THE 1973 BOB HOPE DESERT CLASSIC

INTRODUCTION from The Sports Time Traveler™

I have always been an Arnold Palmer fan. However, I was too young to experience his heyday in the early 1960s, when he dominated the PGA TOUR winning 29 tournaments in the first 4 years of the decade.

In one sensational stretch of 11 majors, beginning with the Masters in 1960, he finished either 1st or 2nd a total of 8 times (winning 5). That's a record neither Tiger Woods nor Jack Nicklaus ever achieved.

It made Arnold Palmer the King of golf.

Palmer's "go for broke" style of play, his habit of hitching up his pants, and the way he attacked the golf ball, instead of applying a sweet, smooth "Snead-like" stroke, endeared him to the everyday sports fan that previously didn't follow the game. It spawned "Arnie's Army," a vocal, passionate and sometimes rude following at every tournament.

Palmer's popularity was such that at the end of the 1960s, he was voted not just golfer of the decade, but athlete of the decade by the AP.

Shortly after Palmer reached his peak, Jack Nicklaus, 10 years younger, came to prominence, and Palmer had a persistent rising challenger to his throne, but not to his fans, for Arnie's Army never ceased to be loyal.

By the early 1970s, Nicklaus had clearly surpassed Palmer as the greatest golfer in the world. And Palmer, in his early 40s, had begun to fade.

In 1972, Palmer failed to win a PGA TOUR event. It was the first time in his professional career, going back to 1955, that he had not won a tournament in a calendar year. His stretch of 17 consecutive years with at least one victory is still tied with Nicklaus for the longest streak ever.

Entering 1973, the king was hungry to win another. His dry spell had reached 18 months.

So I decided to travel back in time to the 1973 Bob Hope Desert Classic in Palm Springs, CA, a tournament Palmer had won 4 times before, to see if Arnie's Army could help him win just one more.

Here's the report from my virtual trip.

PALM SPRINGS, CA - February 7, 1973

The Bob Hope Desert Classic gets underway today. It is an unusual tournament. It's played for 5 rounds, not the traditional 4 – a total of 90 holes. And during the first 4 days, the players travail 4 different courses.

Those first 4 days are also a Pro-Am affair. One pro plays with 3 amateurs in each of 144 groups. This year some of the amateurs included entertainers Bob Hope, Frank Sinatra, Dean Martin and Clint Eastwood. Also playing was the last man to walk on the moon, astronaut Gene Cernan, and future hall of fame baseball player Al Kaline. Even America's Vice President Spiro Agnew will be here on the final day to watch the tournament.

As Shav Glick wrote in the Los Angeles Times, *"The first 4 days of the Bob Hope Desert Classic are not a golf tournament. They are a happening."*

The tournament is also different because it's played in the desert. Jim Murray, L.A. Times sports columnist, wrote that the land around the 4 golf courses, where

Palmer and Nicklaus were planning to design a new course, was, *"so bad the white man didn't even bother to steal it from the Indians,"* and, *"cars sank slowly up to their hub caps in sand."*

Palmer Likes His Chances Despite His Recent Poor Play

Palmer, ranked just 68th in money winnings this year, was asked by Doug Ives of the Long Beach Independent if he could win. Palmer said, *"I don't see why not. The desert seems to bring out the best in me."*

This seems to be true as Palmer won this tournament in its inaugural year of 1960 and again in 1962, 1968 and 1971.

ROUND 1 - February 8, 1973

The perpetually optimistic Palmer may have thought he could win the tournament, but he didn't show any flashes of his brilliant past on Wednesday. He fired a 1 under par 71 on the Indian Wells course, not bad, but he was suddenly spotting the leader, Jack Nicklaus, 7 shots.

Nicklaus is the hottest golfer in the world, having won 2 majors and 7 tournaments overall last year as well as winning the last tournament he played in 2 weeks ago.

Nicklaus shot 64 on the same course as Palmer, on greens that were described by fellow player Bob Rosburg as *"very, very scary."* Yet Nicklaus sank 6 putts of more than 10 feet.

Asked how Nicklaus could have scored so well, Rosburg said, *"You've got to remember one thing about Nicklaus, he plays a different game than the rest of us."*

ROUND 2 - February 9, 1973

Nicklaus struggled with his driver on the 2nd day of the tournament. Playing at the Tamarisk course, Jack could only manage a 70. His 36 hole score of 134 gave him a 2 shot lead over Doug Sanders, Billy Casper and Orville Moody.

Perhaps the biggest surprise of the day was a 66 shot by Arnold Palmer who made 7 birdies. His 2 day score of 137 put him just 3 shots behind Nicklaus. Palmer said, *"Today I made some putts and yesterday I didn't. If I had putted as well yesterday I might have been better than 66."* Palmer also noted that this was the 1st tournament this year in which he used the same putter 2 days in a row.

ROUND 3 - February 10, 1973

Palmer played the LaQuinta course on Friday and shot a 69. This put the King just 1 shot off the lead now held by Nicklaus and journeyman pro Allen Miller, whose 68 earned him all the newspaper headlines. Thus, giving the papers someone else to praise for a day besides Nicklaus.

Palmer did make it into the headlines of one paper, The Palm Springs Desert Sun, which featured an amusing article in which reporters Pamela Landsden and Jolee Edmondson agreed to take an airplane ride with Arnie, and his co-pilot, in Palmer's Lear jet, in order to get an exclusive interview.

With Arnie flying the plane, the terrified reporters, who were imagining their epitaphs, nervously asked him if he was trying to perform some rare acrobatic feat when he swerved the plane. But Palmer said he was just trying to make a left turn.

When they were safely on the ground the reporters told Palmer he was a very good golfer.

ROUND 4 - February 11, 1973

Two big stories emerged from the 4th round on this day.

Another Miller, named Johnny, soared into a first place tie with Jack Nicklaus at 15 under par by blazing a 63 on the Tamarisk course, which many of the pros believe is the toughest of the 4 courses.

But the bigger story was that Palmer, playing at Bermuda Dunes, shot a 68 to remain just one back of the leaders after 72 holes. He holed 4 putts from 15 feet or further. And because Nicklaus and Palmer finished their rounds earlier than Miller, Sunday will feature a Nicklaus-Palmer pairing in the final group.

Arnie could have actually held the 4 day lead if he hadn't double-bogeyed the 11th hole.

After the round Palmer said, *"I'm encouraged. I'm actually making some putts. I made a 20 footer that saved a par and that's a great feeling."*

Hank Hollingworth, writing in the Long Beach Independent, shared a story about Arnie's Army from a Long Beach resident who played in the Pro-Am during the first 4 days. *"When he started to get into contention it swelled like mad. I actually felt sorry for Jack Nicklaus, who's probably the best golfer active today. For the most part, Nicklaus was ignored for Arnie. One thing about Arnie's Army, it's the noisiest throng around any golf course."*

ROUND 5 - February 12, 1973

Palmer and Nicklaus teed off together in the final group at Bermuda Dunes for the last round of play. It was as though Bob Hope had staged a made for TV event. The two greatest active legends in golf were just one shot apart in a duel for the Classic. The final round aired on NBC at 4pm ET.

What wasn't made for TV was the drenching rain. In the 13 year history of the tournament there had never been more than a sprinkle. But today there was a deluge. Johnny Miller, co-leader with Nicklaus at the start of the round said the rain was so bad, *"I just kept thinking the round would be rained out and I couldn't concentrate."* Fortunately, Bermuda Dunes is on the highest ground of the four courses and the greens drained fast enough to keep them playable.

In spite of the rain, Palmer put his 2nd shot on the par 4 opening hole just 8 feet from the pin and sank the birdie putt. While Nicklaus 3 putted for a bogey. Suddenly on the 73rd hole, Arnold Palmer had vaulted into the lead in the tournament for the first time.

Palmer then birdied the 4th to take a 2 shot lead. And Arnie's Army was now on the march.

Shav Glick in the Los Angeles Times was following the two great golfers and wrote, *"The army was in its usual form, cheering mistakes by Nicklaus, and the other leaders, chatting and running while other players shot, and roaring every time Arnie hitched up his pants."*

Palmer played steady from the 5th through the 15th holes. It wasn't until the 16th that he missed a green by hitting his tee shot on the par 3 into a bunker. Meanwhile, Nicklaus hit his tee shot to within 3 feet of the pin. The potential for a 2 shot swing, that would put Nicklaus and Palmer into a tie, looked imminent.

Palmer blasted out of the bunker to within 8 feet of the pin. Still away, Palmer putted first, trying to save par. *"I was sure Jack would make his birdie, so I felt I absolutely had to make my putt just to be even,"* said Palmer. He did make it.

Now, Nicklaus had his 3 footer to move within 1 stroke with 2 holes to play. Nicklaus missed. Palmer remained 2 shots ahead after 16 holes.

Palmer maintained his 2 shot lead over Nicklaus on 17, and the rivals reached the par 5 18th hole. Nicklaus, needing an eagle to tie, reached the green in 2, and his ball stopped just 18 feet from the pin. Nicklaus had hit 2 miraculous shots in the rain and wind to put himself in position to tie.

Palmer's drive was short and he was short of the green on his 2nd shot. But he pitched his 3rd shot to just 7 feet from the pin.

Now Nicklaus had to make the eagle putt to have any chance. His putt grazed by the cup. With a tap in birdie Nicklaus was now 1 shot behind.

"Jack hit a super putt," said Arnie. *"I was sure it was going in and I knew if it went in I had to make mine. When he hit it, I asked him what are you trying to do and he said, 'Trying to beat you.'"*

Palmer now just needed to 2-putt to win. But the version of Arnold Palmer that had been on display on the TOUR over the past 18 months was prone to 3 and even 4 putt greens.

On this day however, Palmer drained the 7 foot birdie putt.

Glick wrote, *"He hurled his visor to the crowd with as much vigor and enthusiasm as any rookie winning his 1st tournament."*

Palmer had finished with a 2 shot victory over Jack Nicklaus and Johnny Miller at 17 under par. Miller had caught Nicklaus with a birdie on the final hole.

Palmer had closed the tournament with a 69, to Nicklaus and Miller's 72. Palmer was the only player to shoot in the 60s for the last 4 rounds.

Nicklaus was the first person to come over and congratulate him. Vice President Agnew, who Palmer often plays with, also came over to congratulate the King.

"It was one of my best finishing rounds. I'm overly excited," said Palmer to Lincoln Werden writing for the New York Times. *"It's always a necessity to win,"* Palmer told Ron Roach of the AP, when asked about the importance of PGA TOUR victories.

He also admitted that before this tournament, he had feared he might never win another PGA TOUR event. Palmer told Shav Glick, *"There were times I had doubts about ever winning again. But I've been thinking more about golf lately. When I was winning that was all I thought about. I've tried to recapture that attitude and I think today I proved it has paid off."*

After Palmer's victory, Nicklaus said, *"I guess after putting up with Arnie's Army for 12 years, I'll have to try and put up with it a few more."*

Jim Murray, sports columnist for the Los Angeles Times, wrote, *"The victory was no more popular than the liberation of Paris... he is to the game what Gable, Cagney, Grant and Bogart were to movies."*

Here is the final leaderboard:

-17   Arnold Palmer

-15   Jack Nicklaus and Johnny Miller

-14   Gay Brewer and Jim Wiechers

-12   John Schlee

-11   Lanny Wadkins

-10   John Mahaffey and Kermit Zarley

POSTSCRIPT from The Sports Time Traveler™

The victory turned out to be the very last one of Arnold Palmer's PGA TOUR career.

While there is no video publicly available from the 1973 Bob Hope Desert Classic, there is one minute of footage of Arnold Palmer's unique golf swing during that era:. You can find the video on YouTube by searching for "Arnold Palmer - Driver (Slow Motion) Classic Footage!"

On a personal note, I last had a chance to march in Arnie's Army during a PGA Senior Tour event in 1987 at Sleepy Hollow country club, a beautiful course along the Hudson River in New York.

That day, I actually got to shake hands with the King. I remember being amazed at his massive hands and powerful grip. His hand was fully twice as wide as mine. He clearly had a physical advantage in the way he could muscle the ball off the tee or out of any trouble.

There may never be another golfer who so singularly captivates the fans as Arnold Palmer.

CHAPTER TWENTY

Snead Destroys the Field at 60

1973 JACKIE GLEASON INVERRARY CLASSIC

LAUDERHILL, FL - February 22, 1973

The Jackie Gleason Inverrary Golf Classic starts today here in Lauderhill, Florida, but there was big news yesterday in the Pro-Am event.

A record crowd of 26,414 was on hand at the Inverrary Golf and Country Club. Those who chose to follow 60 year old Sam Snead, instead of Arnold Palmer, Jack Nicklaus or defending champion Tom Weiskopf, saw something incredibly special. Paired with actor Forrest Tucker, famous for his portrayal of Sergeant O'Rourke in the sitcom "F Troop," Sam Snead shot a course record tying 65 for the best round of the day.

Snead, who is presently 59th on the PGA TOUR money list, beat all his fellow touring pros by a margin of 4 shots!

With a purse of $260,000, this week's tournament is one of the richest in golf and the field includes all the big names with the exception of Billy Casper and Gary Player.

Half the crowd was following Arnold Palmer, a winner less than 2 weeks ago in the Bob Hope Desert Classic. Palmer shot 72. His playing partner yesterday was none other than Bob Hope.

Jack Nicklaus could only manage a 2 over par 74.

Defending champ Tom Weiskopf only shot 73. By the way, when Weiskopf won this event last year he never shot a round better than 68.

In fact, only 12 players broke par yesterday!

All of this makes Sam Snead's 65 seem even more incredible.

Snead hasn't won a PGA TOUR event since 1965, but one for one day yesterday he proved he can still beat the best players in the world.

The Sports Time Traveler is going to stick around to follow the 1973 Jackie Gleason Inverrary Golf Classic.

ROUND 1 - February 23, 1973

Yesterday Sam Snead began the tournament by going 1 under par over the opening 6 holes. Then a 3-putt green on the 7th hole got to him. Snead told Gene Williams of the Miami News, *" When I three-putted seven, it felt like somebody punched a hole in the bag and all the air came whooshing out."* Snead played the remaining 11 holes in 1 over par for a 74. That put him in a tie for 50th. It wasn't too bad considering only 11 players broke par. Snead was tied with Arnie and just a shot behind Jack

But oh, what could have been? Including the Pro-Am, Snead had played 24 holes in 8 under par!

Snead blamed his 74 on his putter, *"It was colder than a brass bra. I don't usually three-putt many greens, but I had three today... that was the difference between my round in the pro-celebrity and today. I made a few putts in that pro-celebrity and the adrenaline was flowing."*

ROUND 2 - February 24, 1973

Yesterday Sam Snead came back with a 69. That shot him up the leaderboard into 12th place, just 1 shot behind Jack Nicklaus. Snead will tee off in the 3rd round at 1:01pm today in a threesome with Jack and Hale Irwin.

Snead is 7 back of the 36 hole leader, Forrest Fezler, who has a 2 shot lead on Lee Trevino.

No reporter interviews of Snead made it into any newspapers this morning.

ROUND 3 - February 3, 1973

Yesterday Sam Snead fired a 68. In his head-to-head match against Jack Nicklaus, Snead outdueled the Golden Bear 68 to 70.

That moved Sam Snead further up the leaderboard into a tie for 6th with Johnny Miller and 1 stroke ahead of Jack Nicklaus for the tournament.

The leader is still Forrest Fezler, who also shot a 68, to take a 3 stroke lead over Lee Trevino. Snead remains 7 shots back.

Fezler is just 23 years old and has never won a PGA tournament.

But he has a big fan supporting him – Sam Snead.

After being shut out in the press yesterday, today Snead took the headlines in the tournament as he told reporters, *"I'd like to see the kid win the darn thing."* The headline at the top of the page in the golf section of the Palm Beach Post this morning read, *"I Know The Pressure That Fezler Feels – Snead."*

Speaking about his own round of 68, Snead said, *"Man would it have been nice to have Wednesday's round on the board. But I can't complain much about today's. That's the most long putts I've had in one round in a long time."* The Palm Beach Post reported that Snead made two 25 footers on the front 9 and a 35 footer on the back 9.

FINAL ROUND - February 26, 1973

After 14 holes yesterday, young Forrest Fezler was in front of Lee Trevino by 2 shots.

Trevino playing in the group ahead of Fezler then birdied the par 5 15th hole to draw within 1 shot.

Fezler was just off the green in the rough on the par 5 in 2 shots. He was in excellent position to get a par or a birdie and come away with a 1 or 2 shot lead. But he hit his shot too hard out of the rough and sent it into a trap. His shot out of the trap landed 30 feet from the hole. His long par putt rimmed the cup and stayed out. Fezler had a bogey 6.

That put Fezler into a tie with Trevino with 3 holes to play.

Both men parred 17. But Fezler missed a 4 foot putt on 17 to fall a shot behind Trevino.

Trevino then made par on 18. Now Fezler needed a birdie to send the tournament to a playoff. Under great pressure, Fezler hit the shot of his life. His 6-iron approach shot on the par 4 landed just 4 feet from the cup. Now Fezler had the biggest putt of his life. Fezler said after the round that his playing partner, Gibby Gilbert said to him, *"try and defy the ball from not going in the hole."* Fezler stroked the putt and he thought it was good. But it rimmed out. Lee Trevino had won the tournament.

Trevino said he had never won before on a missed putt. He shared with reporters how hard it is getting a win on the TOUR. *"I put in 14 hours of practice during the tournament. One night it was dark and I was still hitting. We had to take the car out on the range and turn the lights on to get my practice balls."*

Trevino had won by shooting even par 72 on Sunday. While Fezler only managed a 76.

Sam Snead scored better than both of them finishing the tournament with a 1 under par 71. And that lifted him into a 4th place tie, just 3 shots behind Trevino.

Ray Crawford of the Miami Herald wrote that Sam Snead played, *"probably the best golf of the day from tee to green."* But Snead wasn't hot with his putter. Crawford wrote that Snead had, *"good birdie chances at the second, third, fifth and sixth holes."* But he made none of them.

Still, Snead's 72 hole score of 282 was 1 shot better than the world's best player, Jack Nicklaus and rising star Johnny Miller.

It was 6 shots better than last year's winner Tom Weiskopf.

And Snead was 10 shots better than the recent winner at the Bob Hope Desert Classic - Arnold Palmer.

Snead's 4th place check of $11,440 was more than he earned in the entire year of 1941, when Snead was one of the top golfers in the world and won 6 PGA Tour events.

That's all quite remarkable.

Lee Trevino remarked about Snead, *"He's the most outstanding athlete the world has ever seen."*

Snead's nephew, J.C. Snead, who is also a touring pro, commented on his Uncle Sam's resurgence in the past year, *"The way he's improving, give him 5 more years and he'll be in the top 10 money winners."*

Most of his fellow touring pros also agree that Sam Snead has a super smooth swing. Golf Digest recently reported, here in 1973, on poll results of 25 PGA TOUR players who were posed the question, "Whose swing is best?" The winner was Sam Snead. Nicklaus, Trevino and Weiskopf were tied for 2nd.

FINAL LEADERBOARD

- − 9   Lee Trevino
- − 8   Forrest Fezler
- − 7   Bob Murphy
- − 6   Sam Snead and Bruce Devlin
- − 5   Jack Nicklaus, Johnny Miller, Jerry Heard and Gibby Gilbert

POSTCRIPT from The Sports Time Traveler™

Not a single newspaper report I could find made any special note of Sam Snead's performance at the 1973 Jackie Gleason Inverrary Classic.

Imagine if Snead had shot his score of 65 from the Pro-Am in the opening round, instead of a 74. With those 9 less strokes, he would have won the tournament by 6 shots - at age 60!

And if you include the Wednesday Pro Am in the full 90 hole score of all the pros who played the Pro Am and the 72 hole tournament, Sam Snead actually shot the best 5 day score of anyone in the field, which included nearly all of the best golfers in the world.

In 1988, when Sam Snead was 76, I had a chance to watch him put on a clinic. There were 2 things that stood out from that clinic that I will never forget:

The attention he paid to having a perfect rhythm. As he swung he described how he keeps the rhythm saying to himself *"1, 2 on the backswing and 3, 4 on the downswing."*

He also demonstrated his legendary flexibility by bending down to touch his toes. Only he didn't just touch his toes. He put his palms on the ground without bending his knees! And this was at age 76!

Lee Trevino's comment back in 1973, about Snead, *"He's the most out-standing athlete the world has ever seen,"* actually merits serious consideration. And yet, Sam Snead only ranked #99 on the ESPN list of greatest athletes of the 20th century. Sam Snead is very, very underrated.

Even in the golf world it is seldom noted that Sam Snead is tied with Tiger Woods for most career PGA TOUR victories at 82.

CHAPTER TWENTY-ONE

History and Heartbreak at Oakmont

THE 1973 U.S. OPEN

INTRODUCTION From The Sports Time Traveler™

In chapter 6, I chronicled the classic U.S. Open triumph of Ben Hogan over Sam Snead in 1953 at Oakmont. It was Hogan's 4th U.S. Open victory and solidified his stature as the undisputed best golfer in the world.

In that same 1953 U.S. Open, a young amateur, named Arnold Palmer, whose golf game was well known only in his nearby hometown of Latrobe, Pennsylvania, qualified to play.

Palmer teed it up in his 1st U.S. Open and promptly shot 84 in the opening round, which included a quadruple bogey. He missed the cut the next day.

9 years later, in 1962, the U.S. Open returned to Oakmont. Now Arnold Palmer was the undisputed best player in the world. And just like Hogan

in 1953, Palmer came to Oakmont as the Masters champion and intended to win the U.S. Open and then fly to Scotland to play the British Open.

But Palmer's plans were disrupted by a rookie on the PGA TOUR named Jack Nicklaus. Palmer had the enormous "home course" advantage. Palmer had played Oakmont at least 100 times and Arnie's Army was rabidly rooting for him while shamefully taunting the young Nicklaus as "fat Jack."

The upstart and unappreciated Nicklaus tied Palmer after 72 holes and stunned the golf world the next day by beating him in the 18 hole playoff to capture his 1st major.

You can read more about that equally thrilling, and awkward, U.S. Open from 1962 in chapter 8.

Now I've traveled forward to the 3rd week of June, 1973 as the U.S. Open has returned once more to the hallowed grounds of Oakmont Country Club. And once again, there is an undisputed best player in the world. Now it is Jack Nicklaus. Trimmed and bronzed, Nicklaus is at the peak of his career. He has won 4 majors in the past 3 years, and he arrives as the defending U.S. Open champion.

Moreover, he is now tied with the legendary Bobby Jones for the most major victories in a career at 13. Nicklaus is intent on winning the U.S. Open for the 3rd time and exceeding Bobby Jones' career major total.

Nicklaus had an advantage over many other players in the majors. The majors didn't allow players to use their own caddies until the mid-1970s. While many players relied on their regular caddies for advice during a tournament, Jack Nicklaus did not.

Nicklaus was very clear about this in 2023, when he appeared as a guest announcer on CBS during the broadcast of his Memorial Tournament in Ohio. Jim Nantz asked Jack about whether he took advice on the course from his long time caddie Angelo. Nicklaus bluntly replied that he never did. He explained that he made all his own decisions and that his expectations for Angelo were to, *"Show up. Keep up. And shut up."*

Arnold Palmer is also playing this week in 1973 at the U.S. Open. Now 43 years old and on the backside of his long career, Palmer hopes his "home course" advantage can be leveraged to carry off one more major victory. How sweet it would be for Arnie to win the U.S. Open at Oakmont.

This was a U.S. Open I just had to travel back in time to experience.

OAKMONT COUNTRY CLUB - June 17, 1973

I've been camping out here at Oakmont Country Club virtually this week where the action has been thrilling with all the top names covering the leaderboard. 3 rounds are complete as of this writing. Here's a recap from this week so far.

The Top Name

No name is bigger in golf right now than Jack Nicklaus. And Nicklaus is here to win. On Wednesday, Nicklaus told Lincoln Werden of the New York Times, *"I'm still approaching my peak. I'm still a young man, but I just want to win as many championships as I can."*

Nicklaus seems to be all business this week in his quest to win. Lincoln Werden asked Nicklaus about the hostile galleries during his playoff here with Palmer in the last U.S. Open at Oakmont in 1962. Nicklaus said, *"I didn't hear the galleries or anyone else. I just played golf."*

The Contenders

Phil Gundelfinger, of the Pittsburgh Post-Gazette, ranked the top contenders to win in his article Thursday morning as follows:

1. Jack Nicklaus - Defending U.S. Open champion

2. Tom Weiskopf - Winner of the last 2 PGA TOUR events

3. Bruce Crampton - #2 money winner on TOUR this year (behind Nicklaus)

4. Lee Trevino - 1968 and 1971 U.S. Open champion and 1971 and 1972 British Open Champion

Gundelfinger went on to write, *"Don't entirely discount Arnold Palmer, with the home background somewhat offsetting his age, and Gary Player, despite his recent operations."*

Gary Player, a winner of 6 majors, including last year's PGA Championship, is recovering from a major operation on his bladder in February in which he spent 12 days in the hospital. He missed 6 weeks of golf and has only played in 2 PGA TOUR events this season. But he is healthy now and spent the past week practicing at Oakmont.

Gundelfinger also gave a chance to 3 young players: Lanny Wadkins, Jerry Heard and Johnny Miller.

ROUND 1 - June 15, 1973

Gary Player started the tournament yesterday in the same fashion as Ben Hogan did 20 year ago this week. Just like Hogan, he birdied the 1st hole. Then Player birdied hole no. 2, and went on to shoot a 67 to match the best score in the U.S. Open at Oakmont since Hogan did it.

Player was the only man to break 70 (just like Hogan in 1953) and opened a 3 shot lead.

Player credited his performance to his putter. On Oakmont's notoriously difficult greens, he had 7 one putt greens and no 3 putts. He told Phil Gundelfinger, *"It was not possible for me to putt any better."*

Jack's A Little Further Back

The overwhelming favorite, Jack Nicklaus, started poorly with 2 bogeys in the 1st 6 holes. But he drove the 322 yard part 4 17th green, and sank the putt for an eagle to finish his round at even par 71. The 17th hole was supposed to be impossible to reach as the tees had been moved 20 yards back.

Jack Nicklaus, disappointed with his round, told Lincoln Werden of the New York Times, *"I had a heck of a time getting the ball close. With the greens fast and firm you're scared. You don't trust getting the ball to stop."*

Arnie's Tied With Jack

Arnold Palmer played well matching Nicklaus's score of even par 71 to put him in a tie for 5th place. Palmer told an AP reporter, *"Ever since I lost in 1962 I've been waiting for the Open to come back to Oakmont."*

Here were the top scores on the par 71 course after round 1:

-4   **Gary Player**

-1   **Lee Trevino, Ray Floyd and Jim Colbert**

EVEN   Jack Nicklaus, Arnold Palmer, Johnny Miller and Bob Charles

Tom Weiskopf was further back at +2 while Bruce Crampton was at +4 in a tie with 61 year old Sam Snead who played the opening 9 holes in even par.

Snead told the New York Times, *"I'm not only older than these kids, but I'm older than the officials running the tournament."* This is Snead's 30th try to win the only major that has eluded him in his long career.

Dave Marr on the ABC broadcasting team marveled at Snead in an interview with Al Abrams in the Pittsburgh Post-Gazette, saying, *"Here's a man who played big time golf in the 1930's, 40's, 50's, 60's and 70's. That's 5 decades man. That's quite a feat!"*

Oakmont Challenges the Field

Oakmont was exceedingly difficult for many players in the field in round 1.

31 players shot over 80. Another 16 shot 79. And 17 shot 78.

More than half the field was at least 6 over par in round 1.

ROUND 2 - June 16, 1973

Gary Player shot a 70 to give him a 1 shot lead halfway through the tournament with a 2 day total of 137. Player attributed his success to hard work. He told Ray Kienzl of the Pittsburgh Press, *"I think aside from Ben Hogan, I probably practice more than any golfer who ever lived."*

Of more importance to the crowds was the fact that Arnold Palmer got off to a hot start on Friday. He was 3 under after 11 holes and just off the lead. Don Donovan, wrote in the Pittsburgh Press, *"Palmer was playing like Mr. Golf again and the word spread around Oakmont like sunburn... flocking to Arnie's side so that his playing partners must have thought a new attendance record was set."*

Palmer finished with another even par 71 putting him in a tie for 6th place. One of Palmer's playing partners was Johnny Miller, whose 69, put him in a group at 140, tied for 3rd place and just 3 shots behind Player. Miller told the Pittsburgh Press that when Palmer holed out before him, the gallery would race ahead to the next hole before he putted. And they missed Miller's sensational putting. He told Don Donovan, *"This is the best I have ever putted... fast greens just turn 15 footers into 6 footers. The hole looked as big as this table to me."*

But the biggest news on day 2 was a course record posted by a man who wasn't even supposed to be in the tournament. Gene Borek, a Long Island club professional, made it into the U.S. Open as an alternate when Dave Hill withdrew on Tuesday night. Borek got the call and arrived in Pittsburgh at 3am on Wednesday. After shooting a 6 over par 77 in round 1, Borek shot a 65 yesterday, for a 2 day total of even par 142. It was the lowest score ever at Oakmont and 2 shots better than any round in the history of the U.S. Open at Oakmont. His record round included a hole out from a bunker from 40 yards off the 8th green.

Borek's 2 round total put him in a tie for 6th place with Arnold Palmer, Lee Trevino, Tom Weiskopf, and 2-time U.S. Open champion Julius Boros. Borek told the New York Times, *"That's pretty big company to be in, isn't it?"*

Here were the leading scores after round 2:

− 5   **Gary Player**

− 4   **Jim Colbert**

− 2   **Jack Nicklaus, Johnny Miller and Bob Charles**

EVEN   Arnold Palmer, Tom Weiskopf, Lee Trevino, Julius Boros and Gene Borek

61 year old Sam Snead shot a 74 for a 2 round total of 5 over par 149, and good enough to make the cut which stood at 150.

ROUND 3 - June 17, 1973

Arnold Palmer had a stretch of 8 holes yesterday in which he went 4 under par, concluding with a 50 foot birdie putt on the 11th that electrified his fans. That thrust him to the top of the leaderboard on a day when there was tremendous movement.

Jerry Heard shot a 66 that catapulted him from 7 behind to a tie with Palmer. Also tied with Palmer was John Schlee who had a similar climb with a 67.

And Julius Boros at age 52, shot a 68 to round out a group of 4 tied for the lead. That's the most golfers ever to be tied at the top of a U.S. Open after 3 rounds.

With Palmer at the top of the leaderboard, even if it was as part of a 4-way tie, it was the big story of the day. Ray Kienzl of the Pittsburgh Press started his article about yesterday's 3rd round with a sentence that must have stirred all golf fans, *"Arnold Palmer shot a 3 under par 35-33-68 in the 3rd round of the U.S. Open at Oakmont Country Club yesterday and thereby set himself up for either another heartbreak or one of his most glorious victories."*

Palmer was less excited than the Pittsburgh area fans. Fully aware that a 3rd round tie for the lead doesn't guarantee anything, he told the New York Times, *"There's nothing to be excited about yet."*

On the downside, the leader for the 1st couple of rounds, Gary Player, slid to a 77 to fall 4 shots back of the leaders.

Johnny Miller ballooned to a 76 on Saturday giving him a 3 day total of 216 and tied for 13th place.

Jack Nicklaus slid a little less posting a 3 over 74 and is now 4 shots off. On consecutive holes at 10 and 11 he 3-putted. But Nicklaus is very hopeful. He told the New York Times, *"4 strokes is not too much to make up."*

Here were the leading scores after round 3:

-3 Arnold Palmer, Julius Boros, Jerry Heard and John Schlee

-2 Tom Weiskopf

-1 Lee Trevino, Jim Colbert, Bob Charles

+1 Jack Nicklaus and Gary Player

+2 Gene Littler and Rocky Thompson

+3 Johnny Miller, Miller Barber, Larry Ziegler and Al Geiberger

Gene Borek fired an 80 and was tied with Sam Snead who shot 73 at +9 for the tournament.

After the round, Lee Trevino declared, *"Arnold is going to be the man to beat because he knows the course so well."*

Palmer lives so close by that he has been commuting home in his Cadillac each evening during the tournament. Tonight he will be the only one of the leaders to sleep in his own bed as he contemplates winning his 1st major since the 1964 Masters.

The Sports Time Traveler™ can't wait to experience the final round of the 1973 U.S. Open tomorrow.

FINAL ROUND INTRODUCTION From The Sports Time Traveler™

The excitement here at Oakmont Country Club yesterday, just outside of Pittsburgh was palpable, it was dream-like, it was unreal. Because the hometown hero, Arnold Palmer, was tied for the lead going into the final day of the U.S. Open on his "home course."

Palmer at 43 years old had not won a major title in 9 years and won his only U.S. Open 13 years ago.

He lost the U.S. Open here in a playoff 11 years ago.

And he suffered 2 more heartbreaks, losing playoffs in both the 1963 and 1966 U.S. Opens.

Perhaps it's the heartbreaks even more than the majestic victories that have endeared his legion of fans, that they call Arnie's Army, to this man. For his fans, in their unwavering affinity, are unlike those of any other golfer, perhaps any other athlete. And they were primed to see him make history yesterday by winning the U.S. Open that eluded him here at Oakmont 11 years ago. The one he was supposed to win.

Now let's experience the final day of the 1973 U.S Open.

OAKMONT COUNTRY CLUB - June 18, 1973

Yesterday's final round of the U.S. Open was a thriller. Never before had a U.S. Open final round started with 4 players tied for the lead. And one of them was named Arnold Palmer, who was playing on what could be considered his home course.

The four leaders were split into two groups.

The final group of the today consisted of Jerry Heard and the 53 year old 2-time champion Julius Boros.

The 2nd to last group featured Arnold Palmer and John Schlee.

Schlee's Stressful Start

John Schlee felt less than fortunate to be paired with the legendary Palmer. He told Lincoln Werden in the New York Times, *"Being paired with Arnold Palmer is like a 2 shot penalty. With people yelling all the time for Arnie it was tough and noisy."*

John Schlee must have felt he got that 2 shot penalty right on the opening hole. Possibly rattled by the enormous crowd around him all rooting for Palmer, probably nervous in leading a major in the final round, he needed to take 3 tee shots at the 1st hole. When he hit his 1st tee shot, it was unclear if it had landed out of bounds. So he had to hit a 2nd provisional drive. That was also potentially out of bounds. Schlee, then had to tee it up for a 3rd time.

When Schlee reached the 1st shot he found that it was in bounds but was unplayable. He took a penalty and ended up with a double bogey 6. Instantly he was 2 shots behind the leaders.

Schlee got his 2 shots back when he eagled the par 5 4th. But his playing partner, Palmer, birdied that hole and took over sole possession of the lead for the 1st time on the final round.

Leading scores with Palmer and Schlee through the 5th:

-4 Arnold Palmer (thru 5 holes)

-3 John Schlee (thru 5 holes)

-3 Julius Boros (thru 4 holes)

-3 Jerry Heard (thru 4 holes)

-3 Tom Weiskopf (thru 6 holes)

-2 Lee Trevino (thru 7 holes)

-2 Jim Colbert (thru 7 holes)

-1 Johnny Miller (thru 10 holes)

E Jack Nicklaus (thru 7 holes)

Miller's March

Notice the name at the 2nd from the bottom of the leaderboard. Johnny Miller who started the day at +3, and teed off nearly an hour before the final group, birdied the opening 4 holes to jump to 1 under par for the tournament.

He even narrowly missed an eagle at the 4th that would have put him 5 under for the day after just 4 holes.

Miller's Misfortune

Johnny Miller had finished the 2nd round on Friday in 3rd place just 3 shots behind the leader Gary Player. Then he had the bad fortune to leave his yardage card at the hotel on Saturday morning. When he looked for it on the 1st tee and couldn't find it he panicked. He sent his wife back to the hotel to find it. Without it he was lost and went 5 over on the 1st 6 holes in the 3rd round.

With the yardage book back in hand, on the back 9 of the 3rd round, he played even par. But his 18 hole score of 76 on Saturday had left him 6 shots off the lead in a tie for 13th.

Now with his birdie barrage to begin the final round, Miller was back in contention.

The Old Man and The Lead

Palmer lost his spot in sole possession of first when he bogeyed the par 3 6th. Minutes later, when Julius Boros birdied the hole, the 53 year old 2-time champion found himself alone on top.

With 12 holes to go Julius Boros was in position to possibly become the first man to win a major over the age of 50.

Here was the leaderboard after Palmer and Boros swapped places.

-4 Julius Boros (thru 6)

-3 Arnold Palmer (thru 6)

-3 John Schlee (thru 6 holes)

-3 Tom Weiskopf (thru 7 holes)

-2 Jerry Heard (thru 6)

-2 Lee Trevino (thru 8)

-2 Johnny Miller (thru 11)

The ABC Broadcast and a SPOILER ALERT

Click on the link below to watch the ABC television broadcast of the final round on June 17, 1973 or type "Final Round ABC Broadcast of the 1973 U.S. Open" into the search bar on YouTube.

SPOILER ALERT – Don't open the link or go to the YouTube video if you don't want to know the outcome of the tournament right now.

Final Round ABC Broadcast of the 1973 U.S. Open

In the video link, you can see the above leaderboard on the ABC TV broadcast at the 23:13 mark.

Notice Johnny Miller is now at minus 2 for the tournament. He hit a wedge at the 11th to 14 feet and sank the putt to go to 5 under for his round.

But Boros looked in command as he hit his approach shot on the 7th. Watch him at the 27:44 mark on the video as he lands it inside 10 feet to give him a chance to go up by 2 strokes. At the 32:10 mark you can see his putt slide by the hole and so he remains in front by a single stroke after 7.

Johnny Miller Time

Just before Boros missed his putt for birdie at 7, Miller, still not being shown on the ABC broadcast, made a 15 foot birdie putt at 12. It was his 2nd straight birdie and 3rd in the last 4 holes. It put Miller at 3 under for the tournament and 6 under for the round and vaulted him to a tie for 2nd with Palmer, Weiskopf & company.

Now ABC just had to show Miller. They handed off to Frank Gifford who was covering the 13th. At the 32:37 mark on the video, watch Miller on the tee at the 13th. Miller hits his tee shot on the 185 yard par 3 to just 5 feet from the pin. At the 35:30 mark you can see Miller putt. He cans it for his 3rd straight birdie and his 4th in 5 holes. Johnny Miller has tied Julius Boros for the lead. Miller is 7 under on his round, and no one has ever shot 7 under at Oakmont.

At the 39:50 mark, we see Miller again hitting into the 14th green on the 360 yard par 4. He puts his wedge shot just 12 feet from the hole for yet another great birdie opportunity.

At the 43:05 mark we see Miller miss his putt at 14 to stay at minus 4 for the tournament. Meanwhile, Lee Trevino has now moved up to minus 3 into a tie with Palmer and Weiskopf, just 1 off the lead still held by Miller and Boros.

Palmer Plays Through

At the 43:52 mark on the video you can see something I've never seen before in a professional golf tournament. Arnold Palmer's group has been instructed to play through Tom Weiskopf's group on the 9th hole.

Lincoln Werden in the New York Times described what happened on Tom Weiskopf's 2nd shot that required an official ruling and delayed the group, *"An unbelievable 2nd shot caromed off a vendor selling periscopes on the right side of the 9th green. The ball bounded into a snack bar, skimmed by 3 people who were sitting on the counter and stopped on a shelf next to 3 loaves of bread."*

While the Weiskopf situation was being sorted out by officials, Palmer playing through had an eagle putt attempt on the par 5 9th. You can watch Palmer's long eagle putt at the 45:24 mark on the video. The putt which would have put him back in front by himself fell just short.

At the 47:53 mark you can see Palmer sink his short birdie putt on 9 to move back into a tie for the lead at minus 4. The noise on the course was so loud as the leaderboards were updated with Palmer's name on top, that ABC announcer Chris Schenkel said at the 48:21 mark, ***"This past week Secretariat and Arnold Palmer have received the most applause I've ever heard."*** Schenkel is referring to Secretariat, the triple crown racehorse winner, who had destroyed the field in the Belmont Stakes the prior weekend.

Here was the leaderboard as Arnold Palmer started the back 9 tied for the lead in the U.S. Open:

-4 Arnold Palmer (thru 9)

-4 Julius Boros (thru 8)

-4 Johnny Miller (thru 14)

-3 John Schlee (thru 9)

-3 Tom Weiskopf (thru 8)

-3 Lee Trevino (thru 10)

As a fan of Arnold Palmer, even 50+ years later it's exhilarating to see Arnie's name on top of the U.S. Open leaderboard going into the back 9 on a Sunday.

Miller's Magic

At the 52:51 mark on the tape you can see Miller hit his approach shot on the par 4 453 yard 15th hole. His 4 iron stops just 10 feet from the pin. Miller has now landed his iron shots to within 15 feet on 5 consecutive holes.

Stick with the video and you can see Lee Trevino putt from 10 feet on the 11th. If he makes it he will move into a 4 way tie at the top. But his putt is just short.

Immediately after Trevino misses, you will see Weiskopf finally finish the 9th hole. He cans his birdie putt and now Weiskopf makes it a 4 way tie for 1st.

Skip ahead to the 55:20 mark and you can see Miller putt for birdie on 15. He makes it and Johnny Miller, for the 1st time, has the outright lead in the U.S. Open. He is now 5 under for the tournament and 8 under on the round.

Palmer Presses

At the 1:02:16 mark on the video Arnold Palmer has a crucial putt. It's a 6 footer for par at 10. He makes it and stays 1 shot behind Miller. The announcers described it as one you had to make to win. Palmer tips his cap to the crowd as he walks off the green.

At the 1:07:24 mark we next see Palmer hit a spectacular approach shot on the 11th hole. He puts it less than 5 feet from the hole. He now has a chance to tie for the lead.

Arnold Palmer is clearly feeling in command of the tournament.

It is however at this moment, walking up to the 11th green, that Palmer first sees the leaderboard that indicates Johnny Miller, not Palmer, is in fact in the lead. The board shows Miller is at 5 under thru 16.

John Schlee, Palmer's playing partner, told the Pittsburgh Press, *"When we went to the 11th green Palmer looked totally shocked to see that Miller was 5 under."*

Here are the scores Palmer would have seen when he looked at the scoreboard at the 11th green:

-5 Johnny Miller (thru 16)

-4 Arnold Palmer (thru 10)

-4 Julius Boros (thru 9)

-4 Tom Weiskopf (thru 9)

-3 Lee Trevino (thru 12)

-3 John Schlee (thru 10)

-3 Jerry Heard (thru 9)

At 1:11:33 you can hear Jim McKay make the call as Arnie lines up his birdie putt on 11. Palmer's putt slides by the hole and McKay says, *"He really needed that one."*

Palmer appears clearly dejected as he walks off the green.

After the round Palmer said this about the moment he saw the leaderboard at 11, *"I almost threw up. I couldn't believe anyone was shooting 63 in the Open."*

It was a catastrophic revelation for the King. And it crushed him.

Palmer's next 3 holes were bogey-bogey-bogey. He finished the round with a 37 on the back 9 to end the tournament at minus 2.

Palmer's playing partner, John Schlee, said in the Los Angeles Times, *"When Arnold made those bogeys it was like playing in a morgue."*

Later Palmer told the Pittsburgh Press, *"After all the golf I've played I shouldn't have been that shocked, but it took the fire out of me."*

Miller's Motion

At 1:16:06 on the tape we see Johnny Miller on the 18th tee. It's a great view of his full driver on the par 4 452 yard finishing hole. ABC shows Miller in slow motion after he hits the drive. It's a beautiful thing to see the swing of Johnny Miller at his best.

Byron Nelson says on the video, *"I've never seen him swing through the ball as well as he has today."* You can then hear Nelson's analysis of Miller's swing. It's something we can all learn from.

Miller pars the 18th hole to put his record 63 in the books. And now he waits to see if it will hold up.

Boros has already bogeyed the 10th to drop back to minus 3. Palmer bogeys 13, 14 and 15. Weiskopf bogeys 13, 14 and 17.

Schlee's Second Chance

John Schlee however, playing alongside Arnold Palmer has weathered the "2 stroke penalty" and with the army subdued, Schlee birdies the 16th hole to get to minus 4.

He is now in 2nd place by himself a stroke behind Miller.

He narrowly misses a birdie putt at 17. Then he just misses holing out a birdie chip at 18. When the ball doesn't drop in, he has to settle for a par and finishes at 4 under for the Open, good for 2nd place by himself.

Here is the final leaderboard of the 1973 U.S. Open:

-5 Johnny Miller

-4 John Schlee

-3 Tom Weiskopf

-2 Lee Trevino

-2 Jack Nicklaus

-2 Arnold Palmer

-1 Julius Boros

-1 Jerry Heard

-1 Lanny Wadkins

Nicklaus had birdied 17 and 18 to move up to a tie for 4th. But he still told the Los Angele Times, *"I played atrociously."*

Miller Makes History

Johnny Miller's 63 broke the U.S. Open record for a single round and gave him a 1 shot victory in the 1973 U.S. Open. To do it, he had to pass Jack Nicklaus, Lee Trevino and Arnold Palmer, the biggest names in the game.

After the round Miller explained his incredible 63 to the Los Angeles Times, *"When you're hot you might as well give it a go. I usually make everything or nothing."*

It was a historic round that led some of the leading sports columnists of the time to marvel at Miller. Many were already calling it the greatest round of golf in major tournament history, if not all-time.

Arthur Daley in the New York Times celebrated Miller's final round 63 with this, *"As any intelligent man would be quick to tell you, this kind of shot making on the final round borders on the impossible. Record-breaking in other years was almost always done in early rounds before the pressure tightened."*

Jim Murray, the Los Angeles Times sports columnist, also pontificated on the magnitude of Johnny Miller's 63 with a brilliant piece in today's paper. Here's an excerpt, *"Imagine shooting a 63 in the U.S. Open! That's almost like stoning a church, painting moustaches on statues of saints... you're supposed to look up at the leaderboard and say 'my god, what am I doing, I'm leading a U.S. Open. Where do I come off beating Nicklaus and Arnold Palmer and Lee Trevino and Gary Player.' Then you're supposed to go out and feint."*

POSTCRIPT From The Sports Time Traveler™

Speaking about his sensational 63 at Oakmont decades later, Johnny Miller pointed out that, *"it was not just a 63, it was a 63 with Sunday pins."* Sunday pins at the U.S. Open are notoriously difficult. But as can be seen on the video, on that magical day in 1973, Miller was firing right at the pins and nailing most of them.

50 years after Miller's record round, I was privileged to see, on live television, Rickie Fowler and Xander Schauffle, 2 of my favorite golfers of the present generation, break Miller's U.S. Open record with 62's in the opening round of the 2023 U.S. Open. But it should be noted that they were only 8 under par just like Miller was in 1973, because Xander and Rickie were playing the par 70 L.A. Country Club. Oakmont, in 1973, was a par 71.

And Xander and Rickie did it in the 1st round, not the final round with Sunday pins.

Johnny Miller's 63 in the final round of the 1973 U.S. Open remains one of the most awe inspiring rounds of golf ever played.

CHAPTER TWENTY-TWO

The Game's Greatest Natural Talent

THE 1973 BRITISH OPEN

TROON, SCOTLAND - July 15, 1973

I came here to the Troon Golf Club, on a virtual sports time travel trip last week to experience the 1973 British Open. This is a tournament I didn't watch when I was a kid, so I was eagerly looking forward to see how it unfolded here in 1973.

11 years ago on this course, in 1962, Arnold Palmer set the all-time British Open record score of 276. Sports Illustrated wrote about that performance, ***"Everybody departed saying that Palmer was God and Troon was a beast."***

Now Palmer was back, but at age 43, he was not one of the favorites.

The Favorites to Win

Some oddsmakers picked Lee Trevino to win his 3rd consecutive British Open.

33 year old Jack Nicklaus, very much in his prime, was the favorite to win among most others. Nicklaus has captured 4 majors in the last 3 years, and is the man to beat in every major.

26 year old Johnny Miller, who recently stunned the golf world with a major championship record final round of 63 to win last month's U.S. Open, was another obvious favorite.

And there was also 30 year old Tom Weiskopf. Weiskopf may hold the dubious title of best player in the game to never have won a major.

The Pre-Tournament Odds

Here is how the London Sunday Mirror called the odds to win the 1973 British Open a few days before the start of the tournament:

4 to 1   **Jack Nicklaus, USA**

6 to 1   **Lee Trevino, USA**

10 to 1   **Tom Weiskopf, USA**

14 to 1   **Johnny Miller, USA**

14 to 1   **Bruce Crampton, Australia**

14 to 1   **Gary Player, South Africa**

And Then There's Chi Chi

Another player who was not considered among the top favorites, but is perhaps the most entertaining player in the game, is Chi Chi Rodriguez.

One oddsmaker put Chi Chi at 66 - 1 to which Chi Chi took offense saying in the Miami Herald, *"Who do they think I am, Jose Feliciano* (a famous singer of this time).*"*

Any way you look at it, the Open was expected to be dominated by Americans.

The Oldest Man in the Field

The domination however wasn't expected to extend to the oldest man in the field, who was also an American.

Gene Sarazen, at age 71, was competing in the British Open at Troon exactly 50 years after he competed here in 1923. In that year he failed to qualify for the "competition proper" (in those days qualifying rounds were played immediately prior to the official opening of the tournament).

In the 1st round this week, Sarazen did something he hadn't done in 40 years. He hit a hole-in-one!

Sarazen knocked it in the cup at the famous "postage stamp" hole, the 126 yard par 3 8th. The hole derives its name from its tiny green.

Gene was quoted in the Liverpool Daily Post saying, *"It was the biggest thrill of my life. I'm delighted it's been recorded on film. And I'm going to take the film with me when I go up to see* (Walter*) Hagen,* (Bobby) *Jones and* (Tommy) *Armour, otherwise they are not going to believe me."*

Hagen, Jones and Armour also wouldn't believe that Sarazen shot a 1 under par 35 on the front 9. The London Daily Telegraph wrote, *"Indeed, for a few priceless moments the leaderboards actually had Sarazen's name them."*

ROUND 1 - July 12, 1973

Gene Sarazen was unable to dial back the magic yesterday on the back 9 and finished with a 79. Although, that was still good enough to put him ahead of 34 of the best golfers in the world.

While Sarazen was deep in the middle of the field, several of his American counterparts dominated the top of the leaderboard.

The best score of the day was posted by Tom Weiskopf with a 4 under 68. Weiskopf benefited from a late tee time for the wind abated in the afternoon.

Right behind Weiskopf were 2 other Americans at 69 - Jack Nicklaus and Bert Yancey. And Johnny Miller was just 1 shot further back at 70.

In a tie for 10th place at even par 72, was Arnold Palmer, and 66 - 1 shot Chi Chi Rodriguez.

Playing early in the day, in heavy winds, Lee Trevino, could only manage a 75. A low ball hitter, it was thought that Trevino would have the advantage in the wind. But his low balls were subject to the whims of all the little bumps on the fairways. Trevino told the London Daily Telegraph, *"Unless the wind changes, I have no chance."*

ROUND 2 - July 13, 1973

The wind was not a factor yesterday in round 2. And a light rain made the greens easier.

Weiskopf continued to play at a torrid pace. Michael Williams of the London Daily Telegraph followed Tom Weiskopf and reported, *"No one, not even Sam Snead at his best, has possessed a slower rhythm with such fantastic clubhead speed at impact. He appears to be enjoying a leisurely practice swing when he is delivering the ball the most almighty wallop."*

Weiskopf shot a 5 under 67 to take a 3 shot lead and a 2 round score of 135. Williams wrote, *"His 67 yesterday was near perfection."*

Johnny Miller didn't get his 1st birdie until the 7th hole, but played magnificent after that. His round of 68 put him in a tie for 2nd with Bert Yancey.

And looming 1 shot further back was Jack Nicklaus who followed up his opening round 69 with a 70.

No one else was under 140.

Chi Chi was in a tie for 12th at 145.

Trevino made the cut with a 73. He was at 148, and tied with Arnold Palmer after 2 rounds. However, both of them were out of contention now, 13 shots behind Tall Tom Weiskopf.

Gene Sarazen could only manage an 81 for a 2 round score of 160. He missed the cut by 7 shots.

ROUND 3 - July 14, 1973

Johnny Miller was paired with Tom Weiskopf for round 3 in the final group. Williams wrote in the London Daily Telegraph, *"It was an absorbing struggle between Weiskopf and Miller. At once they became locked in close combat."*

The early advantage went to Miller who is prone to go on hot stretches and produce ridiculously low scores as he did at Oakmont 4 weeks ago. Miller birdied 6, 7 and 8 on his way to a front 9 of 32.

Weiskopf got off to a shaky start with bogeys on 1 and 3. He recovered with birdies at 5, 7 and 8.

And then came the 9th hole in which Weiskopf had a Scottish adventure. Williams described his hole, *"Weiskopf hit an appalling duck hook off the 9th tee. He had to drop under penalty, retired onto a disused tee, knocked a 1 iron short and took 6."*

This gave Weiskopf a 37 for the front 9 and suddenly his 3 shot lead at the start of the round was now a 2 stroke deficit to the U.S. Open champion Johnny Miller.

But Weiskopf remained unfazed by his wayward tee shot on 9 and took out his driver on 10 and blasted it long and straight to restore his confidence. He went on to shoot a 34 on the back 9.

Miller, meanwhile, struggled with his putter and ballooned to a 37 on the back 9.

The lead changed hands again and Weiskopf finished the round with a 1 shot lead.

The pair were now all alone, well ahead of the field.

Nicklaus, reportedly suffering with a strained back, could only manage 76 and dropped well back into a tie for 8th at 215, leaving him 9 shots behind Weiskopf.

Leading Scorers after Round 3

– 10 Tom Weiskopf, USA

– 9   Johnny Miller, USA

– 5   Bert Yancey, USA

– 3   B.W. Barnes, England and Neil Coles

– 2   Lanny Wadkins, USA

– 1   Christy O'Connor, Ireland and Jack Nicklaus, USA

Further down in a 13th place tie were Arnold Palmer and Chi Chi Rodriguez at +2.

ROUND 4 - July 15, 1973

Jack Nicklaus starting 9 shots behind the leader, opened the final round with a birdie at the 1st and another at the 3rd. Before Weiskopf had teed off Jack was now 7 shots behind and seemingly ready to mount a Nicklaus charge.

Britain's Neil Coles, a 38 year old top European professional, who rarely plays in America, also made a charge. Starting 7 shots back he birdied 2, 4 and 5 to pull within 4 shots of the lead.

Weiskopf got off to a good start. He parred 1 and 2. Miller bogeyed the 2nd, missing a short putt.

Then on the 3rd hole, after both players hit brilliant approach shots, Weiskopf drained his 20 foot birdie putt, while Miller on the same line as Weiskopf missed his slightly shorter birdie try.

Weiskopf now led by 3 after 3 holes.

The gap remained 3 shots after the leaders finished the front 9.

Leaderboard After Weiskopf and Miller Finished the 9th

– 12   **Weiskopf**

– 9   **Miller**

– 7   **Coles, Nicklaus and Yancey**

The Back 9

Several holes ahead of the leaders, Nicklaus chipped in on the 13th hole to go to 8 under for the tournament. He was now just 4 shots off the lead.

The gap between Weiskopf and Miller remained at 3 when they arrived at the 13th. Weiskopf hit a wayward 2nd shot and then missed a 10 foot par putt to drop a stroke.

Weiskopf's lead was now down to 2 over Miller and 4 over Nicklaus and Coles.

Leaderboard with 5 holes to play for Weiskopf and Miller

– 11   **Weiskopf**

– 9   **Miller**

– 8   **Coles and Nicklaus**

– 6   **Yancey**

Weiskopf came to the par 3 14th hole and had a critical moment. His prior iron shot on 13 had sailed miserably right. He needed to land this one on the green or else his hold on first would be in peril

He struck a great shot. Although he missed the birdie putt he had steadied his ship and retained a 2 shot lead with just 4 to play.

Nicklaus Takes the Clubhouse Lead

Up ahead, Jack Nicklaus, who had just bogeyed 17, was the first of the leaders to reach the final hole. He drained a birdie putt for a final round of 65, a course record, and one of the greatest rounds in British Open history.

This made Nicklaus the clubhouse leader at - 8.

Coles Surpasses Nicklaus

Next came Neil Coles to the final hole. He was tied with Nicklaus at - 8. Neil had a 6 foot putt in front of him. If he made it he would be the clubhouse leader moving a shot of ahead of the legendary Nicklaus.

Coles, who looks more like Albert Einstein than a top golfer, with his wild graying hair, drained the putt for a final round of 66, capping the best round of golf in his life.

Coles was now the clubhouse leader at 9 under.

The Roar Heard Around the Course

The roar of the crowd for Coles's birdie at 18 was so enormous that back on the 15th green Johnny Miller was rattled while he was standing over a 2 foot par putt. Miller faltered. He missed the 2 footer, giving Weiskopf, who was still at 12 under par, a 3 shot lead with 3 to play.

Miller's missed putt also vaulted Coles into a 2nd place tie with the U.S. Open champ.

Now with a 3 shot lead, it was elementary for Weiskopf, who was playing steady after his mishit on 13. He parred 14 through 17. When he reached 18, he hit his 2nd shot safely onto the green and wrapped up his 1st major championship with 2 putts.

When he sank his final putt he tied Arnold Palmer's British Open record of 276.

Final Leaderboard

- **− 12   Tom Weiskopf**
- **− 9   Johnny Miller and Neil Coles**
- **− 8   Jack Nicklaus**
- **− 6   Bert Yancey**

All others were at least 5 shots further back.

4 of the top 5 players were Americans.

Further down the leaderboard, Lee Trevino, with a final round 68, finished in a tie for 10th, 13 shots behind Weiskopf

Arnold Palmer and Gary Player tied for 14th, 14 shots behind Weiskopf.

Chi Chi finished 29th with a closing 75, 17 behind Weiskopf.

The Key to Weiskopf's Win

Weiskopf's victory might just be the result of an act of sportsmanship he displayed 3 years earlier. In the 3rd round of the 1970 U.S. Open, Weiskopf played himself completely out of the tournament with a 78. That left him 16 shots behind the leader, Britain's Tony Jacklin.

Tony Jacklin finished round 3 of that 1970 U.S Open with a 4 shot lead.

Tom Weiskopf, who was known as a hot headed player, frequently displaying visible anger on the golf course, showed another side to him when he left a note inside Jacklin's locker on the morning of the final round.

As reported in the London Sunday Mirror today, that note delivered 3 years ago simply read, *"stay cool."*

The London Daily Telegraph indicated that the note read one word, *"tempo."*

Either way, Jacklin acknowledged that Weiskopf's note was incredibly helpful for him that day in 1970.

Jacklin stayed cool and shot his 3rd consecutive round of 70 to win the 1970 U.S. Open by 7 shots.

It was a magnificent win for Jacklin. Following his British Open victory in 1969, he was considered one of the game's top players, especially after defeating the entire big 3 of Arnold Palmer, Gary Player and Jack Nicklaus by over 20 shots.

Jacklin Repays the Favor

Flash forward to this week and Tony Jacklin decided to repay the favor.

Tony was 14 shots back after the 3rd round, here at Troon, and out of contention to win. Bill Clark of the London Sunday Mirror reported today that Jacklin placed a phone call to Weiskopf on the morning of the final round yesterday.

Tony told Tom, *"Keep your head and swing it slowly,"* according to the Sunday Mirror.

According to the Daily Telegraph, Jacklin told Weiskopf, *"Play 1 shot at a time and be patient."*

Whatever version of what Jacklin said to Weiskopf is the truth, Tom Weiskopf acknowledged after the round that Jacklin's advice had been instrumental at the most critical time of the final round, when Weiskopf had hit the atrocious approach shot into the 13th hole and bogeyed it.

Weiskopf Uses Jacklin's Advice at the Most Critical Moment

Weiskopf later said, *"I remembered Tony's words when I took my only bogey in the last round. I said to myself, you've made a mistake Tom, now forget it, and swing easy."*

Nicklaus's Advice Helps Too

Weiskopf also received some advice before the final round from fellow Ohio State alumnus Jack Nicklaus.

Tom said that Jack told him before the round, ***"Don't play Johnny*** (Miller)*, **play the course. And that's what I did."***

After the final round, Nicklaus told Fred Tupper of the New York Times that Weiskopf, ***"has more natural talent and more shots than anybody in the game today."***

And that is how the game's greatest natural talent won the 1973 British Open.

POSTSCRIPT From The Sports Time Traveler™

After the 1973 British Open a highlights film of the tournament was produced.
Click on this link below to watch the highlights of the 1973 British Open
https://www.youtube.com/watch?v=NCB5NjjrptQ&t
You can find the video by typing into the YouTube search, "1973 British Open Highlights."

GUIDE TO THE HIGHLIGHTS VIDEO:

At the 1:20 mark on the video watch 71 year old Gene Sarazen's hole-in-one in the 1st round. Sarazen was a winner of 7 major championships, the 1st of which was the 1922 U.S. Open 51 years earlier. Sarazen had 1st played at Troon exactly 50 years ago.

At the 19:25 mark see Jack Nicklaus in the most uncharacteristic outfit you'll ever see him wear, hit a brilliant approach shot during the 3rd round.

At 34:20, Nicklaus opens the final round, wearing more Nicklaus type attire, with a birdie at the 1st hole.

At 35:05 Nicklaus birdies the 2nd hole of the final round. He is now 7 shots behind Weiskopf who has yet to start play.

At 37:00 Nicklaus chips in on the 13th to go 8 under for the tournament. At this point Nicklaus is 4 shots off the lead.

At 37:35 Nicklaus putts on the 18th green. He drains it for a final round of 65, a course record, and one of the greatest rounds in British Open history.

At 38:05 watch Neil Coles putt out for birdie, for his brilliant round of 66, to take the clubhouse lead from Nicklaus at 9 under, capping the best round of his life and thrilling the crowd.

At 39:40 Miller misses a short putt on the 2nd to fall 2 behind Weiskopf after 2 holes.

At 41:10 - after both players hit brilliant approach shots into the 3rd hole, Weiskopf drains his 20 foot birdie putt, while Miller, on the same line as Weiskopf, misses his birdie. Weiskopf leads by 3 after 3.

At 43:00 Weiskopf misses a short putt and falls back to 11 under, just 2 shots ahead of Miller after 4 holes.

At 44:00 Weiskopf sinks a 20 footer for a birdie at 6 to get back to 12 under and take a 3 shot lead over Miller.

At 45:35, Weiskopf has missed the green far to the right of the 13th hole. He hits a fine pitch shot from the high rough but it still leaves him over 10 feet short of the hole and he takes a bogey. Miller is now just 2 shots back with 5 to play.

At 46:00 you can see the leaderboard with Weiskopf ahead by 2 after 67 holes in the tournament. He then hits a fantastic tee shot on the par 3 14th. He misses the putt, but maintains his 2 shot lead with 4 to play and restores his confidence.

At 46:30, Miller is on the 15th green. He is rattled by the roar of the crowd for Coles's final birdie putt up at 18, and Miller misses the 2 footer to fall 3 shots back with 3 to play. The tournament is effectively over as Weiskopf is playing steady.

At 47:05 Weiskopf calmly hits his approach shot safely onto the green at 18 to end any doubt about his 3 shot advantage.

At 48:58, Weiskopf sinks the final putt to tie the British Open record of 276 set by Arnold Palmer.

At 50:40 Weiskopf receives the championship trophy and delivers a short, gracious speech.

CHAPTER TWENTY-THREE

A Family Affair

THE 1974 AMERICAN AIRLINES GOLF CLASSIC

In this chapter I take a break from the PGA TOUR and the nerve rattling major championships for a more relaxing golf tournament.

This is a very personal virtual sports time travel trip to see my parents at a sporting event.

For this trip I dialed the sports time travel machine back to the first week of February, 1974. My mother & father were on vacation in Puerto Rico.

Quite by accident, they found out that there was a sports celebrity golf tournament taking place nearby at the El Conquistador resort.

They went there and had an incredible time as they got to meet some very famous athletes.

One of the celebrity athletes at the tournament was Joe Namath, the quarterback of the New York Jets.

Namath had achieved permanent legend status 5 years earlier when he led the New York Jets to an apocalyptic upset over the Baltimore Colts in Super Bowl III. It was the game that proved the AFL was every bit as good as the NFL.

On February 1, 1974, The New York Daily News had a picture of Joe Namath on the back page of the newspaper (which is the front page of the sports section), as Namath was warming up for the golf tournament.

And wouldn't you know it my parents met Joe Namath at the golf tournament!

Below is a picture of my mother and Joe Namath.

My parents also met Joe DiMaggio.

They asked Joltin' Joe to jot down my name as he signed their program!

Joe DiMaggio. *Baseball Hall of Fame. In his third year won MVP AL took two others in '41 and '47. The greatest feat of his career was when he hit in 56 consecutive games in '41. Lifetime batting average of .325. Inducted to Hall of Fame in '55.*

Thurman Munso *Yankees Catcher. of Year, hitting to the 1971 All played 140 gar home runs and average.*

He wrote, *"To Lenny. Best Wishes, Joe DiMaggio."*

Newspaper Coverage of the Tournament

Articles about the tournament appeared in newspapers across the country from February 1st through the 4th.

An AP photo appeared of Oakland A's star Gene Tenace (MVP of the 1972 World Series) in newspapers across America on February 3, 1974.

NOTE from The Sports Time Traveler

The cool thing about seeing the photo of Gene Tenace at the golf tournament is that in 2023 I interviewed Gene for my book, "The 1973 Mets – You've Got to Believe." Gene played in the 1973 World Series for the Oakland A's against the Mets. On that interview he provided me with some never before heard insights about game 7 won by the A's.

TOURNAMENT RESULTS

The 54 hole, 3 day tournament was won by the team of Jeff Burroughs (outfielder for the Texas Rangers and the 1974 AL MVP) and Bob Anderson (running back for the Denver Broncos) taking first place. The players split $5,000 in prize money for winning.

They were just 1 stroke ahead of 3 teams which included the oldest pair of players in the entire tournament - Joe DiMaggio and hall of fame QB Otto Graham. The three 2nd place teams all split $1,500 in winnings.

MY PARENTS RETURN TO NEW JERSEY

When my parents came home, I remember I had never seen anyone get so tan in one week as they had on their exciting trip in the sun in Puerto Rico.

My dad told me stories about the tournament. One day they were sitting in the buffet for the players and they saw a *"young guy who was alone so we went*

over and talked to him." It turned out to be Reggie Jackson, who recently had earned the nickname, "Mr. October," for his MVP performance against the Mets in the 1973 World Series just 4 months earlier.

A little later that day my mother stopped outside the ladies room to talk to a ball player. Then she hollered over to my dad and said, ***"Come and meet Johnny Bench,"*** (who is arguably the greatest catcher in baseball history). My dad, a big baseball fan from the old Brooklyn Dodgers days, was stunned to hear my mom calling him over to meet Bench. A few months earlier, Johnny Bench, had been the hero of game 1 of the 1973 National League Championship series. His walk off homer against Tom Seaver of the Mets had won the game for the Reds.

After 50 years of hearing about these stories from my parents, I finally got to experience all of this virtually as The Sports Time Traveler.

What a trip!

CHAPTER TWENTY-FOUR

Still Slammin' with the Best

THE 1974 LOS ANGELES OPEN

RIVIERA COUNTRY CLUB – February 18, 1974

The Sports Time Traveler is now in Southern California (virtually, of course) where I experienced the final round of the 1974 Los Angeles Open yesterday.

I had to come back here, 24 years after I was here (virtually) for the 1950 Los Angeles Open because Sam Snead was once again contending to win the tournament. In 1950, Snead defeated Ben Hogan in Hogan's initial comeback attempt (see chapter 1).

Snead also won the Los Angeles Open 5 years earlier in 1945. And he won his first PGA event 9 years before that in 1936.

Now at nearly 62 years old, he's playing against a completely new generation of golfers, some of whom were not even born when Snead beat Hogan in 1950. And the majority of whom were not born when Snead won his first tournament in 1936.

But Snead is being overlooked. That's because here in 1974, the Golf World is in a tizzy. Johnny Miller won the opening 3 tournaments of the season, something no one else has ever done.

SPECIAL NOTE from The Sports Time Traveler

I interrupt this chapter to tell you that I remember watching Johnny Miller on TV in January, 1974, as he crushed the fields at Pebble Beach, Phoenix and Tucson in 3 consecutive weeks.

As a 10 year old boy living in New Jersey where it was freezing and everything looked white outside, I watched those tournaments on our 12 inch Sony Trinitron while I was putting golf balls on the carpet in our home. All the while I was dreaming about being able to play golf in April when the ground would start thawing out. And that's a very long time to wait when your 10.

Now back to 1974.

Snead Wasn't There

But perhaps Johnny Miller's 3 straight wins in January, 1974 should have an asterisk. Because Sam Snead didn't play in those January west coast tournaments that Miller dominated. Snead was in Florida in January playing in senior and club events.

This week, The Los Angeles Open was Snead's first foray back onto the PGA TOUR this season. And he quickly made an impact.

After firing a 2 over par 73 in the 1st round of the Los Angeles Open, Snead showed he was just getting warmed up. He proceeded to have a stellar 2nd round, firing a 68. Only 3 players in the field posted a better score on Friday and one of them was Johnny Miller.

The 68 put Snead in a tie for 16th with Lee Trevino and Arnold Palmer.

In Saturday's 3rd round Snead was placed in a threesome with a couple of 24-year-old Tom "boys" – Tom Watson and Tom Kite. Arnold Palmer yelled to Snead before the round, *"Sam, how does it feel to be playing with your grandsons?"*

Kite shot a 72, Watson shot a 68.

Snead dusted both of them.

He went out in 1 under 34 on the front 9. Then he made consecutive birdies on the 11th, 12th and the 13th holes with putts of 4, 8 and 13 feet. Snead added one more birdie at 17 from just 3 feet. He finished with a sensational 5 under par 66. Even more impressive was that on this 7,028 yard course with three par 5's, Snead was either on or just off the edge of the green in 2 on each one of the par 5's. And he birdied all 3.

With his 2nd and 3rd round scores 68 and 66, Snead's 36 holes in the middle of the tournament totaled 8 under par 134. And that was 2 shots better than anyone else in the entire field for those 2 middle rounds.

And it was a packed field.

Take a look at how the leading golfers in the world fared on those middle 36 holes last week in L.A.:

134 (-8)   Sam Snead
136 (-6)   Tom Weiskopf
137 (-5)   Johnny Miller
144 (+2)   Jack Nicklaus
146 (+4)   Lee Trevino
147 (+5)   Arnold Palmer

A giant picture of Snead using his croquet style putting method was on the front page of the sports section of the Los Angeles Times on Sunday, along with an article titled, ***"Snead Goes 5 Under Par, 5 Over His Age,"*** as the Times was referring to the 66 Snead shot at the par 71 Riviera Country Club.

With that 66, Snead was tied for the lead after 3 rounds in the Los Angeles Open with Dave Stockton, Tom Weiskopf and John Mahaffey.

Snead very nearly had sole possession of the lead going into Sunday. Bill Shirley of the Los Angeles Times, described what happened to Snead on the 18th green on Saturday, ***"He left a 12 foot putt dead center on the edge. He tightened***

up on the putt and scraped his putter on the grass when he heard a kid
yell on his back stroke."

That missed putt on 18 cost Sam a course record tying 65, which is the score
that Tom Weiskopf posted on Saturday. Weiskopf ranks just behind Miller as one
of the biggest young stars on the PGA TOUR. Last year, in 1973, Weiskopf had
a breakout season, winning the British Open and showcasing his capability of
dominating the pros when he had a stretch of 10 weeks in which he won 5 times.

In the clubhouse after Saturday's round, sipping on a beer, Sam Snead told
Shirley, *"I think I can still play, and it's fun to play with these kids."*

Leading scores after 3 rounds:

– 6   Sam Snead, Dave Stockton, Tom Weiskopf and John Mahaf-
fey

– 5   Johnny Miller and Tom Watson

– 3   Jack Nicklaus, Jim Wiechers and Forrest Fezler

– 2   Bert Yancey, Dave Hill, Ken Still, Ben Crenshaw and George
Knudson

– 1   Dale Douglas, Rick Massengale, Bud Allin, Gene Littler and
Tom Kite

Even Craig Stadler, George Archer and Bruce Devlin

On Sunday, Sam Snead was in the second to last group of the day with Dave
Stockton and the hottest player in the world, Johnny Miller. So Snead at nearly
62 years old was going to be able to go head-to-head with the 26 year old phenom,
who wasn't even born the first time Sam won this tournament back in 1945.

Fans were rooting for Snead over Stockton and Miller all day Sunday according
to Mike Waldner of the Los Angeles Daily Breeze. Dave Stockton told Waldner, *"I heard them. Everyone over 25 roots for Sam."* Waldner explained,
"Everyone no doubt feels the old man needs every bit of help against the

younger generation." Stockton replied, *"What they don't realize is that Sam's got a body of someone 20."*

Playing in the final group were Weiskopf, Watson and Mahaffey. Weiskopf faded badly with a 76 in the final round. Watson, who started the day a stroke behind the leaders shot a 1 over 72 and finished 4 shots back. But John Mahaffey was having a good day and remained in contention.

In Snead's group, Johnny Miller, who held the lead briefly early in the round, shot a 2 over 73 and finished 5 shots back. It was the first round of golf in 1974 in a PGA tournament in which Johnny Miller had not broken par. That was a streak of 23 rounds.

Sam Snead and Dave Stockton both played well throughout the day. On 17, Snead drained a 40 foot birdie putt to pull within a single shot of Stockton who was in the lead.

Snead's Gamesmanship

Standing on the 18th tee next to Stockton, Sam Snead deployed a little gamesmanship according to Bill Shirley of the Los Angeles Times.

Snead said to Stockton, *"You know I birdied the last 2 holes to beat Ben Hogan in 1950."*

Snead was referring to a tournament more than a generation ago, that is remembered in the climax of the movie *"Follow The Sun,"* starring A-list actors Glenn Ford and Anne Baxter. The movie told the comeback story of Snead's long time rival - Ben Hogan.

In the movie, Hogan, who had a near fatal accident in 1949, makes his celebrated comeback at the 1950 Los Angeles Open.

You can watch the entire movie for free on YouTube. Sam Snead plays himself at the 1950 Los Angeles Open. And the movie was filmed right on location here at the Riviera Country Club. At the 1:27:40 mark of the movie, Snead sinks the birdie putt at 18 to tie Hogan and force a playoff which Snead won handily.

This is the final birdie putt that Snead was referring to in his gamesmanship with Stockton yesterday.

Stockton Startled but Unphased

To his credit, Dave Stockton was unphased by Snead's remark on the 72nd tee of the 1974 Los Angeles Open.

Stockton birdied the hole and won the tournament by 2 shots over Snead and Mahaffey.

Stockton talked to an AP reporter after the tournament about Snead's comment that he had made 2 birdies to beat Ben Hogan in 1950, *"It kind of startled me. I didn't know what to say, 'Gee that's great Sam? I'm proud of you?'"*

Instead of being rattled, Stockton hit a 245 yard 3 wood into the 18th green that rested 12 feet from the pin. He called it one of the best shots of his life and that sewed up his 7th PGA TOUR victory with an 8 under par 276.

Those 7 prior victories included one major – the 1970 PGA Championship which he won by 2 shots over Arnold Palmer.

Yet, Stockton told Hugh Baker of the Los Angeles Daily Breeze, *"I wanted to win this one more than I ever wanted to win any of the others. I'm extremely pleased with myself because I held up under pressure."*

Stockton told Doug Ives of the Long Beach Independent how proud he was of himself for this win, *"Don't kid yourself, all the big names were in this tournament, and beating them means a lot. I'll bet Johnny Miller would give up his 3 wins at the first of this year to win here. The money spends, but the feeling is different when you beat the superstars."*

Snead made par on the 18th to finish in 2nd place, 2 shots behind with a 278.

Snead's 278 was just 3 shots off the course record by Ben Hogan in the 1948 U.S. Open. In that tournament, 26 years earlier, Snead finished 5th at 283.

Hogan's 275 record in 1948 was so magnificent that the nickname for the Riviera Country Club has been "Hogan's Alley," ever since. And here, 26 years after Snead had finished 5th to Hogan in that U.S. Open, Snead was only 3 shots off Hogan's 72 hole record score.

Snead also beat his two winning scores in the Los Angeles Open. He won in 1945 with a 283 and in the celebrated 1950 playoff over Hogan in 280.

Snead's even par 71 in the final round also made him one of just four players to shoot par or better in the final round yesterday.

Even Johnny Miller, the hottest player on the planet only shot a 73.

Jack Nicklaus, who had won 2 weeks earlier in the Hawaiian Open shot a final round 75.

FINAL SCORES

- 8 **Dave Stockton**
- 6 **Sam Snead and John Mahaffey**
- 4 **Tom Watson**
- 3 **Johnny Miller**
- 2 **Tom Kite and Craig Stadler**
- 1 **Tom Weiskopf**

All of the top 8 players aside from Snead were born after 1940. By 1940 Sam Snead had already won 20 PGA tournaments. Craig Stadler, who finished in 6th place wasn't even born the last time Snead won the Los Angeles Open in 1950.

POSTSCRIPT

A week later at the 1974 Jackie Gleason Inverrary Classic in Florida, Sam Snead managed a 68 on Friday for a 2 round total 140, to put himself just 1 shot back of the lead. Snead was tied for 2nd place with Lee Trevino, and in the final threesome going into the weekend.

Snead's 68 was highlighted by a spectacular 31 on the front 9. He had 4 birdies and an eagle on that magical opening 9 holes in which he only needed 12 putts.

Then on the 10th hole his drive went out of bounds and he recorded a double bogey 6.

Snead told Tom Sears of the Palm Beach Post, *"I love this. I had a dream that I was going to shoot 31 - 41 and that's the second time that's happened. I got the 31, but then when I took the double-bogey on No. 10, I said here it goes."*

Kermit Zarley, the man who led Snead by 1 shot after 2 rounds, told the Miami Herald, *"We all just shake our heads at Sam. You can talk about his swing and his physical condition but to me the amazing thing is that Sam continues to have the desire to win. So many great players lose that in their thirties. But Sam is like a kid."*

The Fort Lauderdale News had fun with Snead's standing in the tournament. An article by sports editor Bernie Lincicome started with this, *"If Sam Snead should win the $52,000 first prize at Inverrary, he would make more money in one tournament than in any one of his 37 years on the pro golf tour."*

Bob Green, a sportswriter for the AP, asked Snead what motivates him to keep playing on tour at nearly 62 years old. Green wrote, *"Snead made a quick, concise, one word reply: 'money.'"*

Then Snead continued, *"With all the money they've got out here now, I just wish for a year or so I had my game, my swing and some 20-year-old nerves. Now, with some 20-year-old nerves and all this money they're playing for, we'd just show 'em something to make 'em sit up and take notice.'"*

Sam's Snead's Stunning Six Rounds

Even more stunning, is the roll that Sam Snead is now on over his first 108 holes of the 1974 PGA TOUR season.

Through the 2nd round of the Jackie Gleason Inverrary Classic, Sam Snead, the oldest player on the TOUR, had the lowest 6 round score of anyone on the entire PGA TOUR.

Here's how Snead's 6 rounds, starting with the Los Angeles Open and continuing into the 2nd round of the Jackie Gleason Inverrary Classic ranked him on the tour:

Last 6 Rounds on the PGA TOUR

- − 10   **Sam Snead**
- − 8   **John Mahaffey**
- − 6   **Tom Watson**
- − 5   **Tom Kite**
- − 1   **Gene Littler, Lee Trevino and Bud Allin**
- Even   **Johnny Miller**
- +2   **Lanny Wadkins and Hale Irwin**
- +4   **Jack Nicklaus**

I found this little stat truly astonishing. Sam Snead at 61 had literally dominated the PGA TOUR for over a week.

It Gets Better!

After I calculated the above scoring stats (they were never reported like this in the newspapers), I kept going and found it got even better.

Although Snead finished 15th in tournament. He scored 3 under for the week, and when combined with his 6 under score the prior week it produced something very, very special.

At the conclusion of the 1974 Jackie Gleason Inverrary Classic, here were the combined scores of the top golfers that had played each of the last 2 tournaments.

Last 8 Rounds on the PGA TOUR:

- − 9   Sam Snead
- − 8   Tom Watson
- − 7   Tom Kite
- − 6   Jack Nicklaus and John Mahaffey
- − 5   Hale Irwin and Gene Littler
- − 4   Lee Trevino and Lanny Wadkins
- − 3   Johnny Miller

I find this absolutely incredible. Over a 2 week span, no one on the PGA TOUR had a better aggregate score than 61 year old Slammin' Sammy Snead! And yet no newspaper I can find pointed this out about Snead.

Sam Snead the Athlete

One reason Snead is able to play competitively at age 61 is that he can do things with his body that most other golfers cannot do at any age.

Lee Trevino told the AP this week that Sam Snead is *"The most amazing athlete the world has ever seen."*

34 year old Jack Nicklaus told Edwin Pope in the Miami Herald, *"I hope I'm in the shape Sam is when I'm 35. You know, that guy can kick the top of a seven-foot doorway. Satchel Snead* (referring to the seemingly ageless baseball player - Satchel Paige). *That's what they ought to call him."*

How does Snead keep playing so well at his age? He gave his own explanation to Edwin Pope in the Miami Herald yesterday, *"The whole thing is, I play every day. If I ever took a few months off my game would shrivel up like a peach-seed."*

A Born Entertainer Too!

Sam Snead is also a source of non-stop entertainment, both in the things he says and what is said about him.

Snead doesn't shy away from the characterization of him as a hillbilly from West Virginia.

Soon to be 62 year old Snead told Edwin Pope in the Miami Herald yesterday, *"I'm really 47. Where I grew up in West Virginia they don't count the years you go barefoot."*

Sam spoke with Bernie Lincicome, the sports editor of the Fort Lauderdale News, and Lincicome reported the following story, *"Legend is, Snead put all his money - more than half a million dollars - in tin cans in the ground. 'That's not true,' said Snead, 'Jimmy Demaret started that story. You know, honest to God, I came home one time and found a man with a pick and a shovel digging up my backyard.'"*

Edwin Pope, relayed another story from the first round of the tournament in yesterday's paper. As Snead putted out on the final hole a fan yelled out, *"Go get 'em Sam. I'm 61 years old, same as you, but I got a cane!"* Another shouted, *"Attaboy, Sam! We're the same age!"* Pope then wrote, *"At lunch Snead is talking about the second voice. 'I look over,' he says a trifle gruffly, 'and that son of a gun must be 90 years old.'"*

My Personal Connection to Sam Snead

I have a soft spot for any story about Sam Snead because of a personal connection I have with him.

In 1988, I was privileged to play in the Duke Children's Classic in Durham, NC. It's a celebrity pro-am type event.

One of the mornings of the tournament, I went to the golf course early to practice. I was taking the event very seriously.

My wife Heather left the hotel to go to the course sometime after me.

The tournament had limo's taking everyone to the course. And when Heather went out in the front of the hotel there was an empty limo waiting. The concierge told Heather she would have to wait in the limo a few minutes until it fills up.

Soon a group of 5 old men came out in front of the hotel and the concierge told Heather that she would need to come out of the limo as these men were going to need this limo.

Heather complied and got out but thought the request was a little odd.

As soon as she got out she saw that the group of men included Sam Snead.

Snead took one look at Heather and said, **"Honey, you can get back in the limo."**

Snead and his buddies were more than happy to ride to the golf course with my wife.

On the ride Snead's entourage cracked jokes the entire time. They also told Heather how they had flown in together from West Virginia in a private helicopter.

Heather told the group that her husband was playing in the tournament and had gone over early to practice on the driving range.

When they got to the course my wife left Snead's group and came over to talk to me at the driving range. Soon I went back to hitting balls.

This was the first time I would be playing in front of a crowd of spectators and I wanted to play well. There were already at least a hundred spectators watching the golfers warming up.

When I hit a couple of wayward shots I got angry at myself and in a lapse of judgement I slammed my club down on the ground.

I kneeled down to grab the club that was on the ground when I heard an old man's voice in a slow southern drawl say sternly, **"Son, pick up that club."**

I looked up. From my crouched position gazing skyward the man seemed to be a giant. And as I made out his face I was in shock. It was a giant. It was Sam Snead. Snead apparently had seen my wife on the range and came over to where I was hitting.

I immediately thought I was going to be subjected to a well-deserved admonishment by Slammin' Sammy Snead for slamming my club in front all the spectators.

Instead, Sam Snead followed up his first sentence with this, **"I'm gonna' to teach you a lesson."**

He proceeded to grab hold of my arms and position them where he wanted them to be at the top of my backswing.

He did this with a large crowd now focused on watching Sam physically altering my club position as I held my arms up high in a stationary backswing position.

Then he said to me, **"Swing down, this is going to be a good shot."**

I was petrified. Everyone had just heard Sam Snead proclaim this was going to be a good shot. I said to Sam softly, **"How do you know it's going to be a good shot?"**

I think he got a tiny bit annoyed at that, and told me to just swing down.

From a stopped point at the top of my backswing, I felt kind of like how a baseball player stands at the plate with their bat back. It was normal for baseball, but alien for a golfer.

I swung down as ordered by one of the game's greatest legends.

Just as Sam Snead had promised I hit the ball high, long and straight.

It was the most beautiful shot I had ever seen myself hit in my life.

The ball went 50% higher than any ball I'd ever hit.

I'd been to many PGA TOUR events and studied the players on the driving range. This shot I hit looked like a pro shot to me. It was the first time in my life I hit a shot that I thought looked like a pro shot.

Sam then took the open spot on the range to the right of me and began his warmup.

My next couple of shots looked similar to the first one, but ever so slightly off. Not quite as high, straight or long.

Then I sliced one.

Sam had his back to me as he was addressing his range ball. He could only have seen my swing if he had eyes in the back of his head. But he yelled to me, *"You're laying off the club."*

I was amazed. He could diagnose my swing fault just by seeing the trajectory of my shot out of the corner of his eye. Unfortunately, I didn't quite know what he meant by "laying off the club." And I wasn't about to interrupt Sam Snead's warm up.

I kept hitting and most of my shots still looked pretty darn good, although none were quite the same as that first one. Overall however, it was the best bucket of balls I ever hit.

As I left the range a spectator came over to me and said, *"You know, you just got a $500 lesson."*

Later that day, after play was completed, Snead gave an exhibition. He explained that he thinks in terms of a dance rhythm as he swings. *"1 - 2 on the back swing, 3 - 4 on the downswing."*

And he demonstrated his legendary flexibility. At age 76, he was able to do a straight leg touching your toes stretch. But he didn't just touch his toes. He kept going. He was able to put his palms flat on the ground without bending his knees. At age 76! Incredible!

The lesson I got from Sam Snead helped me win the closest to the hole contest that day. But the lesson began to wear off after a few weeks. I couldn't retain the muscle memory. Although I still managed to hit my 2nd hole-in-one the following month, on a shot that looked almost as good as that first one on the range when Sam Snead positioned my arms perfectly.

I don't know if I ever properly thanked my wife Heather for her part in enabling that lesson from Sam Snead, so I'm going to thank her now, nearly 40 years later, for that and all the other greatest moments in my life.

Thanks Heather. I love you!

On the next page is a picture of Sam Snead and me that was taken on the driving range that day at the Croasdaile Country Club, in Durham, North Carolina in May, 1988.

Chapter Twenty-Five

Johnny Miller Shoots a 59 – or Did He?

The 1974 Tournament of Champions

INTRODUCTION From The Sports Time Traveler™

In 1974, Johnny Miller got off to the hottest start in PGA TOUR history.

He won the prestigious Bing Crosby National Pro-Am at Pebble Beach on the first weekend in January.

Then he captured the 2nd tournament of the year, the Phoenix Open, by shooting 4 consecutive rounds in the 60s.

One week later he started off the Dean Martin Tucson Open with a bang by shooting a 62 in the 1st round to break the course record and open a 4 shot lead. Miller told the **Arizona Daily Star** after the round, *"I don't know what I've been doing but it must be right."*

Three days later Miller completed the hat trick with a 3 shot victory. And he did it in magnificent style sinking putts of 40, 20 and 20 feet on the 10th, 12th and 13th holes in the final round.

He was hitting putts down the stretch like they were going into an open net in the last minute of a hockey match. He could do no wrong. Every round of the young season had been under par.

And just like that, Johnny Miller became the PGA TOUR's first ever to win the opening 3 tournaments.

It's a feat that has never been duplicated.

Miller had also become the first player on the PGA TOUR to win in 3 consecutive weeks since Arnold Palmer at the height of his career in 1962. Not even the Golden Bear, Jack Nicklaus, had ever done that.

And maybe it could have been 4 in a row to start the season, we'll never know. Because Miller caught a bad cold in Tucson and had to skip the Andy Williams San Diego Open on the 4th week of the season.

In fact, it already was 4 in a row for Miller who had won his last event of the 1973 season, at the World Cup of Golf, where he was paired with Jack Nicklaus in a team event. In doing so, Miller became the first golfer since Jack Burke in 1952 to win 4 straight professional tournaments.

Those opening 3 weeks in 1974 however were electrifying enough. Johnny Miller, who had come from behind to beat Arnold Palmer with a shocker, a 63 final round at the U.S. Open in 1973, for his 1st major, at age 26, had now become one of the top golfers in the world.

NOTE: You can read about Miller's final round 63 at the 1973 U.S. Open in chapter 21.

In real life, in January 1974, at my home in New Jersey, in the dead of winter, and at just 10 years old, I was hooked. I became a big Johnny Miller fan.

I walked like Johnny Miller. And I tried to putt like him. I couldn't play golf outside in January, so I created a makeshift putting green on the carpet in my home, close enough to the TV in the den so I could watch Miller's sweet swing and then practice my putting in between Miller's shots. I loved watching Johnny Miller crush the fields in each of those first 3 weekends in January, 1974.

After he came back from the cold he was good but not dominating. He finished 11th, 4th, 5th and 29th in each of the next 4 events he played.

Then he came to the Heritage at Hilton Head in late March and fired a pair of 67s in the opening rounds to take a 6 shot lead into the weekend. He went on to in wire-to-wire fashion by 3 shots.

With his 4th victory of the year, comparisons were being made to Jack Nicklaus. The confident but respectful Miller was quick to quiet those comments. He told Harold Martin of The State, the Columbia, SC newspaper, *"I have a long way to go to be as good as Nicklaus.. But I know if I'm playing good and he's playing good, I can't even get within sniffing distance of him."*

A few weeks later in the Masters, Miller got a slow start in the first 2 rounds and finished in just 15th place, 4 shots behind Nicklaus and 7 shots back of the winner of the Green Jacket, Gary Player.

Miller, whose putting had been one of the keys to his early season streak, told the Macon Telegraph after the 2nd round, *"You can't get a hot putter on these greens. They're in great shape, but they're hard to read."*

But 2 weeks later, Miller had a great opportunity to prove who was the best on the PGA TOUR.

Miller had qualified to play in the exclusive Tournament of Champions, an event that only included the 25 winners of PGA TOUR events over the prior year.

Nicklaus was the favorite at 7 - 2. Miller despite being the leading money winner so far in 1974 had odds of 8 - 1 to win.

Following Johnny Miller in 1974, was magical to me when I was a kid. So naturally, 50+ years later, as The Sports Time Traveler I just had to go back in time to re-live the Johnny Miller ride and see how he performed at the Tournament of Champions.

Tournament of Champions – April 29, 1974

I'm back here in 1974, virtually, where yesterday, the Tournament of Champions concluded at the La Costa Country Club a little north of San Diego.

Johnny Miller had started this tournament by shooting a 75 to put him in 2nd to last and 9 shots off the lead after the 1st round. It was a very disappointing opening round for Miller, the leading money winner on the PGA TOUR this year.

In today's Times Advocate in Escondido, CA, Miller told sports editor, Dave Hoff, *"After that 75 in the 1st round I thought, 'Okay. That's it for this week.'"*

But by the start of the final round he had pulled himself to within 2 shots of the lead held by Bob Charles.

Here were the leading scores after 3 rounds:

-7 Bob Charles

-6 Bud Allin

-5 John Mahaffey

-5 Hubert Green

-5 Johnny Miller

-4 Jack Nicklaus

-4 Bruce Crampton

-4 Billy Casper

On the final day, Miller was paired with Allin in the 2nd to last group. Nicklaus and Mahaffey were in the group ahead of Miller. And Charles, the leader, was paired with Green in the final group behind Miller.

Bob Charles succumbed to the pressure on Sunday and shot a 38 on the front 9. He finished with a 77 in 8th place.

Jack Nicklaus had an uncharacteristic final round of 75, and never contended. Jack finished in 9th.

Bud Allin wrested the lead from Charles on the 4th hole when he made a 20 foot birdie putt.

Johnny Miller bogeyed 4 and 5 and appeared to be out of contention when he made the turn 4 shots behind Allin.

Then on the 10th hole Miller drilled a 6 footer for a birdie while Allin bogeyed. It was a 2 shot swing and pulled Miller within 2 strokes of the lead. Miller told the Times Advocate, *"I was back in the ball game."*

Miller then pulled to within a single shot with a 14 foot birdie putt on the 14th hole.

And when he canned a 30 footer on 16, Johnny Miller had clawed his way into a tie for the lead with 2 holes remaining.

Up ahead playing with Nicklaus, John Mahaffey birdied the 17th hole and suddenly there was a 3 way tie for the lead.

On the par 4 18th hole, Mahaffey hit his tee shot in the rough. While he was assessing his 2nd shot, Miller and Allin reached the 18th tee.

At this point the 3 players were now tied and all playing the final hole.

The 18th hole was the toughest on the course. Only 1 player across all 4 days had birdied the hole. Lee Elder had done it in the 1st round.

Mahaffey hit his 2nd shot on 18 into the foot tall grass to the left of the green. Mahaffey tried to use a sand wedge to pop the ball out of the high grass. But his shot went 20 feet past the pin. He missed the putt coming back for a bogey.

Mahaffey's chances of winning the tournament had been crushed.

Allin and Miller both drove their tee shots at 18 into the right rough.

After the tournament, Johnny Miller told New York Times reporter Leonard Koppett that as he was walking down the 18th fairway with Bud Allin, *"I was sort of rooting for him."*

Koppett noted in his article, *"Miller is well known for his unorthodox thoughts at unlikely moments."*

Allin, a short hitter, decided to play his favorite club, his 5 wood. He described his shot to Dave Hoff, *"It started out as a career shot, but then the wind caught it."* Allin's shot landed in a greenside bunker.

Miller hit his 2nd shot, a 4 iron from 185 yards, short of the green. But he was able to chip to within 4 feet.

Allin then played his bunker shot. He told Dave Hoff, *"It was a good lie. I just took too much sand."*

Allin had barely gotten his ball out of the trap. It was short of the green.

Allin, who had not looked at a scoreboard all day, was informed by his caddie that he needed to chip the ball in. He nearly did. His shot missed the cup by inches.

That left the tournament up to Johnny Miller. He needed to sink the 4 footer to win.

And he did.

Miller, whose 27th birthday is today, told Dave Hoff, *"2 or 3 years ago you'd have seen a different finish by Johnny Miller. I'm better now under pressure than I used to be. Of course when you've already won $150,000* (for the season) *it makes it a little easier."*

Miller finished the round with a 69 for a final score of 8 under par. His 69 was the only sub-70 round of the day.

It marked the 5th victory of the 1974 season for Johnny Miller. And it was his biggest win over a collection of the world's top golfers since his historic victory last year in the 1973 U.S. Open.

The $40,000 first place prize money increased his PGA TOUR leading money earnings to nearly $200,000 for the season.

Miller has now played in 11 tournaments this season, winning 5, finishing in the top 5 a total of 7 times, and in the top 30 every time.

In addition his scoring average for the year stands at 69.9, just a little behind the all-time lowest season scoring average of 69.8 by Billy Casper in 1968.

Johnny Miller is having a sensational season.

POST TOURNAMENT WRAP UP

As I was reading the final scores in the New York Times this morning something shocking caught my eye.

In the April 29, 1974 New York Times, on page 45, the final scores for the Tournament of Champion are listed.

Johnny Miller's scores for the 4 rounds are listed as 75, 59, 67, 69.

That indicates Johnny Miller shot a 59 on the 2nd day of the tournament.

59!

That's the first time any golfer has ever shot a 59 in a PGA TOUR event.

The prior record of 60 had been shot 7 times, all in the 1950s. The last 60 had been carded by Sam Snead in 1957 in the 2nd round of the Dallas Open.

But that course was only 6,328 yards. La Costa, where Miller had just played, was 6,855 yards.

WAIT A MINUTE!

After about 1 second of pondering all this I realized this must be a mistake in the New York Times - the most trusted source in news.

In my memory I conjured up the image of the man who became known as "Mr. 59," Al Geiberger.

Geiberger had shot a 59 on June 10, 1977 at the Memphis Classic. And this I knew to be the first time that a sub-60 round had been recorded on the PGA TOUR.

Was it possible that Miller's score had simply gone unnoticed?

I didn't think that possible. This had to be a mistake in the New York Times.

I added up the scores of the 4 rounds for Miller. As the New York Times reported them they added to 270, not 280, which was the real final score.

Then I double checked against the scores that were reported in other major newspapers. The Los Angeles Times and the Palm Beach Post both showed Miller with a 69 in the 2nd round.

I further went back to look at the New York Times from 2 days earlier. Surely if Miller had shot a 59 there would have been an article about that. There wasn't any. Because even the New York Times correctly reported on April 27, 1974, that Johnny Miller had shot a 69 (not 59) in the 2nd round.

The Sports Time Traveler™ attempts to protect the future history of golf

I had found a mistake in the New York Times.

But this was more than just a simple typo.

This was a mistake of historical consequence.

Johnny Miller was on such a streak in early 1974 that no one would have been too surprised if his putter got super hot and he shot a 59.

In fact Tommy King, sports editor of the Macon News had written an article less than 2 weeks earlier on April 16, 1974 about how the idea of someone shooting a 59, and the excitement it would generate for the sport. He wrote that day, *"What golf needs is someone to shoot a competitive round in the 50s. It has never been done."*

King posed the question to Johnny Miller himself, while he was at The Masters, about the prospects of someone shooting a round in the 50s. Miller told him, *"If we played the short courses of 20 to 30 years ago you'd see some 50s."*

King then spoke with Sam Snead who agreed with Johnny. Snead said, *"If the guys playing today had played 20 years ago, yes, we would have had some 50s."*

King concluded his article with this, *"Someone is going to sink all those putts and score below 60. It is inevitable."*

And most sports writers would have likely agreed in 1974 that the man most likely to do it would be Johnny Miller.

It then occurred to me that in the distant future, in a world in which no one needs to 2nd guess AI anymore because it has a perfect ability to get the facts right, by leveraging the most impeccable historical sources, such as the New York Times, this "59" by Johnny Miller could be found and accepted.

It is entirely conceivable that in 100 years Johnny Miller could become recognized as the first man to shoot a 59.

SUBMITTING FOR A CORRECTION

And so I resolved to share this with the New York Times and seek a correction.

I sent the following email:

Sent: Monday, April 29, 2024 9:24 AM
To: nytnews@nytimes.com
Subject: Correction for 4-29-1974 New York Times

I write a sports history newsletter called, "The Sports Time Traveler™."

Today, I was reading the April 29, 1974 New York Times. In the coverage of the Tournament of Champions golf tournament on page 45, the final scores indicated that Johnny Miller had shot a 59 in the 2nd round. This is incorrect. Johnny Miller shot a 69.

This is of significance because had Miller shot a 59 in the 2nd round, as the Times incorrectly printed, it would have marked the first time a sub-60 round had ever been shot in a PGA TOUR event.

Accordingly, I feel this deserves a correction 50 years after the fact so that future sports historians, or AI models, don't find this error and not realize it is a mistake.

Best,

Len Ferman
The Sports Time Traveler™

The REPLY from The New York Times

Less than 3 hours later I received the following reply from the New York Times.

From: Senioreditor NYTimes <senioreditor@nytimes.com>
Sent: Monday, April 29, 2024 12:04 PM
To: Len Ferman <Len@fermaninnovation.com>
Subject: Re: Correction for 4-29-1974 New York Times

Dear Len:

Thank you for your note. We make every effort to correct errors when they are brought to our attention in a reasonable period of time. After that, I'm afraid, our general policy is not to alter them.

With an archive of published material dating back to 1851, The Times would be hard pressed to put out the best possible news report today and best possible paper tomorrow if we devoted our time and finite resources to re-reporting old articles. So, as both a practical consideration and a matter of policy, we unfortunately have to resign ourselves to the continued existence of some errors in our digital archives.

At any rate, we appreciate your taking the time to bring this to our attention. Thanks for your close and attentive reading, and for contacting The Times.

Sincerely,

Isabella Paoletto
Assistant, Standards Department
The New York Times

So the New York Times declined to make the correction.

As much of a fan as I've been since I followed Johnny Miller's rise to the top of the golf world in 1974, I hope, for the sake of Mr. 59, Al Geiberger, that the future version of our world, one well beyond our lifetimes, will be able to maintain the proper records so that his 59 continues to be recognized as the first one ever on the PGA TOUR.

CHAPTER TWENTY-SIX

The Greatest Round of Golf

THE 1975 TUCSON OPEN

Introduction from The Sports Time Traveler™

Beginning with Johnny Miller's spectacular 63 in the final round to win U.S. Open in 1973, it was Miller time on the PGA TOUR.

Many golf experts consider Miller's 63 on a difficult Oakmont course, in the height of the pressure of a U.S. Open, to be the greatest round of golf ever played. He came from 6 shots back and passed all of the greatest names of the era: Jack Nicklaus, Gary Player, Lee Trevino, Tom Weiskopf, and finally Arnold Palmer to capture the U.S. Open.

Miller went on to win 8 tournaments the following year in 1974.

It took a quarter century, until Tiger Woods in 1999, before anyone achieved that again.

But Johnny Miller was still getting warmed up.

At the outset of the 1975 season, Johnny Miller had a brief run that just might be the greatest golf ever played.

And it was capped off with a total gem of a round.

I've just returned from my virtual trip to January, 1975 to experience Johnny Miller in the final round of the Tucson Open. Here's my report.

TUCSON, AZ - January 20, 1975

Yesterday was the final round of the Dean Martin Tucson Open. Johnny Miller started the day with a 3 shot lead.

Miller was trying to win the 4th consecutive professional tournament that he has played in. Here are the prior 3:

- 8 shot win over Billy Casper and Lee Trevino in the Kaiser International Open on September 29, 1974.

- 7 shot win in the Dunlop tournament in Japan on December 8, 1974. 4-time major champion Ray Floyd finished 3rd, 9 shots back.

- 14 shot win in the first PGA TOUR event of the 1975 season, the Phoenix Open. The field included Hale Irwin, the 1974 U.S. Open champion. Irwin finished 22 shots back, and Lee Trevino, the 1974 PGA champion, he was 26 shots back.

In the Phoenix Open, Miller's 72 hole score of 260 was the lowest on the PGA TOUR in 20 years.

NOTE from The Sports Time Traveler™

I interrupt this article to share with you that 50 years ago I was a huge Johnny Miller fan.

At 5pm ET on Sunday, January 19, 1975, I was in my home in central New Jersey where the temperatures were in the high 30s. I knew it would be months until I could play golf again, a sport I had recently fallen in love with. But it was just minutes until I would get to see Johnny Miller on channel 4 in New York, in the final round of the Tucson Open. I couldn't wait!

Sadly, there is no video tapes of this incredible round of golf of which I'm aware. If anyone knows of a video tape, even just a few highlights, please share it with me at Len@fermaninnovation.com.

Now back to my virtual time travel trip in 1975.

Prior to the final round, Johnny Miller was asked by Carl Soto of the Arizona Republic about his prospects of winning his 4th consecutive tournament. Miller said, *"It won't kill me if I don't win the tournament, but I'm not going to give it away. It's hard to score bad when you hit it long and straight."*

Miller would need that length. The San Francisco Examiner noted that the par 72, Tucson National Golf Club, at 7,200 yards, is, *"one of the longest layouts the pros play all year and a course strengthened this season by the addition of water on three holes."*

THE FINAL ROUND

John Mahaffey was Miller's closest pursuer starting the day 3 shots back. After the round Miller commented that when he saw that Mahaffey birdied the opening hole, he thought, *"I've got to birdie if I don't want to get down to 2 strokes... I had to get my butt in gear and I just did it."*

Miller didn't just birdie the first hole. He started the day birdie-birdie-birdie.

Two more birdies on the 6th and 7th holes helped him to a 5 under 31 after 9 holes.

That put Miller at 19 under par for the tournament.

When Mahaffey birdied the 11th hole he got to 15 under, and still had a chance.

But then Miller came to the 11th, a par 5, and he put his 2nd shot just 20 feet from the pin. Johnny then made the eagle putt. That put him 7 under for the round and 21 under for the tournament. He had a 6 shot lead with 7 holes left.

Mahaffey told the Arizona Daily Star, *"It was then that I started playing for 2nd place."*

Miller followed up his birdie on 11 with a 14 foot birdie putt on 12.

He was now 8 under on the round and had a 7 shot lead with 6 holes to play.

Two holes later, Miller hit his approach shot on the par 4 14th hole to just 18 inches from the cup. He tapped in for another birdie to go 9 under on the round.

Then it was another 14 foot birdie putt on 16 to go 10 under for the day.

And on 18 he made one final 14 footer for birdie.

Johnny Miller had shot a final round of 61.

He won the Tucson Open by 9 shots over John Mahaffey. 10 shots over Tom Watson. And 20 shots over Arnold Palmer.

It was Miller's 4th consecutive professional victory.

The King expressed great admiration for Miller. He told Sue Hill of the Arizona Daily Star, ***"In all the years I've played I don't think I've ever seen anything like this and I don't think anyone else has either. He's just walking right over the field."***

ASSESSING THE 61

Sportswriters in their pieces today analyzed what Johnny Miller had accomplished in shooting a final round of 61 yesterday.

The round was astounding. Just look at the basic statistics:

– **Every green reached in regulation**
– **1 eagle**
– **9 birdies**
– **0 bogeys**

But the most astonishing aspect of Miller's 61 was that on every hole he had a birdie putt of 15 feet or less, except of course the hole he eagled.

Think about that.

He never hit an approach shot that was farther than 15 feet from the pin.

Johnny Miller was dialed in at a higher level than anyone who has ever played the game.

And this was no pushover golf course. In addition to being a long course, Arnold Palmer described the greens to the AP as, *"the most treacherous I've seen in a long time."*

Miller himself told the AP, *"Without doubt, it was the greatest round of golf of my life... I could have shot in the 50's... It could have been the greatest round of golf I'll ever shoot."* The AP writer noted that Miller said this with, *"a touch of awe in his voice just above a whisper."*

"It Could Have Been a 59"

That's what Miller said.

Indeed, Miller could have shot a 59.

Jack Rickard was following Miller for the Tucson Citizen and he reported, *"Miller dropped* (missed) *a couple of makeable putts, one of 5 feet on the 13th hole and another of 6 feet on the 15th hole."*

Harry Missildine of the Spokane Spokesman Review, wrote in this morning's paper about his first-hand observations of the round, *"Counting the near misses I watched on the last four holes, Miller was maybe three-quarters of an inch away from the first 59 ever shot in an official PGA Tournament."*

Bill Lyon in the Philadelphia Inquirer suggested the round could've been even better *"He missed two putts from five-feet and had one lip out... Those three drop and you've got a neat 58."*

IS MILLER ON THE GREATEST RUN EVER?

Johnny Miller has now won the last 4 consecutive professional tournaments he has competed in by margins of 7, 8, 14 and 9 shots.

He has won the last 2 weeks in Tucson and Phoenix by a combined 23 shots.

He is a combined 49 under par across the last two tournaments.

And in those 2 tournaments, every round was under 70. Here are the scores: 67, 61, 68, 64, 66, 69, 67, 61

As these are the first 2 tournaments of the 1975 PGA TOUR, Johnny Miller presently has a 65.4 stroke average for the season.

In the opening paragraph of their article on the tournament, The New York Times noted that Johnny Miller was, *"playing golf perhaps better than anyone before."* The San Francisco Examiner wrote, *"Right now, Johnny Miller may be playing the ancient game of golf better than anyone has ever played before. His recent accomplishments are the stuff of legends."*

Furman Bisher, writing in the Atlanta Journal, penned this line, *"Johnny Miller has turned out to be something not human."*

In the Tampa Tribune today, sports editor, Tom McEwen wrote that he contacted several former PGA TOUR stars to ask them about Miller's recent play.

Cary Middlecoff, winner of 39 PGA events and 3 majors told McEwen, *"Miller's play in the Tucson and Phoenix tournaments... may represent the best back-to-back 72 hole tournaments EVER played."* Mike Souchak, who holds the record for the lowest 72 hole score ever in a PGA tournament agreed with Middlecoff.

McEwen then called the legendary Gene Sarazen at his condo on Marco Island in southwest Florida. Sarazen, the winner of the 1922 U.S. Open and 7 majors in total said, *"I don't know what the hell is happening to the game of golf. I used to think 72 was a pretty good score."*

POSTSCRIPT - "The best round of golf I ever played"

In a 2021 Golfweek article, Johnny Miller told the magazine, *"That was the best round I ever played. As far as perfect ball-striking, the 61 I had at Tucson... I'm playing with Tom Watson and as we walked off the green he goes, that's the greatest round of golf I've ever seen. Now, Tom Watson does not say that to anybody."*

CHAPTER TWENTY-SEVEN

1975 Masters Preview

A PREVIEW OF THE GREATEST GOLF TOURNAMENT EVER CONTESTED

INTRODUCTION from The Sports Time Traveler™

The 1975 Masters didn't have a lot of lead changes. The names at the top didn't alter much. There were not many great putts made. Yet most who watched it, including myself, came away thinking this was the greatest golf tournament they'd ever seen.

And that's why for the past several years, I eagerly anticipated April, 2025, as the time when I would make the virtual journey, precisely 50 years back in time. I wanted to wait until a special anniversary to experience, once again, the 1975 Masters. I wanted to understand what was it about the playing of this particular Masters that so deeply touched the golfing world and me.

It is of course a totally subjective opinion regarding what is the single greatest golf tournament. It's a designation for which there is no objective standard. Whether or not you personally agree with my opinion about the 1975 Masters, it does not detract from the story of the drama associated with this event.

Now join me as I share the reports from my virtual time travels to the 1975 Masters. Unlike all the other prior chapters, I have split up my reports into 3 chapters:

- Preview of the tournament based on newspaper coverage in the days leading up to the opening round.

- Highlights of the first 3 rounds

- Focus on the 4th round with a deep dive on the final 9 holes on Sunday.

The dates for each of the reports are the dates of the newspapers I read during my virtual journey.

PREVIEW - Thursday, April 10, 1975

In an AP article this morning, Jack Nicklaus made it clear that he thought Gary Player had a better year than Johnny Miller last year in 1974. It's hard to comprehend that statement, because Miller had the most talked about season since Arnold Palmer in 1960.

After Johnny Miller's stunning, come from behind, U.S. Open win in 1973, with the historic 63 in the final round, he got off to the hottest start in PGA TOUR history in January, 1974, capturing the first 3 events of the season (the only player ever to do that).

Johnny Miller went on to win 8 tournaments in 1974, something that hadn't been done since Arnie in 1962, and something Jack has never done. Many in the press started touting Johnny Miller as the new #1 player, taking the unofficial crown from Jack Nicklaus who was starting to be considered by some pundits as the greatest golfer of all-time.

Nicklaus, who has won 12 majors (14 if you include his 2 U.S. Amateur titles), didn't win one in 1974 for the first time in this decade. And that doesn't make for a happy Jack.

Oddly, Lee Trevino told The Charlotte News and Atlanta Journal on Wednesday he's hoping for a happy Nicklaus this week. Trevino, winner of the most recent major, the 1974 PGA, explained the danger for the field if Nicklaus is not happy. He told the press corps at Augusta, *"Y'all made him mad when you put in the paper about Miller replacing him."* Trevino then advised the field about Nicklaus, *"Talk nice to him. Tell him how good he looks. Just don't make him mad. In Florida they made him mad talking about how he hadn't won in 13 months, and he won at Doral. And they made him mad at the Heritage and he shot the lights out."*

Trevino was referring to the most recent 2 tournaments Nicklaus played in, both of which he won.

Nicklaus's mindset however, is that only the majors are important. And Johnny Miller didn't win a major in 1974, while Gary Player grabbed 2. Nicklaus said, *"I would have preferred Player's record over that of Miller last year."*

Back on March 17th, Nicklaus was quoted in an AP article saying, *"I always build my season around the major tournaments. I always try to bring my game to a peak for Augusta."*

And Nicklaus certainly seems to be peaking for the Masters this year. He has been on a tear recently. Since the last week in February, Nicklaus has played in 4 tournaments finishing 3rd, 3rd, 1st, and 1st. Nicklaus is so serious about this year's Masters that after winning 2 weeks ago at the Heritage, he passed up last week's PGA stop, and a certain large check, to get in extra practice as Augusta. He told the Atlanta Constitution last Sunday, *"I'd like to win it. I'd like to get some of that 1972 conversation going again."*

Nicklaus is talking about the year he won both the Masters and the U.S. Open, the first two majors of the year, and fueled massive conversation in the media about a potential grand slam season.

Johnny Miller's hot streak meanwhile has simmered down. After starting 1975 like it was a re-run of 1974, winning 3 of the first 5 tournaments, he's been erratic since then. Last week he finished 8 shots behind Tom Weiskopf and failed to break 70 in any round.

Two weeks ago at The Heritage, Johnny missed the cut with a 2 round score of 151, while Jack Nicklaus blistered the course with a 129, including a 2nd round of 63. Lee Trevino marveled at Jack's 63 on what the merry Mexican called, *"the toughest course in the world."*

NOTE from 2025

I interrupt this article to inform you that Jack Nicklaus's 2nd round score of 63 in the 1975 Heritage was the lowest score he ever posted in a PGA TOUR event. Now back to 1975.

Jack's 2 round total of 129 gave him a 22 shot beat down over Johnny Miller. It also put Jack 6 strokes ahead of the field at the halfway mark. He went on to win the tournament by 3 shots over Tom Weiskopf.

Tall Tom Weiskopf is generally regarded as one of the game's greatest natural talents. That's not just my opinion. It's what Jack Nicklaus said after Weiskopf won the 1973 British Open for his lone major. After the final round, Nicklaus told Fred Tupper of the New York Times that Weiskopf, *"has more natural talent and more shots than anybody in the game today."*

Weiskopf has been knocking at the door of superstar status for a while. In 1973, he showed a flash of true brilliance when he went on a bender, winning 5 of 8 tournaments he played in over a 10 weeks span, that included the British Open.

ANOTHER NOTE from 2025

It was also in this timeframe that Tom Weiskopf finished in the top 8 in 13 consecutive tournaments in which he played. That is a feat that was not matched until Scottie Scheffler, in 2025, finished in the top 8 in 14 consecutive tournaments through the 2025 TOUR Championship. Now back again to 1975.

Tom Weiskopf has also finished 2nd three times at the Masters, including last year.

Weiskopf desperately wants to win a Masters title.

And he looks like he might be ready. After finishing 2nd to Nicklaus 2 weeks ago at The Heritage, Weiskopf played in last week's final event before the Masters, the Greater Greensboro Open. He took command in round 1 with a 64, and won the tournament by 3 shots over a star studded field.

Roy Brown of the Charlotte News & Observer wrote on Monday, *"Tom Weiskopf served notice Sunday that he has grown tired of being kicked around by Jack Nicklaus and Johnny Miller."* Weiskopf said, *"I hit a lot of golf balls for three months trying to get my swing back to where it was in 1973 and I think it is back."*

The Favorites

The Reno Turf Club has set the odds for winning the 1975 Masters as follows:

3 to 1 Jack Nicklaus

6 to 1 Tom Weiskopf

8 to 1 Johnny Miller

8 to 1 Gary Player

8 to 1 Hale Irwin

12 to 1 Lee Trevino

25 to 1 Arnold Palmer

CHAPTER TWENTY-EIGHT

1975 Masters: The First 3 Rounds

THE OPENING 3 ROUNDS OF THE GREATEST GOLF TOURNAMENT EVER CONTESTED

In the prior chapter I shared the preview of the 1975 Masters.

Now I'm excited to share the reports of my virtual time travels to experience the first 3 rounds.

In the next chapter, I will cover the 4th round with in-depth coverage of the thrilling final 9 holes.

The dates for each of the reports below are the dates of the newspapers I read during my virtual journey.

1st Round - April 11, 1975

Light rain slowed down the greens in yesterday's opening round of the 1975 Masters. The conditions were much to the liking of 1964 PGA champion Bobby Nichols, who turns 39 on Monday.

Nichols told George Cunningham of the Atlanta Constitution, *"Rain made us feel we could hit it on the green and hold the ball there. And we could go for the pin. The pin placement was fairly easy... today was ideal for scoring."*

Nichols shot a 5 under par 67 to take the lead.

Most of the rest of the field didn't find the course as easy as Nichols described it. Only 16 of the 75 players broke par. And, only 5 others besides Nichols broke 70.

The closest pursuers were Miller and Nicklaus at 68. But that's not Johnny Miller tied with Jack. It's the "other Miller" on the PGA TOUR - Allen Miller. Allen is 25 years old with 1 PGA TOUR victory and has never finished higher than 62nd on the money list in 4 years on the tour.

The man Miller was tied with, the Golden Bear, Jack Nicklaus, didn't putt well, but was satisfied with his play. He told George Cunningham in the Atlanta Constitution, *"When you have 36 putts and shoot a 68 at Augusta, you have to consider it a good, solid round."*

Note from The Sports Time Traveler

I interrupt this article to ponder what Jack Nicklaus did in the first round - scoring a 68 with 36 putts.

This is an astonishing round of golf for which I'm unable to determine if there is an equal. It wasn't a stellar putting round. Nicklaus didn't make any putts from longer than 6 feet.

But his shot-making was off the charts. Jack Nicklaus took just 32 shots from tee to green. He was on the green in regulation on every par 3 and par 4. And he reached all four par 5's in 2 shots. He birdied 3 of the 4 par 5's and 3-putted one of them (the 8th hole). The 6-foot putt he made was a birdie at the 3rd hole. If Nicklaus had a hot putter, he might have shot a 62. And no one has ever shot a 62 at The Masters.

It's no wonder the often self-critical Nicklaus was pleased with his opening round. It might be the fewest shots ever taken from tee to green.

Now back to 1975.

Like a Ghost from the Past

One shot further back at 69 were some big names: Snead, Weiskopf and Palmer. But the Snead was not Sam, it was his nephew J.C. The 33-year-old J.C. Snead has just 2 lifetime PGA victories, and no major victories, but he is a formidable competitor as he finished 5th on the money list last year in 1974.

J.C.'s uncle Sam had a surprisingly good first round too, shooting a 1-under 71 at age 62. It actually shouldn't be so startling. In the last major of 1974, Sam finished 3rd behind the winner Lee Trevino, and 2nd place Jack Nicklaus.

No other 60+ year old competitor has ever finished in the top 3 in a major.

Weiskopf, a pre-tournament favorite, and winner last week at Greensboro, wasn't a surprise at 69. But 45-year-old Arnold Palmer was. Palmer hasn't won a PGA TOUR event since 1973, and hasn't won a major since the 1964 Masters. But there he was at 69 after the first round. George Cunningham wrote, **"Like a ghost from the past, Palmer returned appropriately in foggy weather for a first-round 69, that had him just two shots out of the lead."**

The Top Story of the Day

However, for much of America, all the interesting storylines from above were not even close to being the big news of the first round of the tournament. The biggest news of the day was that Lee Elder became the first African-American player to compete at the Masters. Elder shot a 2-over-par 74.

Lee Elder qualified for the Masters by winning the Monsanto Open last year. And under the new Masters qualifying rules, anyone who wins a PGA TOUR event in the past year, regardless of the color of their skin, automatically qualifies to play in the Masters.

Prior to the rules changes, Charles Sifford, an African-American PGA TOUR member, won 2 PGA TOUR events in the 1960s, including the prestigious Los Angeles Open in 1969. He had also competed in 10 U.S. Opens, finishing as high as 27th in 1964, yet never received a Masters invitation due to the policies of the Augusta National Golf Club.

THE TOP 16 LEADING SCORES AFTER ROUND 1

-5 Bobby Nichols

-4 Allen Miller and Jack Nicklaus

-3 J.C. Snead, Tom Weiskopf and Arnold Palmer

-2 Bob Murphy, Billy Casper, Tom Watson

-1 Jerry Pate, Sam Snead, Tommy Aaron, Jerry Heard, Lee Trevino, Larry Ziegler and Mac Mclendon

Where's Johnny?

In yet another interesting storyline, notably missing from the top 16 was the phenom of the PGA TOUR - Johnny Miller. Miller has won 11 times on TOUR in the past 16 months, but yesterday he bogeyed 3 of the first 4 holes en route to a 75. Only 17 players shot a higher score, and that puts Miller in danger of missing the cut today.

Like Nicklaus, Miller also took 36 putts. But unlike Jack, Johnny was not happy. He half-joked that he was going to burn his putter. The Atlanta Journal declared that Miller's round had the effect of *"virtually putting himself out of contention after just one day of play."*

Miller told the Macon News, *"I haven't been putting well for four weeks, and if things don't improve, I may be in California Saturday night. We're building a new home and have to select things like door knobs."*

I can imagine Johnny Miller was thinking he would prefer to be selecting golf clubs instead of door knobs on Saturday.

Miller perhaps may have been thrown off kilter by the recent Masters preview issue of Golf World. The cover showed him walking on water.

You can see that magazine cover if you're reading on Kindle by clicking on this link:

Johnny Miller on Cover of Golf World - Walking on Water

Or enter the following words in the search bar in Google images to find the picture: **"1975 APRIL 4 GOLF WORLD MAGAZINE - JOHNNY MILLER FRONT COVER - E 6720."**

In the locker room, other players were kidding Miller about the cover photo, saying things like, *"did you have your rubbers on?"*

2nd Round - Saturday, April 12, 1975

Arnold Palmer caused a stir on the grounds of Augusta early Friday afternoon. Teeing off at 11:39am, and paired with 25 year old Tom Watson, Palmer shot a 2 under 34 on the front 9. And when 1st round leader Bobby Nichols, who teed off at 1pm, started with a bogey on the 1st hole, that gave Arnold Palmer sole possession of the lead in the 1975 Masters. That had to thrill members of Arnie's Army who could see the big board at 18.

Tom Weiskopf, who teed off at 10:26am, also went out in 34, but playing an hour ahead of Palmer, Weiskopf bogeyed the 13th hole when his ball hit a pine tree, and was a shot behind Palmer at that point. Then Weiskopf lost another shot at 15 when he hit into the water.

Jack Nicklaus, teeing off at 1:35pm and Allen Miller, teeing off at 1:56, were also tied with Nichols, 1 shot behind Palmer, as they began play.

THE LEADING SCORERS AS PALMER MADE THE TURN IN ROUND 2

-5 Arnold Palmer

-4 Tom Weiskopf, Jack Nicklaus, Allen Miller and Bobby Nichols

In the New York Times, John Radosta wrote, *"For a few fleeting minutes today, Palmer sent his followers into raptures by holding the lead at five under par after nine holes."*

Arnie Alone in the Lead!

The AP reported that Arnie was, *"alone in the lead for 42 magic minutes."*

Hubert Mizell of the Tampa Bay Times interviewed Palmer's playing partner, Tom Watson, after the round. Tom told him about the galleries, *"They were going ape all day... They yell, 'YEA,' at everything he does, at a noise level of about 10 million decibels... But, Arnold deserves it. He means so much to this game of golf. I was thrilled for him... excited just to be a part of it."*

The magic came to an end when Palmer had a rough patch early on the back 9. Arnold told Milton Richman of the UPI, *"Today out there, I lost my concentration at some point."* Palmer was likely referring to the 11th and 12th holes. Palmer 3-putted from 25 feet on the 11th for a bogey. And when he hit his tee shot into the trap on the treacherous par 3 12th, he bogeyed that hole as well.

Palmer gathered himself back together and finished the day with a 71, for a 2-day total of 4 under par, 140. Right after Palmer's round ended, Jesse Outlar of the Atlanta Constitution noted, *"Glancing over his shoulder at the scoreboard during the Friday interview... at that point Jack Nicklaus was six under par, only two strokes in front of Palmer as he made the turn."*

Jack, like Arnie, went out in 34 on the front nine.

But unlike Arnie, Jack kept his concentration and played masterfully on the back 9. At the 11th, he hit a 6-iron to 28 feet from the pin and sank the birdie putt, his longest of the day. Then on the 12th hole, he put his 7-iron 7 feet from the hole and made that putt. Next, on the par 5 dogleg 13th hole, he hit a 4-iron to 35 feet. He missed the eagle putt, but bagged his 3rd birdie in a row.

Then on the part 5 15th hole, Nicklaus again reached the green in 2, this time just 16 feet from the hole. He missed the eagle putt, but picked up his 4th birdie in just 6 holes on the back 9.

Suddenly, Jack Nicklaus was clear of the field at 10 under par for the tournament.

Nicklaus gave 1 shot back at 18 when he missed a 7 footer for par that rimmed out of the hole. According to Furman Bisher of the Atlanta Constitution, Jack also rimmed out on 14 and 16 as well. Jack finished with a brilliant 67, the best score of the day, but it could just as easily been a record-tying 64 if all 3 rimmed putts had fallen.

Jack was one of only 4 players in the field to break 70 on Friday. The others were Bud Allin (69), Homero Blancas (69), and Pat Fitzsimmons (68). The 24-year-old Fitzsimmons, who won just $10,098 on TOUR in 1974, had qualified for the Masters by winning this year's 1975 Los Angeles Open, his first ever PGA TOUR victory.

First round leader Nichols ballooned to a 74. Allen Miller, who started the day in 2nd place with Nicklaus was even worse with a 75. Of the top 16 scorers from day 1, only Nicklaus shot under 70.

Tom Weiskopf, who started the day with a promising 34 on the front 9, finished the day with a disappointing 72. No press comments from Weiskopf were reported after his round.

Jack Nicklaus's 67 gave him a 5-shot lead over the field. It was just the 2nd time in Masters history that a golfer held a 5-shot lead after the 2nd round. The first was Herman Keiser in 1946, who went on to a 1-shot victory.

LEADING SCORES AFTER ROUND 2

-9 Jack Nicklaus
-4 Arnold Palmer, Billy Casper and Tom Watson
-3 Bobby Nichols, J.C. Snead, Pat Fitzsimmons, Homero Blancas,
Tom Weiskopf and Lee Trevino

After the round, the press was ready to award the tournament to Jack Nicklaus, especially after Nicklaus announced, *"I'm playing as well now as I have played in my life,"* as noted by George Cunningham in the Atlanta Constitution. Cunningham started his article today with this line, *"Jack Nicklaus charged into a class by himself here Friday."*

Horace Billings of the Salisbury, NC Post wrote, *"The Golden Bear, who again is asserting himself as king of golf, destroyed the hopes of his challengers."*

The Raleigh News and Observer posted this assessment *"Jack Nicklaus was turning the Masters into his private show... suddenly, everyone else was playing for second place."*

But Bill Shirley of The Los Angeles Times quoted Nicklaus who spoke words of caution for himself, *"The tournament is not over. I've seen strange things happen at Augusta. I've had five-shot leads here before and lost them."*

Some reporters took Nicklaus's humility with a grain of salt. The Palm Beach Post proclaimed, *"It would take an awful lot of persuading for Nicklaus to convince anybody he's in danger of losing this tournament."*

Where's Johnny - Part 2?

Johnny Miller, Golf World's pick to win this year's Masters, finished the day 11 shots back of Jack. Mark Purdy of the Dayton Journal Herald wrote, *"Johnny Miller has come to Augusta and fallen on his smiling, square-jawed face - almost."*

Purdy wrote *"almost"* because technically Miller was still in the tournament. He had made the cut by 3 strokes. But Purdy was counting Miller out nevertheless, *"He will never recover this weekend from his opening 75... everyone expected that he and Jack Nicklaus would be going blond head to blond head in this tournament."*

And Miller was also counting himself out, *"Sure, this will be a disappointment if I keep on like this and don't do well... And it doesn't look like I'm going to win it."*

Miller was inevitably asked in the clubhouse about the Golf World cover photo showing him walking on water. Miller responded, *"People are trying to make me into something I'm not."*

Lee Elder

Further back of Johnny Miller, and 3 shots outside the cut line, was Lee Elder who could only manage a 78 on Friday. Sam Heys of the Columbus, GA Ledger-Enquirer wrote that Elder, *"seemed unruffled by not being among the top 46 after two-days of the 76 man tournament."*

Elder told the AP, *"I did myself in. I got out of the box bad. I was all over the place. I really did the beautification bit - I saw all the flowers and the trees."*

3rd Round - Sunday, April 13, 1975

Golf fans were treated to a Saturday special at Augusta when tournament officials made the decision to pair Jack Nicklaus and Arnold Palmer in the final group of the day at 2:10pm.

But Jack and Arnie didn't like it according to George Cunningham in the Atlanta Constitution. *"Nicklaus said he and Palmer were so concerned about being paired in the same twosome that they asked Masters officials for a reason."*

Nicklaus told Cunningham, *"Normally I would have played with someone else. But they told us that instead of having two large galleries back to back, they wanted it all at the end of the field. They do things differently here at Augusta."*

So the only two men who had ever won 4 Masters titles were playing mano-a-mano in the final group.

Playing 13 groups ahead of the two legends was Johnny Miller who had teed off at 12:26pm with last year's champion Gary Player. Both men were 11 shots behind the leader, Nicklaus. Miller parred the 1st hole. Then some Miller magic took over. On the par 5 2nd hole, Johnny blasted out of a greenside sand trap to within a foot of the hole for a gimme birdie.

And then Miller went on a birdie barrage the likes of which had never been seen before at the Masters. On 3, 4 and 5, he made putts of 14, 10, and 14 feet. On then on the par 3 6th hole, he hit a 5-iron one foot from the hole for another tap-in birdie.

He wasn't done. On 7, he was just off the green, 35 feet from the hole. He putted and knocked it in.

Miller was in the zone. He told John Radosta of the New York Times, *"When I've got it going and I'm standing over a putt, eight feet looks like four feet and the hole looks bigger. I can't make it happen. It happens by itself."*

Miller's magic took him from +2 for the tournament to -4. Miller had made 6 consecutive birdies. In doing so, Miller had leaped from 28th place all the way to 2nd.

And Miller had clawed his way back from 11 shots behind to just 4 shots back of Jack who bogeyed the 1st hole. It was a stunning comeback.

Miller then parred the 9th hole to post a cool 30 on the front 9.

George Cunningham wrote in the Atlanta Constitution about the reaction of Arnold Palmer and Jack Nicklaus when they saw the leader board as they walked down the fairway on the 2nd hole and saw Miller had shot 30 on the front 9.

According to Arnold Palmer the conversation went like this:

Jack: *"Good nine holes, huh?*

Arnie: *"Yeah, not bad."*

Jack: *"Not bad, right. It's a record. No one has ever done that before."*

Jack was right. Miller's 30 on the front 9 was a new Masters record.

Herman Helms of the Columbia, SC State newspaper was following the *"Gold Dust Twins"* on the course and told the story a little differently. He quoted Nicklaus talking about the first time he saw a leader board with Miller at -5 for the tournament. *"I'm color blind and at first I couldn't tell if that '5' on the scoreboard was a green (over par) or a red (under par). At second glance it seemed to have a darker tint to it, indicating it was red. I said to Arnie, 'That can't be red, can it?' He said, 'I'm afraid so, but that must be for the day not for the tournament.'"*

NOTE from The Sports Time Traveler

I interrupt the article for a moment to inform you that back here in the present time, Johnny Miller's 30 on the front 9 remains the Masters record, although it has been tied by 6 other players.

Miller's record of 6 consecutive birdies has also been surpassed. Steve Pate in 1999 and Tiger Woods in 2005 recorded 7 straight birdies.

Now back to 1975.

Could Have Been a 60

Johnny Miller only got one more birdie on the back 9 to finish with a 65. He told Charles Rhodes of the Columbus, GA Ledger, *"I've been playing well the last three weeks but I just haven't been dropping the putts. I just needed a little inspiration and those early birdies gave it to me. The round could have been a 60 or 61... I threw some strokes away on the back nine and missed some easy putts... I was going for birdie on every hole."*

It was a sensational round that put him at -5 for the tournament. And just after he finished, Jack Nicklaus bogeyed the 9th to drop to -8. Miller had made up 8 shots in one day on the Golden Bear. Johnny Miller had justified the Golf World "walking on water" cover shot.

Tall Tom Takes Charge

Miller wasn't the only player making a moving day charge. Tom Weiskopf, playing with Bobby Nichols, started 6 shots back and 4 groups ahead of Jack Nicklaus. Weiskopf birdied the 6th on an 18 foot putt and the par 5 8th when he chipped his 3rd shot to within 18 inches to get to -5 for the tournament. Then he birdied 10 by draining a 30 footer and birdied the par 5 13th to reach -7.

When Weiskopf dropped a 15 foot putt at the 16th hole, he pulled into a tie for the lead at -8. And one more 15 foot birdie putt at 18 gave Tom Weiskopf the outright lead by a stroke.

When Tom Weiskopf made that putt it was the first time he had ever led the Masters, despite the fact that he has finished as the runner-up three prior times.

Tom told Russ DeVault of the Atlanta Constitution, *"I knew with the way Jack was playing that I had to shoot a super round."* Regarding the task ahead on Sunday, he told George Cunningham, *"I've never led the Masters before. I'm not thinking ahead. If I do have the lead, there are two great players behind me."*

For someone who was the 3rd round leader of the Masters, Tom Weiskopf received shockingly sparse coverage in the press today. Of course, that was because of the marquee matchup that occurred yesterday with Jack Nicklaus playing in the final pairing against Arnold Palmer.

Nicklaus vs. Palmer

It has been 13 years since the two legends first clashed head-to-head in the 1962 U.S. Open. And with Palmer clearly past his prime, yesterday's round was filled with nostalgia and harkened golf fans back to their many battles for supremacy of the golf world in the 1960s.

Arnie's army wanted to see one more charge from the man they still think of as the King of golf. One more chance for their hero to win an unprecedented 5th Masters. One more opportunity to make up for the painful collapses in several prior majors that prevented his total count from reaching double digits like Jack.

If Palmer could pull this one out, it would make up for all those past misses. It would be the glorious crowning achievement to his already sparkling career.

Jack Nicklaus became consumed with defeating the man who has been both his friend and arch competitor. He told George Cunningham, *"We want to beat each other so badly."*

The setting here in Augusta, with two the greatest players of the prior decade, drew an enormous share of the entire crowd watching the tournament. Nicklaus said, *"The crowd following us may have been as big as any I've played before."*

And the crowd relished the rivalry. Jack noted, *"The gallery plays us against each other, and today I think Arnie's gallery was a detriment to him. And the gallery was far more even-handed than it used to be."*

Nicklaus was likely referring to crowds in the early 1960s, particularly at Oakmont, near Palmer's home town in the 1962 U.S. Open, when the crowd was hostile towards Jack, rooting against Nicklaus on the course when the two were paired 3 times in 4 days. It reached a point where it was embarrassing to Palmer and ultimately may have negatively impacted Palmer as he lost in a playoff to Jack.

Ever since then a funny thing happens when Jack and Arnie are paired together. Jack commented on it, *"We have never - in a long time, at least - played well when we played together."*

Arnie was quick to agree, *"Jack and I can't put a finger on why this is. But I suppose it is because we are trying to play each other instead of the golf course."*

And it held true here in the 3rd round. After Nicklaus had shot spectacular rounds of 68 and 67 in the opening rounds, yesterday he shot a lackluster 73. He went out in 37 with bogeys on 1 and 9. And he shot just even par on the back 9, where he notably was unable to take advantage of either the par 5 13th or the par 5 15th. He finished the day at -8 for the tournament. And that left him a shot behind Tom Weiskopf. Jack had not only lost his 5 stroke cushion; he wasn't even leading the tournament.

In addition to the pairing with Palmer, Jack blamed his 73 partly on the conditions. *"The winds were gusty today, and that made it difficult for me."*

But Nicklaus remained upbeat about the tournament despite going into the final day a shot behind Tom Weiskopf. *"I'm not unhappy at all. The position is not all that bad."*

Arnold Palmer also struggled in the pairing with Nicklaus. After starting the day tied for 2nd place, Arnie shot a 3 over par 75. That left him 8 shots behind the leader, Weiskopf, and in a tie for 7th place.

Palmer told Herman Helms of the Columbia, SC State newspaper, *"I played lousy. I was constantly in trouble. I never hit a good iron shot all day.*

He told George Cunningham in the Atlanta Constitution, *"If I wasn't scrambling well I might have shot 80."*

And then he squarely laid blame on the pairing with Nicklaus, *"To be honest about it, if we had our druthers Jack and I would never play together. We always seem to play poorly when we do. I suppose subconsciously we play each other too much."*

Arnie told Russ DeVault, *"Some people want me to beat Jack and some people want Jack to beat me. We feel it. But you can bet I won't be playing with Nicklaus tomorrow. Maybe he'll play better and I'll play better."*

No, Not Nicklaus, Nichols

Almost forgotten by the media on Saturday was 1st round leader Bobby Nichols. Nichols had started the 3rd round tied for 5th at -3. He was playing with Weiskopf. Nichols had a 1 under par round going through 12, and then he eagled the par 5 13th. That vaulted Nichols to -6 for the tournament and just 3 shots off the lead.

Russ DeVault was one of the few to interview Nichols, and Bobby told him, *"I thought I might shoot a pretty good round after the eagle at 13. But I missed too many short putts."*

Nichols bogeyed 3 of the last 4 holes to finish with a round of 72 that placed him 6 back of Weiskopf and tied with Bill Casper, the 1970 champion.

And it put Bobby Nichols in position to be paired with Arnold Palmer for the final round.

Young Tom Watson

One other golfer remained in the mix. 25 year old Tom Watson, who has won just 1 PGA TOUR event, carded a 72 on Saturday after he made the cut in the Masters for the first time on Friday. He had started the day in the group that was 5 shots behind Nicklaus and he ended the day in sole possession of 4th place and 5 shots behind the new leader Weiskopf.

George Cunningham referred to Watson as *"the forgotten man in fourth place."* Referring to the three big names in front of him, Tom Watson told Cunningham, *"They are three tough people to try to pass. I give myself a ray of hope."*

LEADING SCORES AFTER ROUND 3

-9 Tom Weiskopf

-8 Jack Nicklaus

-5 Johnny Miller

-4 Tom Watson

-3 Billy Casper and Bobby Nichols

-1 Arnold Palmer, Lee Trevino, Buddy Allin, Allen Miller and Hubert Green

The Final Round

In the next chapter, I will cover the thrilling final round with in-depth coverage of the back 9.

CHAPTER TWENTY-NINE

The 1975 Masters: The Shootout

THE FINAL ROUND OF THE GREATEST GOLF TOURNAMENT EVER CONTESTED

Watching the 1975 Masters was one of the foundational experiences of my youth. Naturally, as The Sports Time Traveler, I had to go back in time and experience the tournament again.

It was such a classic that during the 2025 Masters broadcast, CBS shared a 3-minute segment to celebrate the 1975 Masters. The segment aired during the final round, while Rory McIlroy was walking up the 8th fairway.

I watched the 1975 Masters on Sunday, April 13, 1975, on Channel 2 WCBS in New York when I was 11 years old. We had a 12-inch Sony Trinitron in our den. The tournament left an indelible impression upon me that has not worn off in 50 years. It had all the dramatic elements of a Hollywood classic movie - an "A-list" cast, a gorgeous set, a compelling plot, and, of course, unexpected twists.

For me, there was an additional allure to the 1975 Masters - my emotional attachment to Johnny Miller. He was my favorite player, and I was at that impressionable age when sports figures are a boy's heroes.

The leading men in the "cast" consisted of the three golfers who began the day at the top of the Masters leaderboard. Here were their scores after 3 rounds:

- **9 TOM WEISKOPF** - 3-time Masters runner-up, including the prior year in 1974, and generally considered to be one of the game's greatest natural talents

- **8 JACK NICKLAUS ("the Golden Bear")** - winner of 14 prior majors (including his 2 U.S. Amateurs) and regarded by many as the greatest of all-time

- **5 JOHNNY MILLER** - hottest player in the world in the past 16 months, winning 11 times, and holder of the major championship record of 63, which he shot on the final day of the 1973 U.S. Open to come from 6 back to capture the title

In addition, the "supporting cast" included nearly every one of the other biggest names in golf at the time:

- **4 Tom Watson** - At 25 years old, he was on the cusp of becoming one of the game's greats, but had not yet won a major (NOTE: Watson went on to win the British Open later that year)

- **3 Billy Casper** - among the all-time leaders in PGA TOUR victories with 50 at the time

- **3 Bobby Nichols** - 1964 PGA Champion and first round leader of the tournament in 1975

- **1 Arnold Palmer** - the man they still called "The King" and the leader of "Arnie's Army," his loyal legion of fans that still swarm him during every round he plays, even though he is well past his prime and has not won a tournament in 2 years

- **1 Lee Trevino** - Winner of 5 prior majors, including the most recent one, the 1974 PGA, and one of the most popular golfers with the fans.

At 11 years old, I was a committed Johnny Miller fan. And I was already a sports sentimentalist. If Miller couldn't come from 4 shots back to win, I wanted Tom Weiskopf to beat out Jack and finally win a Masters after 3 second-place finishes.

I expressly didn't want to see Jack Nicklaus win. In my 11-year-old mind, Nicklaus had already won too many times. I liked the up-and-coming stars rather than the "old" guy (although Jack was just 35).

As I have done throughout this book, the bylines have the dates of the newspapers I read in my virtual sports time travel journey.

Now, I take you back to the final round of the 1975 Masters.

The Final Round - April 14, 1975

Yesterday was set up to be a classic. The weather was ideal. The forecast in Augusta was 68 and dry. Warm enough that the players should have a perfect feel of the clubs. Cool enough that in the high-stakes tension, their palms wouldn't get sweaty.

Here's how the leading scores looked at the start of the final round.

LEADING SCORES AFTER ROUND 3

-9 Tom Weiskopf

-8 Jack Nicklaus

-5 Johnny Miller

-4 Tom Watson

-3 Billy Casper and Bobby Nichols

-1 Arnold Palmer, Lee Trevino, Buddy Allin, Allen Miller and Hubert Green

The Shootout of the 70's

Prior to the start of the round, many newspaper readers across the country, whose papers carried the sports column of Jim Murray of the Los Angeles Times, were treated to a preview from the entertaining journalist. Murray titled his column on Sunday, April 13, 1975, *"The Augusta Gunman."*

Murray, who was in Augusta covering the Masters, opened his article with a vivid depiction of the Masters as an old western movie, *"It was supposed to be the shootout of the 70s. The Clantons vs. the Earps at O.K. Corral... No one noticed the blond, young kid oiling his gun, practicing fast draws in front of a mirror."*

Murray had been captivated by the Saturday pairing of the two greatest legends in the tournament - Nicklaus and Palmer. But his imagination was stirred by the near record round posted on Saturday by Johnny Miller. He continued, *"While Jack Nicklaus and Arnold Palmer were stalking down Main Street at high noon, Johnny Miller was the young gunslinger dreaming of instant glory if he could shoot both of them down... The Augusta National is to golf what Tombstone was to gunfighting."*

Murray then glorified Johnny Miller, *"He's the most dangerous kind of gunfighter - the baby-faced kid... Golf never recovered from the 63 Miller threw at the U.S. Open... NOBODY had ever shot a 63 in a U.S. Open before."*

Murray then tried to explain what happened to Miller during his dreadful opening 2 rounds that had left him 11 shots off the lead and lucky to have made the cut, *"The kid was in with guys who shaved twice a day and drank red-eye whisky."*

Murray conjectured that Arnie being paired with Jack was just the thing Johnny needed, *"Nicklaus and Palmer were shooting each other full of holes... and that's when the kid gunslinger starts feeling cocky and gets to playing around his shooting iron... He sneaked out and said, 'all right everybody... I'm taking over this town. You there, Bad Jack and Awful Arnold! Throw down your guns... I'll show you this is MY territory.'"*

And that pretty much describes what happened in the 3rd round as Miller shot his way back into the tournament with a stunning 65 to pull within 3 shots of Nicklaus. At the end of the article, Murray had a warning for Miller, *"When he becomes No. 1 Gun in the Territory... the next shootout, they'll be watching HIM."*

Oddly, nowhere in the piece did Murray mention the other young "gunslinger" - Tom Weiskopf. Weiskopf had nearly as good a round as Miller on Saturday, shooting a 6 under par 66, to vault him into the lead, one shot ahead of Nicklaus. Weiskopf, not Miller, was the new guy on top of the leaderboard.

The day was set up to be a 3-way dual, a shootout, between the best *"golf-slingers"* in the world today - Jack Nicklaus, Tom Weiskopf and Johnny Miller.

The Pairings

The pairings set by the Masters were again non-conforming with how most tournaments would have it set up.

Most notable was that Jack Nicklaus would NOT be in the final group, despite being in 2nd place. Instead, Johnny Miller, who was 3 shots behind Nicklaus, would be in the final pairing with Tom Weiskopf, the leader. Nicklaus would be paired with the young Tom Watson, who was starting the day in sole possession of 4th place, 4 shots behind Nicklaus and 5 behind Weiskopf. The 25-year-old Watson has won only one PGA TOUR event, and was playing on a Sunday at Augusta for the first time. He had shown some promise however, finishing 5th in last year's U.S. Open.

The 3rd to last group would be an entertaining one. Billy Casper, the 1970 Masters champion and winner of 50 PGA TOUR events, was paired with the merry Mexican, Lee Trevino, a winner of 5 majors. But Casper was starting 6 shots behind Weiskopf, and Trevino was beginning the day tied with 4 others, 8 shots back.

Among those tied with Trevino at 8 shots back was "The King," Arnold Palmer. Palmer would be in the 4th to last group, along with 1st round leader Bobby Nichols.

Play Begins

Early in the round there was a stir when Hale Irwin, the 1974 U.S. Open champion, who started the day well out of the running at +2 for the tournament (11 shots behind Weiskopf), birdied 1, 2 and 3, to join the large group at -1.

Irwin birdied the 8th to get to -2 around the time the leaders were teeing off, but despite going out in 32, and then sinking a 40 footer at the 10th to go 5 under on the day, he was still well off the lead at -3 for the tournament.

The Leaders Tee Off

Jack Nicklaus started poorly. His opening drive went right, hit a tree and bounced further right, according to Al Ludwick of the Augusta Chronicle. Nicklaus, later said that his pre-round practice had not gone well, ***"During practice I couldn't get with it. I couldn't get my tempo and my timing wasn't right."***

Nicklaus's second shot also hit a tree, as observed by Bill Lee of the Hartford Courant. He was lucky to get his 3rd shot on the green and come away with a bogey.

Right away, Tom Weiskopf had a 2-shot lead, and he maintained it when he parred the first hole.

But Jack had too much experience to panic. On the par 5, 2nd hole, Nicklaus reached a greenside bunker in 2 and blasted out to 3 feet from the pin. He made the birdie putt to get back to -8. Nicklaus then hit his approach shot on 3 to within 3 feet and birdied that hole as well, to pull even with Weiskopf at -9.

Weiskopf matched Jack's birdie at 3 with an 18 foot putt and went to -10. Both Jack and Tom were pulling away from Miller, who birdied the 2nd but bogeyed the 3rd to remain at - 5.

LEADERS THROUGH 3 HOLES

-10 Tom Weiskopf
-9 Jack Nicklaus
-5 Johnny Miller

Miller picked up a shot when he birdied the 4th hole to stay within striking distance at -6 for the tournament.

Nicklaus then tied Weiskopf again when he birdied the par 4, 5th hole, by hitting his 5-iron 2nd shot to within 8 feet and sank the putt for his 3rd birdie in 4 holes after the bogey start.

But Tom again took sole possession of the lead on the 6th hole when he and Miller birdied the par 3.

LEADERS THROUGH 6 HOLES

-11 Tom Weiskopf
-10 Jack Nicklaus
-7 Johnny Miller

All 3 parred the 7th. Then Miller birdied the par 5 8th. And Nicklaus birdied the 9th to pull again into a tie with Tom.

At this point, the TV coverage kicked in. Since the original CBS broadcast is available on YouTube, I will now provide you with the highlights of the action that you can watch.

The time stamps represent the time mark on the YouTube video that you can access at this link:

https://www.youtube.com/watch?v=_ojtX1GrIcc

Or you can search on YouTube for "1975 Masters Tournament Final Round Broadcast" to find the video.

0:10 - Vin Scully opens the broadcast with the prescient statement, *"This 4th and final round of the 1975 Masters might very well be a story that will live for many years to come."*

0:25 - The leaderboard is displayed. Here are the scores:

-11 Tom Weiskopf (8 holes completed)

-11 Jack Nicklaus (9 holes completed)

- 8 Johnny Miller (8 holes completed)

- 6 Tom Watson (9 holes completed)

- 5 Bobby Nichlols (9 holes completed)

- 5 Billy Casper (9 holes completed)

- 4 Hale Irwin (14 holes completed)

- 3 Lee Trevino (9 holes completed)

- 2 Dave Hill (12 holes completed)

- 1 Arnold Palmer (9 holes completed)

0:30 - CBS shows the tape of Jack Nicklaus hitting his approach shot on 9 to within 10 feet and canning the birdie putt to tie Weiskopf at - 11.

1:30 - We get our first looks at Tom Weiskopf and Johnny Miller as they hit their approach shots from the 9th fairway. Both are pin high on the green with birdie putts. Miller's ball is about 20 feet right of the pin, while Weiskopf is just 12 feet left.

8:15 - Arnold Palmer gets ready to tee off at the par 3 12th, as the announcer, Jim Thacker, mentions, ***"It was here at Augusta that Arnie's Army was named by a sportswriter, Johnny Hendricks, 15 years ago."***

Palmer's shot hits the flagstick! Then bounces backwards and settles 15 feet short of the pin. It's one of the great moments of the day for Arnie's Army.

10:25 - On tape, see Miller make his 20 footer on 9 for birdie to finish his front 9 in 32 and pull to within 2 shots of the lead held by Nicklaus & Weiskopf. Miller is now -11 for his last 26 holes. He had been 11 shots off the lead after the 2nd round.

Weiskopf, putting next, leaves his ball right of the hole and remains tied with Nicklaus after shooting a 34 on the front 9.

LEADING SCORERS AFTER 9 HOLES
-11 Jack Nicklaus
-11 Tom Weiskopf
-9 Johnny Miller

16:00 - Lee Trevino nearly makes a hole-in-one on 12. His short putt will get him to -3 for the tournament.

18:00 - Arnold Palmer lands a wood shot onto the 13th green where he will have an eagle putt. But Palmer is 10 shots behind the leaders.

19:35 - The announcers, each of whom are broadcasting from a single hole, are introduced on camera. They are:

12th hole - Jim Thacker
13th hole - Pat Summerall
14th hole - Jack Whitaker
15th hole - Ben Wright
16th hole - Henry Longhurst
17th hole - Frank Glieber
18th hole - Vin Scully

This is a stellar group of announcers who are all entertaining to listen to and provide a great variety of accents and styles, as well as individual hole knowledge.

22:55 - Nicklaus tees off on 12 and puts his shot just 10 feet past the pin. At the same time, we learn that Tom Weiskopf has hit into the water on 11. But there is no video coverage of Weiskopf's wayward shot at 11.

25:20 - Palmer nearly sinks his long eagle putt at 13, and the crowd roars. Then the tape cuts back to 11 where Tom Weiskopf is hitting his 4th shot, from the drop zone 30 yards from the green over water on the par 4 hole. His pitch shot lands 3 feet from the pin, assuring him of escaping with just a bogey. Jack Nicklaus, standing on the 12th green as Tom Watson prepares to putt, is aware of Weiskopf's situation.

27:40 - Nicklaus has a 10 foot putt that can give him a 2-stroke lead over Weiskopf, but he slides it just right and has to settle for par.

29:10 - Miller misses a 3 footer at 11. He has 3-putted from just 20 feet to drop back to -8 for the tournament. Both Weiskopf and Miller have bogeyed 11.

LEADING SCORERS
-11 Jack Nicklaus (12 holes completed)
-10 Tom Weiskopf (11 holes completed)
-8 Johnny Miller (11 holes completed)

30:50 - Miller's woes continue as he hits his tee shot on the par 3 12th into the front bunker.

32:50 - Hale Irwin, putting from off the green at 18, narrowly misses setting a new Masters record of 63. He settles for a 64 to tie the existing record. Irwin is now the leader in the clubhouse at -6, but he is still 5 shots behind the leader Nicklaus, who is on the 13th hole.

NOTE from the Sports Time Traveler

Back here in 2025, 64 remains the record score at the Masters despite all the advances in golf club technology in the past 50 years.
  Now back to 1975.

35:00 - As Weiskopf studies his long birdie putt on 12, Jim Thacker makes note that the top 8 golfers on the leaderboard are all major champions, with the exception of Tom Watson.
  Weiskopf just misses his birdie putt and remains a shot behind Nicklaus.
  36:50 - The leaderboard is shown on TV for the first time since the start of the broadcast

-11 Jack Nicklaus (12 holes completed)

-10 Tom Weiskopf (12 holes completed)

- 8 Johnny Miller (12 holes completed)

- 6 Hale Irwin Finished

- 6 Bobby Nichols (13 holes completed)

- 5 Billy Casper (13 holes completed)

- 5 Tom Watson (12 holes completed)

- 4 Dave Hill (16 holes completed)

- 3 Lee Trevino (13 holes completed)

- 2 Tom Kite (17 holes completed)

40:20 - Nicklaus pars the 13th hole after being just off the green in 2, losing an opportunity to gain another shot on Weiskopf. But Tom Watson converts the birdie at 13 and moves to - 6. He is 5 shots behind Nicklaus and moves into a tie for 4th place. Watson has never finished this high in a major.

43:00 - After Weiskopf hits a layup shot on 13, Johnny Miller put his 2nd shot squarely on the green and will have a makeable eagle putt that could bring him within 1 shot of Nicklaus.

46:20 - Weiskopf's 3rd shot on the par 5, a 50 yard pitch over the water, runs through to the back of the green, but leaves him with a makeable birdie putt of only about 15 feet.

47:30 - Miller's 40-footer for eagle stops about 2 feet short of the hole.

48:25 - Nicklaus hits his 9-iron approach shot into 14 from the middle of the fairway and leaves the ball short of the green about 55 feet from the pin. Nicklaus is visibly upset.

49:10 - Weiskopf strokes his birdie putt attempt at 13, a makeable 15-footer, too hard. It runs through the break and stops 2 feet past the hole. He remains a shot behind Nicklaus.

49:35 - Bobby Nichols is in the sand trap on the front right of the green at 15. His 3rd shot stops just a few feet from the pin. He will have an opportunity to get to -7. But he misses the short putt. He's squandered an opportunity to get within striking distance of the lead.

50:00 - Miller makes his 2-footer for birdie at 13. He is now at -9, just a shot behind Weiskopf and 2 back of Nicklaus. Weiskopf makes his 2 foot par putt to stay at -10.

51:00 - Jack, putting from off the front of the 14th green, hits the putt way too hard and it goes completely off the back of the green and into the rough. The ball is sitting up, so he could chip or putt for his par. Nicklaus elects to putt, but leaves it short and takes a bogey. The lead is tied again.

LEADING SCORES AFTER NICKLAUS FINISHED 14:

-10 Jack Nicklaus (14 holes completed)

-10 Tom Weiskopf (13 holes completed)

- 9 Johnny Miller (13 holes completed)

- 6 Hale Irwin (Finished)

- 6 Tom Watson (14 holes completed)

- 6 Bobby Nichols (15 holes completed)

56:50 - Miller is making a mess of the 14th. His tee shot landed left behind a tree, and his 2nd shot hit a tree and landed well short of the green.

Just after Johnny hits his second shot on 14, Jack tees off on 15. It's a perfect drive. He will have an opportunity to go over the water and try to reach the green in 2. Immediately, the camera cuts back to the 14th hole for Weiskopf's approach shot from the middle of the fairway. Jack Whitaker describes it, *"a magnificent shot."* Tom Weiskopf is inside of 6 feet and has an excellent chance to re-gain the lead.

59:08 - Johnny Miller's 3rd shot on 14 hits the flagstick and drops just 2 feet from the hole. CBS misses the shot, but shows you the result. Miller will be able to escape the 14th with a par.

1:00:00 - Nicklaus takes a long time to ponder his 220-yard 2nd shot over water. Ben Wright provides extra drama by calling the upcoming shot, *"one of the most vital strokes of his distinguished career."* Nicklaus drills a spectacular long iron that rolls right by the hole and stops 15 feet past.

1:00:50 - As Nicklaus walks towards the 15th green, watch as he pats his caddy on the head and his caddy briefly wraps his arm around Nicklaus in a celebratory moment while Ben Wright exclaims, *"What a marvelous golf shot!"*

1:01:10 - Back at the 14th green, Weiskopf coolly cans his 6-foot birdie putt and he is back in the lead by himself at -11. Jack Whitaker describes it as, *"a brilliant bird here at 14."* Tom doesn't know it yet, but the lead could be temporary since Nicklaus has a short eagle putt coming ahead on 15.

Leading Scores After Weiskopf & Miller Finished 14:

-11 Tom Weiskopf

-10 Jack Nicklaus

- 9 Johnny Miller

1:02:10 - Nicklaus is walking towards the 15th green. Ben Wright tells the CBS audience, *"There's going to be a standing ovation, I'm sure. There certainly should be for a stroke of that majestic violence that has just been reeled off by Nicklaus."* Wright is right, there is a standing ovation for the Golden Bear.

   1:03:45 - As Nicklaus surveys the 15th green, back on the tee over 500 yards away, Weiskopf and Miller both hit superb tee shots with what appear to be fairway woods. At least the clubheads are so tiny they look like fairway woods to me. They will both have a chance to reach the green in 2.

   1:06:30 - CBS creates some dramatic flair as they show Nicklaus putting for eagle on 15, while displaying an inset of a facial closeup of Tom Weiskopf as he marches down the 15th fairway. It doesn't appear that Weiskopf can see Nicklaus putting, as Tom has no reaction when Nicklaus narrowly misses the eagle putt. Nicklaus has a tap-in birdie and moves into a tie with Tom on top yet again.

LEADING SCORES AFTER NICKLAUS FINISHES 15:

-11 Tom Weiskopf

-11 Jack Nicklaus

- 9 Johnny Miller

- 6 Hale Irwin

- 6 Bobby Nichols

- 6 Tom Watson

- 5 Billy Casper

1:08:20 - Now that Nicklaus and Watson have cleared the 15th green, Tom Weiskopf hits a long iron over the water. He lands the ball smack in the middle of the green, but it bounces and rolls off the back into the rough. Miller, who outdrove Weiskopf, is hitting a wood into the green. He initially thinks his ball is headed right, but it catches the right corner of the green and sits. Miller will have a 25-foot putt for eagle that could create a 3-way tie at the top.

1:10:00 - Nicklaus has waited until Miller's shot to have quiet on the 16th tee, which is near the 15th green. But Nicklaus is disappointed when his tee shot lands 40 feet short of the pin at the par 3.

1:10:40 - Tom Watson hits his tee shot on 16. Minutes earlier, Watson had missed a 3-foot putt for birdie on 15 that would have put him in sole possession of 4th, and just 4 shots behind the lead. Now you can hear Tom clearly on the tape talking to himself out loud, *"Aw, get up! Aw, Tom!,"* as he watches his ball land short of the green and in trouble. Henry Longhurst, from his vantage point behind 16, can't tell if it's in the water or in the trap just beyond the water.

1:12:00 - Weiskopf chips his 3rd shot about 15 feet past the pin. He will still have a chance for a birdie to re-take sole possession of 1st place, but to do that he will need to make a difficult putt.

1:13:20 - As Miller studies his eagle putt that could tie him for the lead, look at Tom Weiskopf. He is looking over at the 16th hole, where he sees Tom Watson hitting his 3rd shot from the front of the tee box, which is the drop zone. Watson's initial tee shot did indeed land in the pond. For Watson, it's a nightmare in his prime time debut as he puts the next shot in the water again. He will now be hitting 5, and he is still on the tee box.

Back on the 15th green, Miller pauses his putting preparation until Watson hits his 3rd "tee shot" (his 5th shot) on 16. Watson's ball lands on the green this time, but rolls back, leaving him over 40 feet uphill to the hole. Watson's ball has settled a little behind the spot where Jack Nicklaus has marked his ball. Thus giving Jack a chance to see the break when Watson putts.

1:14:55 - Miller's eagle putt on 15 seems right on line, but it just slides past the hole. He will have a 3-footer coming back for birdie to get within a shot of the lead.

1:16:20 - Weiskopf's ball lies half the distance to the hole as Miller's was and on the same line. His putt drops in the hole and ignites the crowd. Ben Wright exclaims, *"Oh! What a tremendous putt by Tom Weiskopf!"*

Even before Wright has finished the sentence, the CBS producers quickly cut to a close-up of Nicklaus standing on the 16th green, watching the fireworks back on the 15th green. Nicklaus looks disturbed, almost as if he can hear Ben Wright saying that the crowd noise is, *"going to be evil music ringing in Nicklaus's ear."*

1:16:37 - Immediately after showcasing Nicklaus's reaction, CBS cuts to a close-up of Weiskopf. Watch as Weiskopf looks in the direction of Nicklaus at the 16th green. Tom momentarily assumes a posture that sends a message, *"Take that, Jack!"*

Tom Weiskopf has just put himself in the lead of the Masters by a stroke over Jack Nicklaus. Weiskopf is 3 holes away from the Green Jacket that he so dearly covets. While Johnny Miller makes his short birdie putt to keep himself in contention.

NOTE from The Sports Time Traveler

I can't remember if I noticed the two quick close-ups of Nicklaus and Weiskopf as they peered over towards each other right after Weiskopf re-took the lead with his putt on 15. On the tape, the fiery look on Jack's face, coupled seconds later with Tom's look of bravado towards Jack is clear. And CBS caught it brilliantly. It's such great drama. It should be a lesson for all golf broadcasts here in the present time.

Now, back to 1975.

Leading Scores After Weiskopf & Miller Finished 15:

-12 Tom Weiskopf

-11 Jack Nicklaus

-10 Johnny Miller

1:17:45 - Now that Nicklaus is assured of some quiet again, he prepares to strike his uphill 40-footer on the 16th green as his caddy holds the pin in the cup. The line looks good, but as his caddy pulls the pin out and backs up, he blocks off the camera.

The first indication that the ball is going in is when the caddy fist pumps high over his head and leaps. Then there is the roar of the crowd as Jack Nicklaus uncharacteristically leaps in the air, putter high over his head.

Whether it is by design or not, Jack is now facing the 16th tee as he celebrates his miracle putt. Weiskopf and Miller are forced to witness the spectacle on the green as they stand waiting to hit their tee shots.

When Jack lands, he does a little jig and jogs several steps and again raises his hands over his head, and yet again, holds his club towards the sky, in celebration. Henry Longhurst says, *"ah-ho! Did you ever see one like that! I think that's one of the greatest putts I've ever seen in my life!"*

And then Nicklaus quickly returns to a state of calm, and deliberately walks off the green to the 17th tee.

It's as if the golfers are in an old western saloon in a heated poker game. Jack, without saying a word, pushes out a stack of chips to call Tom's bet and then another stack to raise him.

The CBS producers quickly cut to a shot of Tom Weiskopf on the 16th tee, who had watched the theatrics unobstructed. Weiskopf now has his head down. He is looking for a spot to tee from, but perhaps, he is also attempting to gather himself after enduring this swipe from the Golden Bear.

LEADING SCORES AFTER NICKLAUS FINISHES 16:

-12 Jack Nicklaus

-12 Tom Weiskopf

-10 Johnny Miller

1:19:45 - Weiskopf is visibly disappointed when his tee shot lands about 45 yards short of the flag and doesn't even reach the front of the green. It's a devastating mishit.

Seconds later, Nicklaus drills a perfect drive down the center of the par 4 17th hole. Miller's tee shot on 16 is the best of the three leaders on that hole, but it is still about 30 feet left of the flag.

1:23:05 - Weiskopf elects to try a long distance putt from off the green. His putt starts out well but near the end it catches the slope to the left of the hole and drifts a long way down towards the water. His ball comes to a rest 18 feet from the pin. He will need to make the putt to maintain his tie with Nicklaus.

1:23:50 - Nicklaus puts his 2nd shot safely on the green just 20 feet from the pin at 17.

1:25:35 - Weiskopf's putt to save par looks good, but coming up hill it loses steam and stops just shy of the hole. Weiskopf has bogeyed the 16th. That puts Jack back in front by 1 shot over Weiskopf and 2 over Miller, who narrowly missed his birdie putt moments earlier.

Leading Scores After Weiskopf & Miller Finish 16:

-12 Jack Nicklaus

-11 Tom Weiskopf

-10 Johnny Miller

1:27:55 - Johnny Miller's tee shot on 17 lands safely on the left side of the fairway.

1:28:30 - Nicklaus' birdie putt on 17 falls just short. Nicklaus remains 1 shot in front.

1:29:25 - Nicklaus is safely in the fairway on his tee shot at 18.

1:31:00 - CBS switches back to the 17th fairway where Miller is getting ready for his approach shot. The producers have created a split screen in which we see an up close view of Miller on the left and a long distance view looking back from the green on the right. This provides viewers with multiple perspectives and is something I've not often seen in TV productions back in the 2020's. We have a great dual view throughout the shot as Miller's ball lands on the green just 15 feet from the pin.

1:31:55 - Oddly absent from the action on the CBS broadcast for the past 6 minutes is Weiskopf who apparently hit a great tee shot at 17, and is hitting his approach shot from the middle of the fairway. He lands his ball pin high 15 feet to the right. Both Miller and Weiskopf have makeable birdie putts.

1:33:30 - Nicklaus hits his approach shot on 18 pin high and just 12 feet right of the pin. Vin Scully proclaims, *"A magnificent approach for Jack Nicklaus, and he is in birdie country."*

1:35:10 - Weiskopf's birdie putt at 17 falls just short. He remains a shot back.

1:36:30 - As Miller watches his putt roll towards the hole he is certain it is going in and begins to raise his arm skyward when the ball still has 5 feet left to go. It falls in. And the crowd roar is enormous for Miller who is now tied with Weiskopf for 2nd place just a shot behind the Golden Bear.

Now continue watching as CBS cuts to a close up of Jack Nicklaus standing on the 18th green, listening to the crowd. Frank Glieber alertly says on air, *"Now Nicklaus has got to be wondering exactly what did happen on 17."*

If the roar is for Weiskopf it would mean Tom has tied Jack for the lead.

But if the roar is for Miller, then Jack is still a shot in front.

Leading Scores After Weiskopf & Miller Finish 17:

-12 Jack Nicklaus

-11 Tom Weiskopf

-11 Johnny Miller

1:37:20 - Tom Watson putts first on 18 and he drills home his 20 foot birdie putt resulting in a large ovation.

Now Weiskopf and Miller are left to wonder if the roar up ahead is for Watson or for Nicklaus. A roar for Nicklaus would mean Jack has just put the tournament out of reach with a birdie to go 2 shots up.

A few seconds later Vin Scully tells us that Nicklaus looked up at the leaderboard before he began to line up his putt. This means that Jack knows he holds a 1 shot lead, and that if he can sink this birdie putt, he will effectively wrap up the 1975 Masters.

1:38:00 - Out of sight of the 18th green, Miller and Weiskopf tee off on 18. Both men hit their drives in the fairway, but Weiskopf has blasted his tee shot and is considerably closer to the green. It is the longest drive at 18 by anyone in the 4 days of the tournament.

NOTE from The Sports Time Traveler

I interrupt the article to tell you of my first-hand memory of Weiskopf's tee shot at 18. I recall feeling the frustration of Weiskopf, who was tied for 2nd, a shot behind Nicklaus, and now must birdie the final hole to force a playoff.

Weiskopf had been in the lead to start the day. He had sole possession of the lead after 15 holes. And he has been 2nd in this tournament 3 prior times.

In my memory, I saw a look of ferocity on Weiskopf's face as he unleashed everything he had on that 18th tee shot, knowing he must boom a

drive out there to set up an approach shot that would give him a makeable birdie putt.

And I was pulling hard for Miller and Weiskopf on that final hole. Now back to 1975.

1:39:30 - Nicklaus just misses on his birdie putt. He pars the 18th. He must now wait to see if either Miller or Weiskopf can birdie the 18th and force a playoff.

LEADING SCORES AFTER NICKLAUS FINISHES 18:
-12 Jack Nicklaus
-11 Tom Weiskopf
-11 Johnny Miller

1:41:10 - Johnny Miller's approach shot lands in the middle of the 18th green, 15 feet from the pin. He will have a chance for a birdie to force a playoff with Nicklaus. Vin Scully says, *"A bird is certainly a possibility. He has a chance to tie."*

1:42:40 - Weiskopf now has one of the most important wedge shots of his career and he hits a marvelous one. Vin Scully yells, *"He's inside of Miller! Oh! What a horse race!"*

Weiskopf is perhaps 8 feet away from sending the Masters to an 18-hole playoff on Monday.

Indeed a playoff appears imminent as 2 of the greatest players in the world at this time both have strong birdie opportunities.

1:44:50 - Johnny Miller putts first. His ball looks dead on track for the hole, but just fades left at the end. Vin Scully says, *"And one birdie flew away. Johnny Miller, a gallant effort."* Miller will end the Masters 1 shot short of Nicklaus, after he had been 11 shots behind the Golden Bear after 2 rounds.

A Record Final 2 Rounds

Johnny Miller finishes with weekend rounds of 65 - 66. His 131 score on the final 2 rounds is a new Masters record. Miller has scorched Nicklaus 131 to 141 for the weekend. But, for the entire 4 rounds of the Masters, he finished a shot behind Jack Nicklaus.

Miller walks away holding his putter with his hands over the back of his head and the putter dangling down his back. Miller mopes around the green in a display of devastating disappointment.

1:45:15 - Vin Scully says, *"And now there is one last shot left in the arsenal and it belongs to Tom Weiskopf."*

1:46:20 - After carefully studying the putt, Weiskopf strokes the ball. Miller's ball had faded left. Weiskopf putts it a little to the right. And the ball doesn't break. It moves past the hole on the right. Vin Scully says, *"And so the heartbreak and the disappointment registers on Tom Weiskopf's face and on the lips of those who had cheered him for 4 days. And hail to the victor. Jack Nicklaus wins his 5th Masters' green coat."*

Tom Weiskopf tied a Masters' record he never wanted. He has come in 2nd place for the 4th time.

All 3 of the *"golf-slingers"* have proven themselves worthy. Miller had shot a 66, Nicklaus 68, and Weiskopf 70 on this pressure-packed, legacy-making day.

FINAL SCORES of the 1975 MASTERS

-12 Jack Nicklaus

-11 Tom Weiskopf

-11 Johnny Miller

- 6 Hale Irwin

- 6 Bobby Nichols

- 5 Billy Casper

- 4 Dave Hill

- 3 Tom Watson

- 3 Hubert Green

- 2 Lee Trevino

- 2 J.C. Snead

- 2 Tom Kite

- 1 Arnold Palmer

- 1 Larry Ziegler

BUTLER CABIN INTERVIEWS and THE GREEN JACKET CEREMONY

1:54:35 - The winner and the 2nd place golfers are interviewed in Butler cabin by Augusta National member, Frank Broyles. Broyles introduces Johnny Miller by saying, *"Johnny, what a comeback. The last 2 days of golf is the most fantastic that's probably been played ever in the history of golf. 131, I think Jack mentioned, in the last 2 days."*

Johnny Miller responded, *"I was 3 over par after 4 holes on the 1st day and that's no way to start a golf tournament, but I just sort of stuck with it... I just kept plugging away... but it was a real thrill for me to be here and also a great thrill to have a putt on the last hole to tie or to win a golf tournament, you can't imagine how exciting that was, and I'll never forget it... I really congratulate Jack Nicklaus. That was a super clutch putt he made at 16.... I look up to him and he's a great player. And I congratulate Tom. I know how he feels right now."*

1:56:20 - Frank Broyles next utters a phrase that spoke directly to viewers just like me back in 1975, *"There is no question that for the young golfers of America, you are their idol right now and they can identify with you."* Broyles couldn't have phrased that more perfectly.

Then Broyles moves on to have the difficult conversation with Tom Weiskopf. He looks at Tom and says, *"Tom, I don't know what to say. I know our comments for the last 2 or 3 years have been one of somewhat disappointment, but you made a great run at it and played tremendous golf all week long."*

1:56:40 - Weiskopf responds in a gracious manner, *"Well, thank you Frank... It's a tremendous pleasure for me to be able compete in what I think is one of the greatest spectacles in all of sports... I know one thing, and I believe it, I will win this golf tournament someday."*

1:58:05 - Weiskopf is asked to describe the putt on 18 that could have forced a playoff, *"Well, I watched John's putt from just about on the same line and his broke very quickly to the left. I probably had about an 8-foot putt there, and I thought I'm just going to try to hit it firm on the top edge of the hole, and it has to break. I felt like I stroked it good."*

As they watch the tape of the putt, Weiskopf says, *"It never even turned, you can see right there. It looks like it has to turn... You know, you make a lot of putts you don't think you'll make at times, too. That's the way it goes."*

1:59:00 - Now Frank turns to speak to Jack Nicklaus who is sitting on the far left side of the couch (right side of the TV screen) with Weiskopf in the middle and Miller on Tom's right. Broyles says, *"Jack, what can we say, 5th Masters, great day, congratulations."*

Nicklaus responds, *"Thank you very much... I was obviously delighted, and I wanted to win this tournament very badly... I said the beginning of the week... the 2 guys I felt that had more talent in the game today, and the 2 guys that are going to dominate this game as time goes on are Johnny and Tom. As it turned out, Johnny got a bad start... I really didn't think anybody could play this golf course the way he played it the last 2 days to come back into contention. He just played fantastic golf."*

Then Nicklaus talked about Tom Weiskopf, *"I knew he was ready* (to win). *After yesterday, after losing my lead, and Tom going ahead, I knew it was going to be a tough day. But I've been here before, been in that position before, and I felt just play good solid golf and see what happens. Well, I played real good golf and kept making birdies, but these guys kept making right behind me too."*

"I don't think I've ever been involved in all the years that I've played golf, about 15 on the TOUR now, a more exciting day of golf, I don't think there ever was at least since I've been involved... Anyone of the 3 of us could've won. That is the fun of the game... They'll win their tournaments, they'll win their Masters. These guys are going to win several of them."

2:01:45 - After Frank Broyles asks Nicklaus to describe the par 5 15th hole, Nicklaus says this about his approach shot from 245 yards to the green, *"I took a 1-ron out which I knew I had to just hit all of it... I think it may be the finest 1-iron I've ever it in my life... and I guess it almost went in the hole."*

2:02:55 - Nicklaus describes what it was like standing on the 16th hole watching Miller and Weiskopf play the 15th, *"I saw Tom hit his pitch at 15 and I knew he didn't hit the pitch the way he wanted to. He ran it by the hole about 8 - 10 feet."* Nicklaus turns to look to Weiskopf to confirm the distance and Weiskopf tells him about 12 feet. Then Nicklaus continues, *"Then I heard him make his putt."*

Then Nicklaus describes the putt of the tournament, his 40-footer at 16. *"It was really funny as I stood over my putt at 16. You know how sometimes you have the feeling that you might make something?... I had the feeling that I might make it. And I hit the darn thing and it went right in. I knew what it was going to do as far as break, because I just watched Tom Watson putt. And obviously, that was the tournament... I figured Tom had bogeyed 16 from the reactions as I was walking up 17."*

2:04:05 - Nicklaus then describes his approach on 18, *"I hit a good shot. I just tried to take a little 6-iron and just bump it on the green."* Then, Nicklaus, who is one of the longest hitters in the history of the game, smiled, and turned to Weiskopf, and in a fitting ode to the man who finished 2nd for the 4th time, Nicklaus said, *"I saw where Tom drove, what did you hit, a pitching wedge?"* Nicklaus was referring to the club selection for Weiskopf's approach shot. Having just a pitching wedge left into the 18th green at Augusta is astonishing.

2:04:55 - Frank Broyles announces the Green Jacket ceremony and we see defending champion Gary Player put the jacket on Jack.

2:07:20 - Listen to Vin Scully's closing comments on the broadcast, *"It would defy the writing of a Hemmingway, or you name the author, to tell you what transpired here today, but to use the word 'unforgettable' I think will hold up."*

MORNING PRESS TODAY

Newspapermen today tried to top one another with their grandiose descriptions of what they saw yesterday.

Harley Bowers in the Macon Telegraph titled his article, *"The Greatest Finish."* He began with this paragraph, *"The Masters had had many great finishes, but never has there been one that involved three players of the caliber of Jack Nicklaus, Johnny Miller and Tom Weiskopf, the trio battled right to the final hole."*

Jesse Outlar of the Atlanta Constitution wrote this, *"Millions in TV land observed one of the greatest tournaments ever staged anywhere. The 39th Masters was the Cardiac Open... Veteran experts such as author Herbert Warren Wind called it, 'the greatest Masters ever.'"*

Outlar also had this amusing paragraph:

"The Golden Bear, who rarely shows any emotion, did a victory jig as the putt plunked (at the 16th). *When Miller was later asked if he saw the putt, he said, No, but I saw the bear prints."*

John Husar of the Chicago Tribune wrote, *"This was one of those days that will be carved in the granite of sports history. For 18 nail-biting holes, three of the finest players in the game played as well as possible, and it was a work of art."*

Perhaps none of the writers could top the hyperbole that Jim Murray poured out in his syndicated column in the Los Angeles Times this morning. Here's my favorite parts, *"It was the Super Bowl of golf. The three registered titans of the game were out there on a course as treacherous as an ice floe in the North Atlantic... It was Rockne against Pop Warner in football, Babe Ruth facing Lefty Grove and Dizzy Dean, Red Grange trying to move the ball against the Seven Blocks of Granite, Dempsey toe-to-toe with Tunney."*

Murray continued:

"My God, what a golf tournament! You can talk of Hogan and Snead, Jones and Sarazen, Hagen at Holylake, but I think when I remember golf in the 1970s for the rest of my life, the general conversation will begin with 'Let me tell you that year when Nicklaus and Weiskopf and Miller hit the Amen Corner at Augusta.'"

"... This was one sporting event where 200,000 people, who weren't, will one day say, 'I was there when Nicklaus, Weiskopf and Miller came down to the last holes at Augusta birdie-birdie-birdie-par and it's a shame any of them had to lose it.' In a sense, none of them did. It was not only one of the greatest golf tournaments I have ever seen, it was one of the greatest sporting events. In fact, it was one of the greatest events. Period."

And of course, the lasting legacy of the tournament was the reference to it being a "shootout." Will Grimsley of the AP, in an article that ran in hundreds of papers across America wrote, *"Thousands pouring over Augusta's floral acres and millions viewing on television watched the battle go down to the final hole - a no-quarter, no-choke shootout involving the three finest golfers of the age."*

Many newspaper sports editors across America took Grimsley's AP article and put the word, "shoutout," in the title.

POSTSCRIPT

Vin Scully's description of the final day of the 1975 Masters as "unforgettable" has proven to be true here 50 years later in 2025.

A Golf Magazine article on April 2, 2025, had the headline, *"50 years later, we've still never seen anything quite like the 1975 Masters."*

Despite Jack Nicklaus's prediction in the Butler Cabin interview that Johnny Miller and Tom Weiskopf would win the Masters neither of them ever did. But Jack himself did win one more, 11 years later at age 46.

Johnny Miller would play in 13 more Masters tournaments. His highest finish was 2nd place, giving him 3 2nd place finishes in his career, one short of the record still held by Tom Weiskopf.

Tom Weiskopf would play in only 8 more Masters tournaments. His highest finish would be just 9th place.

During the CBS broadcast of the 1986 Masters, in which Nicklaus won his record 6th Green Jacket, Tom Weiskopf was the color commentator. When Nicklaus was on the 16th tee, CBS broadcaster Jim Nantz asked Tom what Jack was thinking. Weiskopf delivered one of the greatest lines I've ever heard from a golf commentator, *"If I knew what was going through Jack's mind, I would have won this tournament."*

Jim Nantz, in a 2022 Golf Digest article about that specific moment with Weiskopf wrote, *"He then added, as though it were Jack talking to himself, 'Make a good golf swing. Your destiny is right here.' Jack very nearly aced the hole, scoring a 2, and the memory of that exchange in the tower alongside Tom gives me chills to this day.'"*

CHAPTER THIRTY

Never a More Dramatic Finish

THE 1922 BRITISH OPEN

INTRODUCTION from The Sports Time Traveler

In this final chapter of volume 1, I take you back over 100 years to the 1922 British Open that was played at Royal St George's Golf Club in Sandwich, England. It's a little seaside town in the southeast of England that I'm personally very familiar with as I went to college in 1983 – 1984 just a few miles away at the University of Kent in Canterbury.

The British Open has been played since 1860. The first 29 championships were all won by Scots where the game was invented. That streak was broken in 1890 by John Ball of England. Ball began a stretch in which 16 of the next 26 British Opens were won by Englishmen, 9 by Scots and 1 by a Frenchman.

No American had ever won the British Open until 1921 when Jock Hutchison, an American citizen who was born in Scotland captured the Claret Jug in a playoff at St. Andrews. Hutchison actually grew up in St. Andrews, and learned how to play golf there. He emigrated to the USA as an adult, becoming a naturalized citizen just the year before in 1920.

So aside from the one Frenchman, Arnaud Massy, in 1907, a golfer born outside of the U.K. had never won the British Open.

But 1922 was shaping up to be a foreign assault on the British Open. Several golfers from outside of Great Britain were looking like they would be contenders. And the most recent champions from the U.K. were getting old as the war had crippled the development of a new generation of British golfers.

Here's an introduction to the biggest names in golf that were entered in the 1922 British Open:

JOE KIRKWOOD of Australia

The 25 year old Kirkwood emerged as a factor on the world stage when he finished tied 6th in the 1921 British Open. In the past few weeks, Kirkwood has established himself as the man to beat after 4 shocking victories. First he destroyed a field of professional golfers in a 72 hole event, in Lossiemouth, Scotland, by 13 shots. Then he humiliated the highly regarded George Duncan of Scotland in a match in Glasgow 6 and 5. Next, he smothered a field of professional golfers in an 18 hole event at Gleneagles, in Scotland, as reported in the June 7, 1922, London Daily Telegraph. Finally, he defeated defending British Open champion Jock Hutchison in an exhibition match at the Leven Links in Scotland as reported in the June 13, 1922, London Daily Mirror.

Kirkwood is also a renowned trick shot artist. D.J. McGuiness of the Boston Globe, in an article on September 8, 1921 called Kirkwood, *"The magician of the links."* McGuiness also described in great detail the entire show Kirkwood puts on. Here are some of the "acts" I thought were particularly noteworthy:

- *"Driving for distance right or left-handed"*
- *"Teeing balls on top of each other and hitting whichever one picked"*
- *"Driving off partner's foot, and from under, off watch, golf bags, etc."*

Kirkwood is planning an around the world exhibition tour with American golfer Walter Hagen to begin right after the 1922 British Open.

WALTER HAGEN of the USA

The 29 year old is a 2-time winner of the U.S. Open in 1914 and 1919. And he won the PGA Championship in 1921. He also was tied 6th in the 1921 British Open. In an April 21, 1922, article, The New York Times wrote, *"Hagen has long been regarded as one of the greatest golfers in the world and easily the ranking home-bred pro."* He is also a favorite of American sportswriter Grantland Rice. In his February 1, 1922 column, Rice described Hagen, *"Powerfully built with a slashing, confident style, always willing to hit for the pin and take his gamble with fate."*

JIM BARNES of the USA

36 year old Jim Barnes was born in England, but has lived in the USA since 1906. He recently won the U.S. Open in 1921 by 9 shots. And he finished in a 6th place tie in the last 2 British Opens in 1920 and 1921. Francis Ouimet, the man who famously defeated the two top players in the world in 1913, Harry Vardon and Ted Ray, to win the U.S. Open, said in a May 13, 1922 article in the San Francisco Examiner, *"Jim Barnes stands a better chance of being crowned 'Golf Champion of the World' this summer than any man has ever stood heretofore."*

JOCK HUTCHISON of the USA

At 38 years old, Hutchison, the defending British Open Champion, is back again. He had announced that he was NOT going to make the trip because he could not afford it, as reported in the May 15, 1922 Boston Globe. But just a week later the Boston Globe announced he had reversed his decision. For the past year, British officials had feared that Hutchison would not return across the Atlantic with the Claret Jug, which has been kept in the possession of the winner each year since 1872. Hutchison told the Chicago Tribune on July 11, 1921, after he had returned to the USA with the silver jug, how badly he had been treated in Scotland (his original home) during the 1921 British Open, *The British were peeved because I renounced my citizenship and became an American. This is my country* (America) *and I love it more than ever."*

GEORGE DUNCAN of Scotland

38 year old Duncan won the 1920 British Open and finished 5th last year. Despite his recent match play loss to Joe Kirkwood, the June 8, 1922 London Daily Mirror reported Duncan to be playing superb in the tournament at Gleneagles, *"Duncan was in his most brilliant form... so smooth and graceful was his swing."* He came in 2nd in that event with many of the top players in the field, and if not for 2 missed putts of 2 feet in length, he would have tied Kirkwood at the top.

HARRY VARDON of England

At 52, Vardon is past his prime, but he can't be counted out. He has played in the Open every year it's been contested since 1893. He has won it 7 times, most recently in 1914. He finished tied for 23rd last year. But Vardon has something going for him that no one else in the field does. He won the British Open the last time it was played at Royal St. George's back in 1911.

Yet, Harry Vardon himself has picked Jim Barnes to win the 1922 British Open. He explained why in a Boston Globe article he authored on June 11, 1922. He wrote, *"he drives as far as anybody on earth... nobody can beat him at putting."*

TED RAY of England

The 45 year old has played in every British Open in this century. He won the British Open in 1912 and finished 3rd as recently as 1920. He also won the U.S. Open in 1920.

J.H. TAYLOR of England

At 51 years old, Taylor, is one of the senior statesmen of golf. He is a 5-time winner of the British Open. His first victory was in 1894, here at Royal St. George's, and his most recent in 1913. In 1921, playing in his 24th British Open, he finished in 26th position.

JAMES BRAID of Scotland

The elder statesman of the game in Scotland, Braid is 52 years old and is also a 5-time winner of the British Open. He won all his Opens from 1901 to 1910. In 1921 he finished in a tie for 16th.

   Naturally, as The Sports Time Traveler, I had to go back in time virtually to Sandwich, England in June of 1922 to experience the British Open.
   Here are my reports:

Sandwich, England – June 18, 1922

I'm reporting virtually from Royal St George's Golf Club where the 1922 British Open qualifying rounds will begin tomorrow.

The London Sunday Dispatch had the odds today for the favourites to win:

6 to 1 - Joe Kirkwood of Australia

8 to 1 - George Duncan of Scotland

9 to 1 - Walter Hagen, USA Jock Hutchison, USA and Jim Barnes, USA

The qualifying rounds will take place today and tomorrow. All 225 players that are entered in the British Open must first go through the two days of 18 hole qualifying. Each player will play 18 holes one day at Royal St. George's and 18 holes the other day at nearby Prince's Golf Club.

1st Qualifying Round – June 20, 1922

George Greenwood of the London Daily Telegraph spent the entire day yesterday at the Prince's Golf Club where most of the favourites were playing. He began his article today with this, *"The first of the two qualifying rounds for the British Open championship has provided no sensations. Kirkwood, the Australian, and the three Americans, Hagen, Barnes and Hutchison have lived up to their splendid reputations and their stock has risen still higher."*

Jock Hutchison posted the best score on either course with a 71 at Prince's. It may sound hard to fathom, but Greenwood noted that Hutchison's score broke the course record at the 6,880 yard course by 6 strokes! Greenwood also made mention that Prince's, *"is the longest and certainly the most difficult course in Great Britain."*

Also inside the old course record were both Hagen and Kirkwood who shot 75s, which put them in a tie for the 4th best score at Prince's course. I'm not sure however, why Greenwood included Barnes in his opening, as Jim could only manage an 82, which puts him in jeopardy of not making the top 80 scores after today's 2nd day of qualifying. Only the top 80 will qualify for what they call "the championship proper." And more than 100 golfers had scores of 81 or better on the 1st day.

Greenwood did indicate however, that Barnes's situation could be even worse. He reported that on the 458 yard 12th hole, Barnes's 2nd shot went far off line and landed (wait for it) inside a toolshed whose doors had been left open (I shed you not)!

Here's where the controversy begins. Barnes simply picked the ball up from inside the toolshed and, *"dropped it alongside the shed without incurring any penalty."* It is possible that penalty strokes may yet be added to Barnes's score.

Fortunately for Barnes, the Royal St. George's course, that he will play in today's 2nd round of qualifying, is the shorter and easier course. He will need a solid round to qualify for the championship proper.

Greenwood noted that among the crowds of fans attending the 1st qualifying round at Prince's, *"Interest was centered purely in the doings of the Americans and Kirkwood."* Greenwood mentioned a funny reaction he overheard by one of the patrons, *"I heard one lady say to her friends, 'who's that?'"* as she tried to determine the identity of a golfer. Upon learning it was the Englishman, Abe Mitchell, she said, *"Mitchell, I don't want to see him. I want to look at Kirkwood."*

As highly touted as Kirkwood has been, and rightfully so given his play over the past few weeks, Greenwood reported something interesting he heard among the players, *"Although Kirkwood has been established favourite by the masses, Hagen is regarded by the professionals as the man possessing the best chance."*

Supporting the professionals opinion was Greenwood himself. After following the American yesterday, Greenwood wrote, *"Walter Hagen played very convincing golf, and was hitting his drives farther than any other player I saw."*

Hagen had great praise for the Prince's links. Greenwood reported Hagen told him, *"outside America, Prince's is the best course he has played."*

What Greenwood did not get to see yesterday was the big news at Royal St. George's, where 52 year old Harry Vardon tied the top score of the day at that course with a 72.

Here were the top scores across the two courses in yesterday's 1st qualifying round:

71   **Hutchison, USA (Prince's)**

72   **Vardon, England (Royal St. George's) and Boomer, France (Royal St. George's)**

73   **9 tied (only 1 of the 9 was at Prince's)**

74   **T. Walton (Prince's)**

75   **Hagen, USA (Prince's), Kirkwood, USA (Prince's) and 3 others at Royal St. George's**

Other favourites:

79   **Braid, Scotland (Royal St. George's)**

80   **Taylor, England (Prince's)**

81   **Ray, England (Prince's) and Duncan, Scotland (Prince's)**

82   **Barnes, USA (Prince's)**

Overall, only 19 players broke 80 at Prince's, while 51 golfers broke 80 at Royal St. George's.

2nd Qualifying Round – June 21, 1922

George Greenwood of the London Daily Telegraph wrote, *"It has been a chastening day for English golf."* The overseas challengers thoroughly outplayed the British.

"Joe Kirkwood played many masterful shots, some of which Vardon in his irresistible days, twenty years ago, would have been proud of," wrote Greenwood. Kirkwood played the opening 9 holes at Royal St. George's in just 34. On the back 9 he made a great 3 at the 439 yard 13th hole, and he reached the green on the 457 yard 15th hole hitting into a steady wind. However he bogeyed each of the last 2 holes after hooking his drive and finished the day with a 72 for a 2 day score of 147.

The Bristol England Western Daily Press reported that, *"Hagen played perfect golf, and certainly produced better shots than he has ever before in this country."* Hagen played the opening 9 at Royal St. George's in 35. At the 16th he holed a 30 foot putt for a 2. At that point he needed two 4's to finish with a 69, but he took a 5 and a 6 and had to settle for a 72, tied with Kirkwood for the 2 days at 147.

Hutchison played conservatively just doing what he needed to assure a qualifying score. The Western Daily Press commented about his play, *"There was no need for Hutchison to attempt the spectacular, and he was content to play steadily for a safe round."* He finished with a 78 for a 2 day score of 149.

These three, all from overseas were the only golfers of the 216 playing to score under 150 in the qualifying rounds.

Jim Barnes could not be comfortable with his position starting out yesterday the Royal St. George's. After an 82 the first day he needed to play more aggressively. Greenwood wrote about his play yesterday, *"Barnes was hitting the ball with consummate accuracy and his driving was terrifically long. There were very few holes where he required a wooden club for his second shot."* But Greenwood was most impressed with Barnes's chipping, *"The man who invariably gets dead from 25 yards and has merely to tap the ball into the hole backhanded is a very dangerous fellow."* Barnes matched Kirkwood and Hagen with 72, the low score of the day at Royal St. George's, and that gave him a 2-day total of 154, and good enough to qualify. He was not assessed any penalty for moving his ball from the toolshed on day 1.

Harry Vardon, played the tougher Prince's course yesterday. Greenwood noted that the wind made the scoring 2 or 3 strokes tougher than the 1st day. And starting with a 6 and a 5 didn't help. But Vardon made a 3 on the 3rd, and then a string of 4's from the 4th to the 11th put Vardon in good shape. On the final holes, The Western Daily Press noted, *"he made one or two mistakes, but he could afford to do so, and though the round cost him 80, he was never in danger of getting outside the pale of qualification."* Combined with his fine score of 72 on the 1st day at Royal St. George's, his total of 152 was good for 8th overall. Harry Vardon, at age 52, had qualified for the championship proper for the 25th consecutive time.

Ted Ray shot a 75 at Royal St. George's. Added to his 81 on day 1 he was in safely at 156.

J.H. Taylor followed up his 80 at Prince's with just a 79 at Royal St. George's for a 159, which was a mere 2 shots inside the cut line.

George Duncan followed up his 81 on day 1 with a 79 for a 160, to make the cut with only a single stroke to spare.

James Braid was done in by his putting. He 3-putted 6 holes and 4-putted on another hole. His 2nd day score of 83 gave him a 162 for the 2 days and that was 1 shot outside the qualifying line. That broke his string of 21 consecutive years he had qualified for the championship proper.

After a day of domination by competitors from Australia and America, The London Daily Mirror concluded, *"There is no doubt that a British golfer will have to rise to a great height to save the cup."*

Fortunately, for the British, the scores from the qualifying rounds don't count. Tomorrow, when the championship proper starts everyone will be back to even.

Here were the top scores from qualifying:

147   Joe Kirkwood, Australia and Walter Hagen, USA

149   Josh Hutchison, USA

150   A.J. Miles, England

151   Aubrey Boomer, France, Tom Walton, England and Jack Ross, England

152   Harry Vardon, England and 4 others

Other favourites to qualify:

154   Jim Barnes, USA

156   Ted Ray, England

159   J.H. Taylor, England

160   George Duncan, Scotland

The only favourite to miss the qualifying:

162   James Braid, Scotland

The Long Driving Contest – June 22, 1922

Yesterday was a day off from competition as the championship proper gets started today. But a long driving contest was held yesterday. 50 players took part in the contest which was billed as *"World's Long Driving Championship."*

Each entrant took 6 shots. The rules called for 3 shots to be taken with balls of *"permissible size and weight,"* and 3 additional shots with any size or weight balls.

George Greenwood of the London Daily Telegraph was there reporting. He was clearly hoping to see some great new innovations but was instead disappointed that, *"The inventors of secret and freak balls failed to put in an appearance."*

The 15th hole was used for the contest because the ground there is fairly level. The scoring for the contest involved adding the 2 longest drives from each golfer.

The winner was John Smith of nearby Sussex. He drove 272 yards with a legal ball and 260 yards with a ball that weighted *"31 pennyweights,"* according to George Greenwood for a total of 532 yards. Greenwood described Mr. Smith, *"A man of small stature, who puts every possible ounce into the shot. But I think the secret of his power lies in the beautiful timing of the stroke."*

Among the tournament favorites, Walter Hagen was the only American to partake in the contest. His longest drives were 252 yards with the legal ball and 259 yards with another ball of unknown composition to the sportswriters.

J.H. Taylor drove 249 yards with a legal ball. And James Braid's longest shot with the legal ball was 248 yards.

Ted Ray and Joe Kirkwood did not participate.

FIRST HALF of the Championship Proper – June 23, 1922

Here in 1922, the British Open is a grueling affair. The entire 72 hole championship proper takes place in just 2 days. The 80 players must complete 36 holes each day.

The weather was fine and warm with only a light breeze for the start of the tournament yesterday, but the wind increased making for difficult afternoon conditions according to the London Daily Mirror.

The first man to tee off at 8:30am was Alec Herd, the 1902 champion. Herd, who is now 54, had qualified with the 13th lowest score, and may have been the oldest qualifier.

Herd's playing partner was George Duncan who started out with a great opening 9 holes to take an early lead. But Duncan couldn't maintain his play on the back 9 and finished the opening round with a 76.

Despite all the signs up till yesterday that the overseas challengers were going to dominate, the morning round yesterday belonged to the old British guard. 51 year old J.H. Taylor got off to a magnificent start with a 33 on the front 9. He couldn't sustain that but still finished with a fine 73. That was the same score as 45 year old Ted Ray. This led George Greenwood to write, *"There was hope after all."* But Greenwood tempered that enthusiasm by noting, *"Ray's 73 was not convincing because his recoveries, although executed as only Ray can execute them, were far too frequent."*

Walter Hagen got off to a steady start posting 38s on the front and back 9 for a 76 1st round. Jock Hutchison could only manage a 79 in the opening round. Jim Barnes had the best opening round of the Americans shooting a 75 despite a 4-putt green.

Joe Kirkwood was a bit of a mystery in the morning round. After having been the co-leader of the qualifying, he looked awful yesterday. Greenwood wrote, *"For some unexplained reason, his wonderful control in the long game seemed to have departed. The shots would not fly straight or as he had intended."* He ended up with a 79.

Here were the leading scores after the opening 18 holes:

73   **Ted Ray (England), J.H. Taylor (England)**

74   **Gus Faulkner (Wales)**

75   **Jim Barnes (USA) and 7 others**

76   **George Duncan (Scotland), Alec Herd (Scotland), Walter Hagen (USA) and 4 others**

Other favourites:

79   **Jock Hutchison (USA), Harry Vardon (England), Joe Kirkwood (Australia)**

Afternoon Round of First Half – June 23, 1922

The pangs of patriotism that must have been felt after the morning round by British fans extended early into the afternoon. George Duncan of Scotland was the first to begin play and he emerged as the British hope. The Liverpool Daily Post reported that Duncan went out in a 35, that could have been even better if not for a 3-putt on the 3rd green and, *"one or two strokes on the subsequent greens,"* that were lost.

George Greenwood watched Duncan on the 17th hole as he, *"played two of the most perfect wooden club shots I've ever seen."* Although a weak chip shot led to a 5 on the hole, it was emblematic of a solid round. Duncan shot a 75 to come in at 151 for the day. He was the early mid-way leader for the rest to shoot at.

But unlike the Scotsman Duncan, neither of the Englishmen in the lead after the morning round were able to maintain their level of play in the afternoon. Taylor came back with a 78 and Ray soared to an 83. The Liverpool Daily Post wrote of Ray's afternoon round, *"Gone was his boyish confidence and gone was the accuracy that came of it."*

Little known Gus Faulkner of Wales could not build on his surprising 74 in the morning and came back in 81.

Harry Vardon, who had shot a 72 in the qualifying round at Royal St. George's, was a bit of a disappointment all day, shooting a second 79 in the afternoon for a first day score of 158.

Joe Kirkwood's game improved a little bit in the afternoon. He went out in 37 on the front 9. Greenwood wrote about the Australian showman, *"He was steering the ball better."* He shot a 76 for the round to keep himself in contention.

A special to the New York Times described the 2nd rounds for Barnes, Hutchison and Hagen, *"the luck of the draw sent the Americans out late when a strong wind had sprung up and introduced a considerable handicap."*

Yet in spite of the more difficult conditions the Americans improved their game. Hagen suddenly found his putting stroke after struggling on the greens in the morning. The Times wrote, *"in the afternoon he made ample amends by taking a single putt on several greens."* That included a 36 foot putt on the 12th and an 18 footer on the 17th. In spite of a wind so strong that, *"several of his long shots got badly punished,"* Hagen managed to shoot a 73 in the afternoon, to tie Taylor and Ray for the low 18 hole score of the day.

Jock Hutchison, who also had scored 79 in the morning, was able to pull himself together in the afternoon with a 74. The Times reported, *"His score of 74 for the second round might easily have been a few less. He failed to reach the green in two on the ninth and tenth and he took three putts on the thirteenth."*

Jim Barnes had a sensational start to the afternoon with a 33 on the front 9, and combined with his 75 in the morning, he assumed the 27 hole lead. But he had a disastrous 43 on the back 9 to shoot 76 for the day.

Here were the leading scores at the end of the first day:

149   Walter Hagen (USA)

151   Jim Barnes (USA), George Duncan (Scotland), J.H. Taylor (England)

153   Jock Hutchison (USA), Percy Aliss (England), Tom Walton (England), Jean Gassiat (France)

Other favourites:

155   Joe Kirkwood (Australia)

156   Ted Ray (England)

158   Harry Vardon (England)

SECOND HALF of the Championship Proper – June 24, 1922

The golfers had to contend with gusty winds on the second and final day according to Arthur Draper writing in a special cable to the New York Tribune.

In the morning round, Hagen 3-putted the 2nd hole, but a 36 foot putt on the 9th enabled him to make the turn in just 36 strokes. But this wasn't good enough.

Taylor went out in a brilliant 34, that was marred by a 6 on the 9th, yet was good enough to pull the 51 year old into a tie for the lead with Hagen.

2 shots back at the turn was Hutchison who also had a 34 by, *"not making any mistakes,"* according to Greenwood.

The Frenchman, Jean Gassiat was out in 36, keeping him in contention just 4 shots off the lead at the turn.

Jim Barnes, who was just 2 shots behind Hagen at the beginning of the day, had a poor start to the 3rd round. He lost 5 shots on the first 5 holes. He made the turn in 38, putting him 4 shots off the lead.

George Duncan had a fair start to the day with a 37 on the front 9, keeping him 3 shots off the lead.

Here were the leaders' scores when each of them had 27 holes remaining in the Open:

185   Walter Hagen (USA) and J.H. Taylor (England)

187   Jock Hutchison (USA)

188   George Duncan (Scotland)

189   Jim Barnes (USA), Jean Gassiat (France)

On the back 9, Hagen started well with 4, 4, 4. Then he hit a bad stretch of 5, 5, 5. After a 4 at 16, he hit his drive at 17 into a bunker that was 10 feet deep. He made a 6 on the hole. On 18 he was no better. He took 4 shots to reach the hole and carded another 6. It added up to a 43 on the back 9, which was devastating to his chances of winning. He had shot a 79 for the round.

Hutchison could only manage a 39 on the back 9, but given Hagen's collapse, that moved him from 2 shots behind Walter, to 2 in front of him.

Taylor's putter betrayed him on the back 9 where he three-putted 4 times. On the 10th green he missed a short putt. Greenwood wrote, *"a spectator laughed when he missed... Taylor glared at the unfortunate individual, and after a stony silence, remarked, 'I'm glad you find it amusing.'"* In addition to his putting woes, a poor drive at 16 led Taylor to require 4 shots to reach the green. He shot a 42 on the back 9 for an 18 hole score of 76 in the 3rd round.

Gassiat of France came home in 38, giving him a fine 74 for the 3rd round and a great opportunity going into the final round just 1 shot off the lead.

Barnes came back with a 39 which left him tied with Hagen after his 43.

But even worse than Hagen's back 9 was George Duncan's. W.I. Hunter wrote of Duncan, *"He was weak with his approaches and also with his putts, and this proved very expensive."* Yes, it was expensive, Duncan had shot a 44 on the back 9 to score 81 for the 3rd round.

One more golfer, who was well back after the first day was Charles Whitcombe of England. He had the best round of the morning with a 72 and that brought him within 2 shots of the lead after 3 rounds.

Leading scores after 3 rounds:

226   Jock Hutchison (USA)

227   J.H. Taylor (England) and Jean Gassiat (France)

228   Walter Hagen (USA), Jim Barnes (USA) and Charles Whitcombe (England)

Other favourites:

232   George Duncan (Scotland) and Harry Vardon (England)

235   Joe Kirkwood (Australia)

241   Ted Ray (England)

FINAL 18 HOLES – Afternoon of June 24, 1922

Hagen played the final 18 holes earlier than many of the other contenders, although he was in the group right behind Hutchison the 3rd round leader. According to George Greenwood of the London Daily Telegraph, *"By means of a messenger he* (Hagen) *knew exactly what the other fellow* (Hutchison) *was doing at every hole."*

At the 4th hole this information feed became valuable for Hagen, who had lost a stroke and was now 3 behind his fellow American. Hutchison got into trouble when his 2nd shot, *"plunged headlong into the kitchen garden beyond the small wooden fence,"* according to Greenwood. Hutchison took a 7 on the hole. Greenwood wrote further about Hutchison's bad fortune at the 4th, *"That awful garden, with its cabbages and onions, and the scoffers sitting on the fence, will live long in Hutchison's memory."*

Hutchison himself penned an article after the round for The New York Herald. He wrote, *"My heart and spirits sank as I saw that fated second shot* (at the 4th hole) *fly over the green and drop out of bounds costing me a seven."* Yet Hutchison managed to maintain his lead as Hagen took a 5 on the hole. The New York Times noted about Hutchison, *"Nevertheless, he persevered splendidly, the feature of his game again being his uncanny pitching and putting."*

A little while later at the 484 yard 7th, Greenwood watched Hagen play a brilliant 2nd shot that landed just 3 feet from the pin. This helped him make the turn in just 35 strokes, but he was still a shot behind the leader Hutchison.

As the back 9 started, Greenwood wrote, *"the excitement now became fast and furious."* At the 10th hole Hagen tied Hutchison, but he lost the tie at the 11th when he 3-putted, only to take the lead outright at 12, when Hagen made 3 after Hutchison had taken 5. Then on 13, Hagen took 5 while Hutchison made 4 and the pair were tied once more.

Then they came to the 505 yard 14th hole. Hutchison took a 5. Hutchison described how Hagen played the hole, *"He drove well and then taking out a brassie* (2 wood)*, hit the master stroke of the tournament. He smashed a terrific shot, low and long and straight for the flag and with so much power and stuff on the ball that it cut the breeze, held the line and ran up to within 4 yards of the pin. He played it for a sure 4."*

Hagen had again taken the outright lead from Hutchison. At 15, Hutchison lost another stroke and now Hagen led by 2. On 16, perhaps with his confidence boosted, Hagen hit his tee shot on the short hole to within 4 feet of the pin, although he didn't make the putt. But Hutchison had taken a 4, so Hagen further increased his lead to 3 shots.

Both men took 4's at the 17th. Hutchison took 4 again on 18. But Hagen pulled his 2nd shot to the left of the green, and his 3rd shot left him 12 feet from the cup. His putt, *"trembled on the very brink of the hole,"* according to Greenwood, but did not go in. Hagen had finished with a 5 for an 18 hole score of 72 and a total of 300 for the championship.

Hagen was now the leader in the clubhouse. Hutchison at 302 was in 2nd place at this juncture. But there were many players on the course with plenty of golf to play that still had a chance. Barnes was only on the 9th and Duncan, the last man out in the afternoon was even farther behind.

Barnes finished the front 9 in 36. He now needed a 36 to tie Hagen. Arthur Draper in the New York Tribune wrote, *"Even fours for the difficult inward journey would give him a 72 and when he had reached the eighteenth he had kept his task."* Barnes needed a 4 on the 18th to tie and force a playoff, or a 3 to take the clubhouse lead. He hit his tee shot down the middle and had a good lie. His 2 wood 2nd shot landed right of the green in the rough. His chip landed on the far side of the green. And his putt stopped 2 feet shy of the hole. Barnes was in at 301.

At this moment, Americans were in the clubhouse holding the top 3 spots in the British Open. Draper wrote, *"With the Americans holding first, second and third places, the great gallery gathered around the last green grew deeply despondent as one after another of the British possibilities drew in."*

Taylor was the next to come in. He had made a 6 at the first hole in the final round, and that seemed to take him out of contention. However Taylor played on diligently and when he made 3's at 15 and 16 he was even with Hagen. Greenwood wrote about Taylor, *"he stuck manfully to his guns and when he came to the last he required a couple of 4's to tie."* On 17, he had a 15 foot putt for a 4. The London Guardian reported that he missed by a, *"fraction of an inch."* On 18, he had a disastrous *"visit to a bunker"* and lost 3 strokes. In spite of this disappointing finish Draper wrote that Taylor, *"merited all the applause he received at the last green for he played marvelous golf over the course where he won the championship twenty-eight years ago."* Taylor was in at 304.

Whitcombe had finished 3 shots behind Hagen and Gassiat had faded to 6 shots behind.

The last player out on the course, who had seemed completely out of the running after the morning round, still had a chance. George Duncan had shot 81 in the morning to start the final round 6 shots back. But perhaps Duncan knew that he was Britain's last hope because he was doing something special. Greenwood declared, *"the greatest sensation of all came at the very end when Duncan, starting out in the late afternoon, required a 68 to tie - a score which seemed impossible of accomplishment on a links such as St. George's. Playing inspired golf as only George Duncan knows how to play it, he reeled off fours and threes with amazing regularity."*

Duncan shot a 34 on the front 9. He now needed another 34 to tie Hagen. Like Taylore before him, Duncan came to the 17th hole needing two 4's to tie Hagen. He got the 4 on 17. Now a 4 on 18 would force a playoff with Hagen.

On 18, his 2 wood shot into the green, *"swerved slightly in its flight and it rolled off the green into a little hollow on the left,"* according to Greenwood.

Greenwood at this point was standing near Hagen, whom he called, *"an anxious spectator."* Hagen whispered to him, *"If Duncan knew as much about that shot as I do he is certain to get the ball dead."* Hagen meant he would pitch it up and get the ball to stop near the cup.

Draper was at the 18th green following the action in this tense moment. He wrote, *"One of the markers begged the huge crowd to get down on its knees and pray. They obeyed the first injunction and probably the second."*

Greenwood indicated that Duncan decided to hit the ball with a mashie (3 wood). Draper wrote, *"Duncan, who unquestionably was feeling the strain, made a rather feeble putt."* Apparently, rather than pitch the ball as Hagen felt was in order, Duncan tried to putt it with a 3 wood.

The ball stopped 20 feet short of the pin. Greenwood wrote, *"the club fell from his hands to the ground and a deep groan of disappointment went up from the expectant crowd."*

Still he had a 20 foot putt to tie. 3 inches before the cup the putt stopped. George Duncan had made a 5 on the 18th hole and had to settle for a course record 69 in his final round. Hutchison called it, *"one of the really great rounds in the history of championship golf; a 69 under pressure."*

Draper wrote, *"his 69 will be remembered by Britons for many a day as it was a truly gallant effort."*

With Duncan's missed putt at 18, Walter Hagen had won the 1922 British Open.

Greenwood declared, *"It was a dramatic ending to a great championship."*

H.H. Hilton of the London Evening Standard opened his article with this, *"In the whole history of the professional golf championship there has never been a more dramatic finish than at Sandwich yesterday, and the miracle attempted and almost achieved by George Duncan will rank as one of the most gallant efforts ever made."*

FINAL SCORES:

300   Walter Hagen (USA)

301   Jim Barnes (USA) and George Duncan (Scotland)

302   Jock Hutchison (USA)

303   Charles Whitcombe (England)

304   J.H. Taylor (England)

306   Jean Gassiat (France)

307   Harry Vardon (England) and Tom Walton (England)

Other favourites:

313   Joe Kirkwood (Australia)

321   Ted Ray (England)

Many newspapers across the USA today had Walter Hagen on the front page including the New York Times, The New York Tribune, The Cleveland Plain-Dealer, The Washington Herald, and The Miami Herald.

POSTSCRIPT

Walter Hagen returned to America on July 1st, and received a hero's welcome.

Hagen arrived in New York onboard the ocean liner Aquitania. *"He was accorded a welcome home that set a new record in lavish enthusiasm,"* stated the New York Times story which continued, *"it was the greatest reception ever accorded a returning athlete. Hagen received an ovation that no other golfer has ever received here or anywhere."*

The Times noted that acting mayor of New York, Murray Hulbert, *"presided over the occasion. The band struck up a martial tune and pennants waved to and fro."* All of this took place while Hagen was still on the deck of the Aquitania along with the other American golfers, Jim Barnes and Jock Hutchison. When Hagen came down the gangplank, *"there was an outburst that drowned out the band which was doing its best to render, Hail the Conquering Hero."*

Advance arrangements were made so the golfers didn't have to go through customs and were immediately taken in automobiles to the mayor's office where Mayor Hulbert, *"congratulated Hagen on his victory, acclaiming him the greatest golfer in the world."*

Next the party moved to the Hotel Biltmore for lunch. Hagen remarked about his trip across the Atlantic to the British Open, *"I wasn't going over to try to steal the cup but really wanted to show that one could be a good sportsman whether winner or loser."*

Hagen's picture appeared on the front page of the New York Herald sports section on July 2, 1922 while onboard the Aquitania as he returned home from England.

NOTE from The Sports Time Traveler

I have a couple of personal connections to this story that made it very compelling for me to make the virtual journey back to 1922.

The 1922 British Open took place in Sandwich, England, which is very close to the University of Kent. I spent a year attending the University in the early 1980s. While there I was a part of the cross country running club. One morning for practice we went to Sandwich and ran 10 grueling miles along the seaside, often right near giant cliffs that drop down to the English Channel. On that run with us was Mike Gratton, the winner of the 1983 London marathon. Mike ran me into the ground that morning. I finished so far behind that I got lost on the way back. When I did make it back to the gym we all had tea, as was the custom.

My other connection involved the ocean liner Aquitania that Walter Hagen returned on to the USA after the 1922 British Open. Hagen sailed onboard the Aquitania in first class. Two years earlier, on August 21, 1920, my great grandmother Eva arrived in America in the steerage class section of the Aquitania after a courageous journey with her two little daughters, Mary and Jennie (my grandmother). They had fled war torn Ukraine in the middle of the Russian Revolution after having survived World War I, various epidemics, pogroms and general lawlessness. Escaping from Ukraine (no one was allowed to leave the Soviet Union at the time) and traveling across Europe to England to board the Aquitania to America was a harrowing experience which I have documented for my family and to which all of my great grandmother's direct descendants owe a deep debt of gratitude, as well as our lives.

My great grandmother was such a strong willed woman that she became a successful entrepreneur and lived to 90, long enough that I got to know her very well. And so I end this book by saying, *"Thank you great grandma. Without your courage and perseverance I would not be here, and of course would never have had the opportunity and pleasure of writing this book."*

COMING SOON!

Now that this book is complete, I am starting work on "Great Golf Tournaments – Volume 2." There are many more golf tournaments with incredible and dramatic stories to tell. The focus will be on great events from 1920 – 1979 and will include Bobby Jones, Gene Sarazen, Walter Hagen, Byron Nelson, Arnold Palmer, Jack Nicklaus, Tom Watson, Johnny Miller and probably a bit of Ben Hogan and Sam Snead as well.

I hope you enjoyed the journey back in time with me to some of the greatest golf tournaments of the past. I would love to hear your feedback and your selections for tournaments that will make the list for coverage in volume 2.

Please send feedback to: Len@Fermaninnovation.com

For more information visit: www.thesportstimetraveler.com